THE COMPLEXITY OF COOPERATION

PRINCETON STUDIES IN COMPLEXITY

THE COMPLEXITY OF COOPERATION

AGENT-BASED MODELS OF
COMPETITION AND
COLLABORATION

Robert Axelrod

PRINCETON UNIVERSITY PRESS   PRINCETON, NEW JERSEY

Library of Congress Cataloging-in-Publication Data

Axelrod, Robert M.
The complexity of cooperation : agent-based models of competition
and collaboration / Robert Axelrod.
p. cm. — (Princeton studies in complexity.)
Includes bibliographical references and index.
ISBN 0-691-01568-6 (cloth : alk. paper). — ISBN 0-691-01567-8
(pbk. : alk. paper)
1. Cooperativeness. 2. Competition. 3. Conflict management.
4. Adaptability (Psychology) 5. Adjustment (Psychology)
6. Computational complexity. 7. Social systems—Computer
simulation. I. Title. II. Series.
HM131.A894 1997
302'.14—dc21 97-1107 CIP

This book has been composed in Sabon

Princeton University Press books are printed
on acid-free paper and meet the guidelines
for permanence and durability of the Committee
on Production Guidelines for Book Longevity
of the Council on Library Resources

Printed in the United States of America

10 9 8 7 6 5 4 3 2 1

10 9 8 7 6 5 4 3 2 1
(Pbk.)

To Amy, Lily, and Vera

Contents

Tables and Figures _____

Tables

Figures

Preface _____

THIS BOOK is a sequel to *The Evolution of Cooperation* (Axelrod 1984). That book had a single paradigm and a simple theme. The paradigm was the two-person iterated Prisoner's Dilemma. The theme was that cooperation based upon reciprocity can evolve and sustain itself even among egoists provided there is sufficient prospect of a long-term interaction. The theme was developed from many different angles, including computer tournaments, historical cases, and mathematical theorems.

The two-person iterated Prisoner's Dilemma is the *E. coli* of the social sciences, allowing a very large variety of studies to be undertaken in a common framework. It has even become a standard paradigm for studying issues in fields as diverse as evolutionary biology and networked computer systems. Its very simplicity has allowed political scientists, economists, sociologists, philosophers, mathematicians, computer scientists, evolutionary biologists, and many others to talk to each other. Indeed, the analytic and empirical findings about the Prisoner's Dilemma from one field have often led to insights in other fields.[1]

The Evolution of Cooperation, with its focus on the Prisoner's Dilemma, was written during the Cold War. Indeed, one of its primary motivations was to help promote cooperation between the two sides of a bipolar world. My hope was that a deeper understanding of the conditions that promote cooperation could help make the world a little safer. The work was well received in academic circles, and even among scholars interested in policy-relevant research.[2] Nevertheless, I was keenly aware that there was much more to cooperation than could be captured by any single model, no matter how broad its applications or how rich its strategic implications.

The present book is based on a series of studies that go beyond the basic paradigm of the Prisoner's Dilemma. It includes an analysis of strategies that evolve automatically, rather than by human invention. It also considers strategies designed to cope with the possibility of misunderstandings between the players or misimplementation of a choice. It then expands the basis of cooperation to more than a choice with a short-run cost and a possible long-run gain. It includes collaboration with others to

---

[1] For reviews, see Axelrod and Dion (1988) and Axelrod and D'Ambrosio (1995).

[2] For example, in 1990 I received the National Academy of Sciences' new Award for Behavioral Research Relevant to the Prevention of Nuclear War. On the Soviet side, several senior defense intellectuals and scientists involved in arms-control policy reported that they read the book with interest, and had passed it around to their friends.

build and enforce norms of conduct, to win a war or to impose an industrial standard, to build a new organization that can act on behalf of its
members, and to construct a shared culture based on mutual influence.

Expansion of the potential forms of collaboration implies the expansion of the potential forms of competition. The present volume therefore
considers more than whether or not two players cooperate. It includes
the conflicts between violators and enforcers of a norm, the threats and
wars among nations, competition among companies, contests among organizations for wealth and membership, and competing pulls of social
influence for cultural change.

This book includes work done from 1986 to 1996, a period in which
the Cold War was coming to an end and a new era was taking shape. My
own research agenda was deeply affected by these dramatic and unexpected transformations. The transformations of this decade were especially salient because during this period I was fortunate to have had opportunities to participate in international activities aimed at promoting
cooperation, first between the United States and the Soviet Union, and
then among the various warring groups in the former Yugoslavia. It is
ironic that my theoretical work on two-person games led to my participation in international activities just as the bi-power world of the Cold War
was coming to an end.

In 1986, I joined a committee of the National Academy of Sciences
examining the relevance of behavioral and social sciences to the prevention of nuclear war. Among other projects, this committee promoted parallel and collaborative research with Soviet scholars on topics of mutual
interest.

My participation in this committee also led to my joining a second
committee of the National Academy of Sciences, the Committee on International Security and Arms Control. This committee consisted mostly of
physical scientists and worked with a counterpart Soviet group. Our mis-
sion was to consider fruitful avenues for arms-control initiatives that
would go beyond what was currently being negotiated between the two
governments. Among the members were scientists with decades of experience in arms control and a former Chairman of the Joint Chiefs of Staff.
The Soviet counterpart committee included several key science advisors
to the Soviet leader, Mikhail Gorbachev.

Participating in these social science and arms-control forums taught
me a great deal about how international politics was viewed by leading
scholars and policy activists. In particular, I was impressed by the intellectual efforts of leading thinkers on both sides to formulate concepts and
recommendations that would capitalize on the new opportunities of the
era as well as deal with the new dangers of instability. The difficulties
faced by these talented, experienced, and practical leaders reinforced my

own faith in the potential value of research into fundamental political and social processes.

I was also affected by what was happening outside our committee meetings. Our work brought me to meetings in Uzbekistan in 1988 and Estonia in 1989, as well as Russia. In Estonia, I asked our Soviet hosts if they could find a way for us to meet with both the Estonian nationalists, who were then accelerating their demands for independence, and the ethnic Russians who opposed them. Having them meet in one room was impossible, I was politely told, but separate meetings were arranged for our benefit. This gave me a firsthand feel for the depth of nationalist sentiment and heightened my interest in cultural conflict and nationalism as fundamental forces in the world. These interests in turn led to work included in this book on how new political actors are formed and how social influence promotes cultural change as the foundation of political change.

In 1989, however, I accepted the validity of the quip that if it came to a conflict between Estonia and Moscow, the winner would be the Red Army. Yet within two years the Soviet Union had collapsed and Estonia as well as all the other republics had their independence.

As democracy was developing in Russia, Yugoslavia disintegrated. In Bosnia, a bitter civil war ensued, marked by a level of atrocities not seen in Europe for fifty years. At the height of the fighting, in the summer of 1995, I was invited by the United Nations to talk about my work on cooperation at a conference designed to bring together nongovernmental representatives of all the warring factions in the former Yugoslavia. The participants had many critical questions about how my Prisoner's Dilemma work applied to the complexity of their conflicts, with its unequal power, with fifteen rather than two sides to the conflicts, and with violations of widely held norms of conduct.

Many of the issues raised by the participants did not have simple answers, but they were ones on which I had been actively working. The present volume includes models that deal with unequal power, with multisided as well as two-sided conflict, with misunderstandings and misimplementions, with the enforcement of norms, with newly emerging political entities, and with the cultural basis for political affiliation and polarization. Although I have no solutions, I believe that analyzing large-scale outcomes in terms of the interactions of actors can enhance our understanding of conflict and cooperation in a complex world.

The seven chapters of this book were first published in journals and edited volumes of political science, conflict studies, organizational science, and computer science. The separate articles originally appeared in such a wide range of places that people who may have read one or two of them are unlikely to be aware of the others. Publishing these articles as a collected set may be of special value to three partly overlapping groups of readers: those who want to learn about extensions to the two-person Prisoner's Dilemma, those who are interested in conflict and collaboration in a variety of settings, and those who are interested in agent-based modeling in the social sciences.

To place the work in a wider context, I have added a variety of new material:

1. An introductory chapter describing the common themes of the volume and showing how the individual chapters relate to each other.

2. Introductory material for each chapter showing how it grew out of my long-term interests, recounting experiences related to the project, and describing how the work was received.

3. An appendix providing resources for students and scholars who wish to do their own agent-based modeling.

With the supplementary material, the volume should be accessible to an advanced undergraduate interested in fundamental aspects of political and social change. Readers unfamiliar with the iterated Prisoner's Dilemma may wish to consult any standard game-theory text, or Axelrod (1984, 1–15). In the few places where specialized knowledge is used, the argument is also explained in simpler terms.

I acknowledge with pleasure the encouragement and helpful criticism of the BACH research group: Arthur Burks, Michael Cohen, John Holland, Rick Riolo, and Carl Simon. It has been an education, a joy, and an honor to have been part of the BACH group for well over a decade. For editorial help with this volume, I would like to thank Amy Saldinger. For the index I thank Lisa D'Ambrosio. I would also like to thank all those people and institutions who helped with chapters of this book. Their names are given in the appropriate places. Finally, for financial help in completing this book, I would like to thank the Defense Advanced Project Research Agency for its assistance through the Santa Fe Institute, and the University of Michigan for its assistance through both the LS&A College Enrichment Fund and the School of Public Policy.

References

Axelrod, Robert. 1984. *The Evolution of Cooperation*. New York: Basic Books.

Axelrod, Robert, and Lisa D'Ambrosio. 1995. "Announcement for Bibliography on the Evolution of Cooperation." *Journal of Conflict Resolution* 39:190.

Axelrod, Robert, and Douglas Dion. 1988. "The Further Evolution of Cooperation." *Science* 242 (9 Dec.):1385–90.

THE COMPLEXITY OF COOPERATION

Introduction

THE TITLE of this book illustrates the dual purposes of the volume. One meaning of "The Complexity of Cooperation" refers to the addition of complexity to the most common framework for studying cooperation, namely the two-person iterated Prisoner's Dilemma. Adding complexity to that framework allows the exploration of many interesting and important features of competition and collaboration that are beyond the reach of the Prisoner's Dilemma paradigm.

The second meaning of "The Complexity of Cooperation" refers to the use of concepts and techniques that have come to be called complexity theory. Complexity theory involves the study of many actors and their interactions. The actors may be atoms, fish, people, organizations, or nations. Their interactions may consist of attraction, combat, mating, communication, trade, partnership, or rivalry. Because the study of large numbers of actors with changing patterns of interactions often gets too difficult for a mathematical solution, a primary research tool of complexity theory is computer simulation. The trick is to specify how the agents interact, and then observe properties that occur at the level of the whole society. For example, with given rules about actors and their interactions, do the actors tend to align into two competing groups? Do particular strategies dominate the population? Do clear patterns of behavior develop?

The simulation of agents and their interactions is known by several names, including agent-based modeling, bottom-up modeling, and artificial social systems. Whatever name is used, the purpose of agent-based modeling is to understand properties of complex social systems through the analysis of simulations. This method of doing science can be contrasted with the two standard methods of induction and deduction. Induction is the discovery of patterns in empirical data.[1] For example, in the social sciences induction is widely used in the analysis of opinion surveys and macroeconomic data. Deduction, on the other hand, involves specifying a set of axioms and proving consequences that can be derived from those assumptions. The discovery of equilibrium results in game theory using rational-choice axioms is a good example of deduction.

Agent-based modeling is a third way of doing science. Like deduction, it starts with a set of explicit assumptions. But unlike deduction, it does

[1] Induction as a search for patterns in data should not be confused with mathematical induction, which is a technique for proving theorems.

not prove theorems. Instead, an agent-based model generates simulated data that can be analyzed inductively. Unlike typical induction, however, the simulated data come from a rigorously specified set of rules rather than direct measurement of the real world. Whereas the purpose of induction is to find patterns in data and that of deduction is to find consequences of assumptions, the purpose of agent-based modeling is to aid intuition.

Agent-based modeling is a way of doing thought experiments. Although the assumptions may be simple, the consequences may not be at all obvious. Numerous examples appear throughout this volume of locally interacting agents producing large-scale effects. The large-scale effects of locally interacting agents are called "emergent properties" of the system. Emergent properties are often surprising because it can be hard to anticipate the full consequences of even simple forms of interaction.[2]

There are some models, however, in which emergent properties can be formally deduced. Good examples include the neoclassical economic models in which rational agents operating under powerful assumptions about the availability of information and the capability of optimizing can achieve an efficient reallocation of resources among themselves through costless trading. But when the agents use adaptive rather than optimizing strategies, deducing the consequences is often impossible; simulation becomes necessary.

Throughout the social sciences today, the dominant form of modeling is based upon the rational-choice paradigm. Game theory, in particular, is typically based upon the assumption of rational choice. In my view, the reason for the dominance of the rational-choice approach is not that scholars think it is realistic. Nor is game theory used solely because it offers good advice to a decision maker, because its unrealistic assumptions undermine much of its value as a basis for advice. The real advantage of the rational-choice assumption is that it often allows deduction.

The main alternative to the assumption of rational choice is some form of adaptive behavior. The adaptation may be at the individual level through learning, or it may be at the population level through differential survival and reproduction of the more successful individuals. Either way, the consequences of adaptive processes are often very hard to deduce when there are many interacting agents following rules that have nonlinear effects. Thus the simulation of an agent-based model is often the only viable way to study populations of agents who are adaptive rather than fully rational.

Although agent-based modeling employs simulation, it does not aim to

---

[2] Some complexity theorists consider surprise to be part of the definition of emergence, but this raises the question of surprising to whom?

provide an accurate representation of a particular empirical application. Instead, the goal of agent-based modeling is to enrich our understanding of fundamental processes that may appear in a variety of applications. This requires adhering to the KISS principle, which stands for the army slogan "keep it simple, stupid."

The KISS principle is vital because of the character of the research community. Both the researcher and the audience have limited cognitive ability. When a surprising result occurs, it is very helpful to be confident that we can understand everything that went into the model. Although the topic being investigated may be complicated, the assumptions underlying the agent-based model should be simple. The complexity of agent-based modeling should be in the simulated results, not in the assumptions of the model.

Of course there are many other uses of computer simulation in which the faithful reproduction of a particular setting is important. A simulation of the economy aimed at predicting interest rates three months into the future needs to be as accurate as possible. For this purpose the assumptions that go into the model may need to be quite complicated. Likewise, if a simulation is used to train the crew of a supertanker or to develop tactics for a new fighter aircraft, accuracy is important and simplicity of the model is not. But if the goal is to deepen our understanding of some fundamental process, then simplicity of the assumptions is important, and realistic representation of all the details of a particular setting is not.

My earlier work on the Prisoner's Dilemma (Axelrod 1984) illustrates this theme. My main motivation for learning about effective strategies was to find out how cooperation could be promoted in international politics, especially between the East and the West during the Cold War. As it happened, my tournament approach and the evolutionary analysis that grew out of it suggested applications of which I had not even dreamed. For example, controlled experiments show that stickleback fish use the TIT FOR TAT strategy to achieve cooperation based upon reciprocity (Milinski 1987).

At a political science convention, a colleague came up to me and said she really appreciated my work and found it helpful for her divorce. She explained that my book showed her that she had been a sucker during her marriage, always giving in to her husband. I asked whether the book helped save her marriage. "No," she replied. "I didn't want to save my marriage. But it certainly helped with the divorce settlement. I started to play TIT FOR TAT, and once he learned that I couldn't be pushed around, I got a much better deal."

The fact that a single model, in this case the Prisoner's Dilemma, can be useful in understanding the dynamics between foraging fish and between divorcing people is not due to the accuracy of the model in representing the details of either situation. Instead it is due to the fact that an extremely simple model captures a fundamental feature of many interactions. What the Prisoner's Dilemma captures so well is the tension between the advantages of selfishness in the short run versus the need to elicit cooperation from the other player to be successful in the longer run. The very simplicity of the Prisoner's Dilemma is highly valuable in helping us to discover and appreciate the deep consequences of the fundamental processes involved in dealing with this tension.

A moral of the story is that models that aim to explore fundamental processes should be judged by their fruitfulness, not by their accuracy. For this purpose, realistic representation of many details is unnecessary and even counterproductive. The models presented in the volume follow this same logic of simplicity. The intention is to explore fundamental social processes. Although a particular application may have motivated a given model, the primary aim is to undertake the exploration in a manner so general that many possible settings could be illuminated.

Taken as a whole, this book presents a set of studies that are unified in three ways. First, they all deal with problems and opportunities of cooperation in a more or less competitive environment. Second, they all employ models that use adaptive rather than rational agents. Although people may try to be rational, they can rarely meet the requirements of information or foresight that rational models impose (Simon 1955; March 1978). Third, they all use computer simulation to study the emergent properties of the interactions among the agents. Thus they are all agent-based models. The simulation is necessary because the interactions of adaptive agents typically lead to nonlinear effects that are not amenable to the deductive tools of formal mathematics.

The chapters can be read either separately or as a whole. The order of the presentation represents a progression from variations on the Prisoner's Dilemma paradigm (Chapters 1 and 2), to different strategic models (Chapters 3, 4, and 5), to an examination of the emergence of new political actors and shared culture (Chapters 6 and 7). The order of the chapters is also the order in which I did the work, with the exception that Chapter 2 represents later work on an earlier theme.

The first project represents my effort to go beyond the tournament approach to generating a rich strategic environment. The tournament approach solicited entries from professionals and amateurs, each trying to develop a strategy for the Prisoner's Dilemma that would do well in the environment provided by all the submissions. Having done two rounds of the tournament, I wondered whether the amount of cooperation I observed was due to the prior expectations of the people who submitted the rules. Fortunately, a colleague, John Holland, had developed an automated method for evolving a population of strategies from a random start. The technique is called the genetic algorithm. I tried it, and it performed far beyond my expectations. The results are in Chapter 1.

An important extension of the basic Prisoner's Dilemma is consideration of what happens when a player might misunderstand what the other did on the previous move or might fail to implement the intended choice. These kinds of "noise" can have a big impact on the performance of a given strategy, and hence on the best means of attaining cooperation among egoists. Several suggestions had been proposed in the literature for dealing with noise, including adding generosity or contrition to reciprocity, as well as a completely different strategy based upon learning through reward and punishment. I wanted to see how these different approaches would work in a noisy environment. A postdoctoral visitor from China, Wu Jianzhong, and I found that generous or contrite versions of the classic TIT FOR TAT strategy did very well in a variegated noisy environment, even better than the Pavlovian strategy. Chapter 2 explains how these strategies performed and why.

For a long time, I had been eager to move beyond the two-person format of the basic Prisoner's Dilemma. I especially wanted to find out how cooperation could emerge when many people interacted with each other in groups rather than in pairs. It was well known that the straightforward extension of the Prisoner's Dilemma to an *n*-person version will not sustain cooperation very well because the players have no way of focusing their punishment on someone in the group who has failed to cooperate. Nevertheless, social norms do emerge and are often quite powerful means of sustaining cooperation. So I developed a "norms game" that allowed players to punish individuals who do not cooperate. It turned out that another twist was needed lest all the cooperators be tempted to let someone else be the one to bear the costs of disciplining the noncooperators. This led to a wide-ranging study of the mechanisms for promoting norms (Chapter 3).

Another form of cooperation occurs when people organize themselves into groups to compete with each other. This is clearly an example of collaboration in the interests of competition. It takes place in many forms, including alliances among nations, strategic partnerships among businesses, and coalitions among political parties in parliamentary democracies. Having worked on the problem of coalition formation in Italy as part of my dissertation in the late 1960's, I was struck by how political parties wanted to work with others who were similar to themselves (Axelrod 1970). Two decades later, I returned to this theme of choosing sides based upon affinity rather than strategic advantage. Working with a graduate student, Scott Bennett, I developed a model for how players choose sides. We found that the model actually did a good job of accounting for how European countries were aligned in World War II (Chapter 4).

The same model even worked well in accounting for how computer companies took sides in the competition to develop standards for the UNIX operating system (Chapter 5). This was work done with Scott Bennett and three collaborators from the Michigan Business School: Will Mitchell, Robert E. Thomas, and Erhard Bruderer.

An even deeper problem is how independent actors sometimes cooperate to such an extent that they give up most of their independence. The result is a new level of organization that behaves as an independent actor in its own right. Multicellular organisms evolved this way, and so have many large business organizations. My approach to analyzing how new levels of political actors can arise uses a model of war, threats, and commitments. The agent-based model and its results are provided in Chapter 6.

Whereas the model in Chapter 6 attributes the emergence of new actors to the dynamics of coping with conflict, I also wanted to study an even more fundamental question: how people become more alike so that they find it easier to work together in the first place. This led to a study of the process of social influence and the emergence of shared culture. Once again, the transformations of the post-Cold War environment helped emphasize the importance of returning to some very fundamental issues about the basis for cooperation within as well as between societies. The resulting model of social influence and cultural change is given in Chapter 7.

Two appendixes provide supporting material about agent-based modeling. Appendix A develops the concepts and methods of comparing agent-based models through a process called "alignment." Alignment is needed to determine whether two modeling systems can produce the same results, which in turn is the basis for critical experiments and for tests of whether one model can subsume another. The work provides a case study of alignment, using the model of social influence presented in Chapter 7. The project was done with Robert Axtell, Joshua Epstein, and Michael Cohen. Appendix B provides resources for students and scholars who wish to do their own agent-based modeling. It includes advice on programming such models, exercises to develop one's skills, and suggested readings for applications of complexity theory and agent-based modeling to the social sciences.

Associated with this volume is an Internet site.[3] The site includes the source code and documentation for most of the models in this book. It also provides links to many topics related to complexity theory, agent-based modeling, and cooperation.

---

[3] http://pscs.physics.lsa.umich.edu/Software/ComplexCoop.html

References

Axelrod, Robert. 1970. *Conflict of Interest.* Chicago: Markham.
———. 1984. *The Evolution of Cooperation.* New York: Basic Books.
March, James G. 1978. "Bounded Rationality, Ambiguity and the Engineering of Choice." *Bell Journal of Economics* 9: 587–608.
Milinski, Manfred. 1987. "TIT FOR TAT in Sticklebacks and the Evolution of Co-operation." *Nature* 23: 434–35.
Simon, Herbert A. 1955. "A Behavioral Model of Rational Choice." *Quarterly Journal of Economics* 69: 99–118.

1

Evolving New Strategies

THIS CHAPTER began with a hammer and a nail. The nail was a problem I wanted to solve. The hammer was a tool I wanted to try out that looked well suited to driving my nail. The problematic nail was the question of whether the success of the TIT FOR TAT strategy in my computer tournaments depended in large part on the prior beliefs of the people who submitted strategies about what the other submissions would be like. In other words, would the tournament results be influenced by what people believed others would be doing, or would something like the reciprocity of TIT FOR TAT succeed in a tournament setting without any preconceptions about the tendencies or even the responsiveness of others?

Answering this question would require a method of generating new strategies that would not involve human preconceptions. A tool for doing precisely this was developed by John Holland, a computer scientist at Michigan. I knew John well from a small research group we were both part of for years. This was the BACH group, named after its original members: Arthur Burks, myself, Michael Cohen, and John Holland. John's genetic algorithm technique (Holland 1975) was inspired by the ability of evolution to discover adaptive solutions to hard problems. By the mid-1980's, the genetic algorithm had proven to be an effective search technique for discovering effective solutions in highly complex computer problems (Goldberg 1989; Mitchell 1996).

My own interest in evolutionary simulation dates back to 1960, when I did a high school science project on computer simulation of hypothetical life forms and environments. At the University of Chicago I was a math major, but also spent a summer with the Committee on Mathematical Biology reading about evolutionary biology. Despite these interests in computers, mathematics, and evolution, I chose to go to graduate school in political science. The problems I most wanted to work on dealt with the prevention of conflict between nations, especially nuclear war. After getting my Ph.D. from Yale, I taught international politics at Berkeley and then moved to the University of Michigan, where I took a joint appointment in the Department of Political Science and what is now the School of Public Policy.

At Michigan, Michael Cohen became my closest colleague. He kept suggesting that I meet John Holland and learn about his work. Eventually I succumbed—to my great joy and benefit. Among other things, I learned about the potential of John's genetic algorithm as a method of discovering highly adaptive responses even in complicated contexts. So when I had the nail of needing to study the evolution of Prisoner's Dilemma strategies and the hammer of the genetic algorithm, it seemed like a perfect match.

The first thing I did was to test the genetic algorithm to see if it could perform well in an environment I thought I knew fairly well, namely, the rules submitted to the second round of my tournament. The algorithm performed beyond my wildest expectations, evolving strategies that were more effective than what I thought was even possible in this environment. Having convinced myself that this was indeed a hammer that could pound my kind of nails, I next used it on my real problem. I started with a population of strictly random strategies (chosen from a huge universe of possible strategies that had no bias toward either cooperation or reciprocity), and let the population evolve using the genetic algorithm. Within a very short time, the population evolved toward strategies that behaved very much like TIT FOR TAT, and were certainly achieving cooperation based upon reciprocity. This demonstrated that the success of reciprocity in my two rounds of human submissions was not a fluke that depended upon particular prior beliefs about what other submissions would look like.

I was pleased that earlier claims about reciprocity were even more robust than I had imagined. I was also pleased because I would not have to devote my life to conducting more and more rounds of the computer tournament, as a number of people had requested that I do.

The resulting paper was first published as a chapter in a book on the genetic algorithm and related computer techniques. It is widely cited in the computer science literature on the genetic algorithm. The reason seems to be that the Prisoner's Dilemma provides a task that is easy to understand, and the performance of the genetic algorithm on this task is quite impressive. In addition, this was the first application of the genetic algorithm to evolving strategies in an interactive setting. Unfortunately, the appearance of this paper in a computer science collection has meant that it has not been very accessible to social scientists.

This project has an interesting sequel that deals with the adaptive value of sexual reproduction. The story involves William D. Hamilton, with whom I had previously worked on biological applications of my work on the Prisoner's Dilemma (Axelrod and Hamilton 1981).[1] As I was completing my paper on the genetic algorithm, Bill told me about his theory that sex was an adaptation to resist parasites. Bill is one of the world's leading evolutionary biologists, so when he suggested a novel theory, I

---

[1] Our paper is also included in revised form as Chapter 5 of Axelrod (1984).

took it seriously, no matter how bizarre it sounded at first. He pointed out that virtually all large animals and plants reproduce sexually, even though sexual reproduction can be very costly. In mammals, for example, the cost can be as large as two-for-one when half the adults, the males, do not give birth. What advantage conferred by sex makes up for this huge cost is one of the great unsolved puzzles in evolutionary biology. Bill's idea, roughly stated, was that all large animals and plants have the problem of resisting parasites by being able to distinguish their own cells from parasites that evolve to fool them. Parasites, being much smaller, reproduce much faster than the hosts, so they can evolve faster than the hosts. Sex, Bill reasoned, allows the offspring of the hosts to be different from either the mother or the father, and thereby makes it hard for parasites that have adapted well to a host to be well adapted to the host's offspring. By juggling the genes of two parents, sex allows a host species to resist its rapidly evolving parasites.

This was a fascinating idea. Bill told me, however, that he had trouble working out a mathematical model that could be solved. The problem was that the model would have to include many genes, but mathematical models of genetics typically became quite unmanageable when there are more than two interacting genes. "No problem," I said. I had a technique based on Holland's genetic algorithm that could easily handle dozens of interacting genes. Moreover, it could easily represent the competition between hosts and parasites. So Bill and I worked with a graduate computer science student, Reiko Tanese. We adapted the genetic algorithm to test whether sexual reproduction of the hosts could indeed overcome the two-for-one disadvantage compared to asexual hosts who also had to deal with evolving parasites. It worked. The resulting paper was a review of alternative explanations of the origin of sex and a demonstration that Bill's own explanation was theoretically sound (Hamilton et al. 1990). To this day, I am delighted that a political scientist was able to adapt a tool from computer science and thereby contribute to evolutionary biology. About the origins of sex, no less. Clearly John Holland's "hammer" is effective for quite a variety of nails.

The use of the genetic algorithm to study the evolution of strategies has had many other applications recently. Here are two of my favorites:

> Instead of starting with a random selection from a very rich set of strategies for the Prisoner's Dilemma as I did, Kristain Lindgren (1991) began with the simplest possible strategies and used an extension of the genetic algorithm to evolve more and more complex possibilities. The result was an alternation of periods of stability and instability as one dominant pattern of strategies was eventually invaded by another. The dynamic behavior of the population is highly complicated with long transients and punctuated equilibria. This is

one of my favorite uses of the genetic algorithm because it diplays the evolution of strategies from simple to more complex.

In a completely different setting, Smith and Dike (1995) used the genetic algorithm to evolve air combat tactics for a new kind of fighter plane. The resulting maneuvers allowed the X-31 research plane to exploit its ability to maintain control after a stall in simulated combat against a conventional fighter opponent. The project demonstrates that the genetic learning system can discover rules for novel and effective maneuvers without flying a prototype in costly test flights.

The effectiveness of the genetic algorithm and its evolution toward reciprocity in a population playing the Prisoner's Dilemma help validate the robustness of reciprocity as an effective strategy that does not depend on the prior beliefs of the other players.

References

Axelrod, Robert. 1984. *The Evolution of Cooperation.* New York: Basic Books.

Axelrod, Robert, and William D. Hamilton. 1981. "The Evolution of Cooperation." *Science* 211: 379–403.

Goldberg, David E. 1989. *Genetic Algorithms in Search, Optimization, and Machine Learning.* Reading, Mass.: Addison-Wesley.

Hamilton, William, Robert Axelrod, and Reiko Tanese. 1990. "Sexual Reproduction as an Adaptation to Resist Parasites (A Review)." *Proceedings of the National Academy of Sciences (USA)* 87: 3566–73.

Holland, John H. 1975. *Adaptation in Natural and Artificial Systems.* Ann Arbor, Mich.: University of Michigan Press. 2d ed., 1992.

Lindgren, Kristain. 1991. "Evolutionary Phenomena in Simple Dynamics." In *Artificial Life II,* ed. C. G. Langton, C. Taylor, J. D. Farmer, and S. Rasmussen, 295–312. SFI Studies in Complexity, vol. 10. Reading, Mass.: Addison-Wesley.

Mitchell, Melanie. 1996. *An Introduction to Genetic Algorithms.* Cambridge, Mass.: MIT Press.

Smith, Robert E., and Bruce A. Dike. 1995. "Learning Novel Fighter Combat Maneuver Rules Via Genetic Algorithm." *International Journal of Expert Systems* 8: 247–76.

Evolving New Strategies

THE EVOLUTION OF STRATEGIES IN THE ITERATED PRISONER'S DILEMMA

ROBERT AXELROD

Adapted from Robert Axelrod, "The Evolution of Strategies in the Iterated Prisoner's Dilemma," in *Genetic Algorithms and Simulated Annealing,* ed. Lawrence Davis (London: Pitman; Los Altos, Calif.: Morgan Kaufman, 1987), 32–41. © Robert Axelrod

In complex environments, individuals are not fully able to analyze the situation and calculate their optimal strategy.[1] Instead they can be expected to adapt their strategy over time based upon what has been effective and what has not. One useful analogy to the adaptation process is biological evolution. In evolution, strategies that have been relatively effective in a population become more widespread, and strategies that have been less effective become less common in the population.

Biological evolution has been highly successful in discovering complex and effective methods of adapting to very rich environmental situations. This is accomplished by differential reproduction of the more successful individuals. The evolutionary process also requires that successful characteristics be inherited through a genetic mechanism that allows some chance for new strategies to be discovered. One genetic mechanism allowing new strategies to be discovered is mutation. Another mechanism is crossover, whereby sexual reproduction takes some genetic material from one parent and some from the other.

The mechanisms that have allowed biological evolution to be so good at adaptation have been employed in the field of artificial intelligence. The artificial intelligence technique is called the "genetic algorithm" (Holland 1975). Although other methods of representing strategies in games as finite automata have been used (Rubinstein 1986; Megiddo and Wigderson 1986; Miller 1989; Binmore and Samuelson 1990; Lomborg 1991), the genetic algorithm itself has not previously been used in game-theoretic settings.

This essay will first demonstrate the genetic algorithm in the context of a rich social setting, the environment formed by the strategies submitted

[1] I thank Stephanie Forrest and Reiko Tanese for their help with the computer programming, Michael D. Cohen and John Holland for their helpful suggestions, and the Harry Frank Guggenheim Foundation and the National Science Foundation for their financial support.

to a Prisoner's Dilemma computer tournament. The results show that the genetic algorithm is surprisingly successful at discovering complex and effective strategies that are well adapted to this complex environment. Next the essay shows how the results of this simulation experiment can be used to illuminate important issues in the evolutionary approach to adaptation, such as the relative advantage of developing new strategies based upon one or two parent strategies, the role of early commitments in the shaping of evolutionary paths, and the extent to which evolutionary processes are optimal or arbitrary.

The simulation method involves the following steps:

1. the specification of an environment in which the evolutionary process can operate,

2. the specification of the genetics, including the way in which information on the simulated chromosome is translated into a strategy for the simulated individual,

3. the design of an experiment to study the effects of alternative realities (such as repeating the experiment under identical conditions to see if random mutations lead to convergent or divergent evolutionary outcomes), and

4. the running of the experiment for a specified number of generations on a computer, and the statistical analysis of the results.

The Simulated Environment

An interesting set of environmental challenges is provided by the fact that many of the benefits sought by living things such as people are disproportionately available to cooperating groups. The problem is that although an individual can benefit from mutual cooperation, each one can also do even better by exploiting the cooperative efforts of others. Over a period of time, the same individuals may interact again, allowing for complex patterns of strategic interactions (Axelrod and Hamilton 1981).

The Prisoner's Dilemma is an elegant embodiment of the problem of achieving mutual cooperation, and therefore provides the basis for the analysis. In the Prisoner's Dilemma, two individuals can each either cooperate or defect. The payoff to a player affects its reproductive success. No matter what the other does, the selfish choice of defection yields a higher payoff than cooperation. But if both defect, both do worse than if both had cooperated. Table 1–1 shows the payoff matrix of the Prisoner's Dilemma used in this study.

In many settings, the same two individuals may meet more than once. If an individual can recognize a previous interactant and remember some aspects of the prior outcomes, then the strategic situation becomes an iterated Prisoner's Dilemma. A strategy would take the form of a decision

TABLE 1-1
The Prisoner's Dilemma

		Column Player	
		Cooperate	*Defect*
Row Player	Cooperate	$R = 3, R = 3$ Reward for mutual cooperation	$S = 0, T = 5$ Sucker's payoff, and temptation to defect
	Defect	$T = 5, S = 0$ Temptation to defect and sucker's payoff	$P = 1, P = 1$ Punishment for mutual defection

Note: The payoffs to the row chooser are listed first.

rule that specified the probability of cooperation or defection as a function of the history of the interaction so far.

To see what type of strategy can thrive in a variegated environment of more or less sophisticated strategies, I conducted a computer tournament for the Prisoner's Dilemma. The strategies were submitted by game theorists in economics, sociology, political science, and mathematics (Axelrod 1980a). The fourteen entries and a totally random strategy were paired with each other in a round robin tournament. Some of the strategies were quite intricate. An example is one that on each move models the behavior of the other player as a Markov process, and then uses Bayesian inference to select what seems the best choice for the long run. However, the result of the tournament was that the highest average score was attained by the simplest of all strategies, TIT FOR TAT. This strategy is simply one of cooperating on the first move and then doing whatever the other player did on the preceding move. Thus TIT FOR TAT is a strategy of cooperation based upon reciprocity.

The results of the first round were circulated and entries for a second round were solicited. This time there were sixty-two entries from six countries (Axelrod 1980b). Most of the contestants were computer hobbyists, but there were also professors of evolutionary biology, physics, and computer science, as well as the five disciplines represented in the first round. TIT FOR TAT was again submitted by the winner of the first round, Anatol Rapoport. It won again.

The second round of the computer tournament provides a rich environment in which to test the evolution of behavior. It turns out that just eight of the entries can be used to account for how well a given rule did with the entire set. These eight rules can be thought of as representatives of the full set in the sense that the scores a given rule gets with them can be used to predict the average score the rule gets over the full set. In fact,

98 percent of the variance in the tournament scores is explained by knowing a rule's performance with these eight representatives. So these representative strategies can be used as a complex environment in which to evaluate an evolutionary simulation. What is needed next is a way of representing the genetic material of a population so that the evolutionary process can be studied in detail.

The Genetic Algorithm

The inspiration for how to conduct simulation experiments of genetics and evolution comes from an artificial intelligence procedure developed by computer scientist John Holland and called the genetic algorithm (Holland 1975; Holland 1980; Goldberg 1989). For an excellent introduction to the genetic algorithm, see Holland (1992) and Riolo (1992). The idea is based on the way in which a chromosome serves a dual purpose: it provides both a representation of what the organism will become, and also the actual material that can be transformed to yield new genetic material for the next generation.

Before going into details, it may help to give a brief overview of how the genetic algorithm works. The first step is to specify a way of representing each allowable strategy as a string of genes on a chromosome that can undergo genetic transformations, such as mutation. Then the initial population is constructed from the allowable set (perhaps by simply picking at random). In each generation, the effectiveness of each individual in the population is determined by running the individual in the current strategic environment. Finally, the relatively successful strategies are used to produce offspring that resemble the parents. Pairs of successful offspring are selected to mate and produce the offspring for the next generation. Each offspring draws part of its genetic material from one parent and part from another. Moreover, completely new material is occasionally introduced through mutation. After many generations of selection for relatively successful strategies, the result might well be a population that is substantially more successful in the given strategic environment than the original population.

To explain how the genetic algorithm can work in a game context, consider the strategies available for playing the iterated Prisoner's Dilemma. To be more specific, consider the set of strategies that are deterministic and use the outcomes of the three previous moves to make a choice in the current move. Since there are four possible outcomes for each move, there are $4 \times 4 \times 4 = 64$ different histories of the three previous moves. Therefore, to determine its choice of cooperation or defection, a strategy would only need to determine what to do in each of the

situations that could arise. This could be specified by a list of sixty-four
C's and D's (C for cooperation and D for defection). For example, one of
these sixty-four genes indicates whether the individual cooperates or defects when in a rut of three mutual defections. Other parts of the chromosome would cover all the other situations that could arise.

To get the strategy started at the beginning of the game, it is also necessary to specify its initial premises about the three hypothetical moves that
preceded the start of the game. To do this requires six more genes, making a total of seventy loci on the chromosome.[2] This string of seventy C's
and D's would specify what the individual would do in every possible
circumstance and would therefore completely define a particular strategy.
The string of seventy genes would also serve as the individual's chromosome for use in reproduction and mutation.

There is a huge number of strategies that can be represented in this
way. In fact, the number is 2 to the 70th power, which is about 10 to the
21st power.[3] An exhaustive search for good strategies in this huge collection of strategies is clearly out of the question. If a computer had examined these strategies at the rate of 100 per second since the beginning of
the universe, less than 1 percent would have been checked by now.

To find effective strategies in such a huge set, a very powerful technique
is needed. This is where Holland's "genetic algorithm" comes in. It was
originally inspired by biological genetics, but was adapted as a general
problem-solving technique. In the present context, it can be regarded as a
model of a "minimal genetics" that can be used to explore theoretical
aspects of evolution in rich environments. The outline of the simulation
program works in five stages. See Table 1–2.

1. An initial population is chosen. In the present context the initial
individuals can be represented by random strings of seventy C's and D's.

2. Each individual is run in the current environment to determine its
effectiveness. In the present context this means that each individual
player uses the strategy defined by its chromosome to play an iterated
Prisoner's Dilemma with other strategies, and the individual's score is its
average over all the games it plays.[4]

3. The relatively successful individuals are selected to have more offspring. The method used is to give an average individual one mating, and

---

[2] The six premise genes encode the presumed C or D choices made by the individual and
the other player in each of the three moves before the interaction actually begins.

[3] Some of these chromosomes give rise to equivalent strategies because certain genes
might code for histories that could not arise, given how loci are set. This does not necessarily make the search process any easier, however.

[4] The score is actually a weighted average of its scores with the eight representative rules,
the weights having been chosen to give the best representation of the entire set of strategies
in the second round of the tournament.

TABLE 1-2
The Basic Simulation

I. Set up initial population with random chromosomes
II. For each of 50 generations
  A. For each of 20 individuals
    1. For each of the 8 representatives
      a) Use premise part of the chromosome as individual's assumption about the three previous moves
      b) For each of 151 moves
        (1) Make the individual's choice of cooperate (C) or defect (D) based upon the gene that encodes what to do given the three previous moves
        (2) Make the representative's choice of C or D based upon its own strategy applied to the history of the game so far
        (3) Update the individual's score based upon the outcome of this move (add 3 points if both cooperated, add 5 points if the representative cooperated and the individual defected, etc.)
  B. Reproduce the next generation
    1. For each individual assign the likely number of matings based upon the scaling function (1 for an average score, 2 for a score one standard deviation above average, etc.)
    2. For each of 10 matings construct two offspring from the two selected parents using crossover and mutation

to give two matings to an individual who is one standard deviation more effective than the average. An individual who is one standard deviation below the population average would then get no matings.

4. The successful individuals are then randomly paired off to produce two offspring per mating. For convenience, a constant population size is maintained. The strategy of an offspring is determined from the strategies of the two parents. This is done by using two genetic operators: crossover and mutation.

a. Crossover is a way of constructing the chromosomes of the two offspring from the chromosomes of two parents. It can be illustrated by an example of two parents, one of whom has seventy C's in its chromosome (indicating that it will cooperate in each possible situation that can arise), and the other of whom has seventy D's in its chromosome (indicating that it will always defect). Crossover selects one or more places to break the parents' chromosomes in order to construct two offspring each of whom has some genetic material from both parents. In the example, if a single break occurs after the third gene, then one offspring will have three C's followed by sixty-seven D's, while the other offspring will have three D's followed by sixty-seven C's.

b. Mutation in the offspring occurs by randomly changing a very small proportion of the *C*'s to *D*'s or vice versa.

5. This gives a new population. This new population will display patterns of behavior that are more like those of the successful individuals of the previous generation, and less like those of the unsuccessful ones. With each new generation, the individuals with relatively high scores will be more likely to pass on parts of their strategies, whereas the relatively unsuccessful individuals will be less likely to have any parts of their strategies passed on.

Simulation Results

The computer simulations were done using a population size of twenty individuals per generation. Levels of crossover and mutation were chosen averaging one crossover and one-half mutation per chromosome per generation. Each game consisted of 151 moves, the average game length used in the tournament. With each of the twenty individuals meeting eight representatives, this made for about 24,000 moves per generation. A run consisted of fifty generations. Forty runs were conducted under identical conditions to allow an assessment of the variability of the results.

The results are quite remarkable: from a strictly random start, the genetic algorithm evolved populations whose median member was just as successful as the best rule in the tournament, TIT FOR TAT. Most of the strategies that evolved in the simulation actually resemble TIT FOR TAT, having many of the properties that make TIT FOR TAT so successful. For example, five behavioral alleles in the chromosomes evolved in the vast majority of the individuals to give them behavioral patterns that were adaptive in this environment and mirrored what TIT FOR TAT would do in similar circumstances. These patterns are:

1. Don't rock the boat: continue to cooperate after three mutual cooperations (which can be abbreviated as *C* after *RRR*).
2. Be provocable: defect when the other player defects out of the blue (*D* after receiving *RRS*).
3. Accept an apology: continue to cooperate after cooperation has been restored (*C* after *TSR*).
4. Forget: cooperate when mutual cooperation has been restored after an exploitation (*C* after *SRR*).
5. Accept a rut: defect after three mutual defections (*D* after *PPP*).

The evolved rules behave with specific representatives in much the same way as TIT FOR TAT does. They did about as well as TIT FOR TAT did with each of the eight representatives. Just as TIT FOR TAT did, most of the evolved rules did well by achieving almost complete mutual cooperation with seven of the eight representatives. Like TIT FOR TAT, most of the evolved rules do poorly only with one representative, called ADJUSTER, that adjusts its rate of defection to try to exploit the other player. In all, 95 percent of the time the evolved rules make the same choice as TIT FOR TAT would make in the same situation.

Although most of the runs evolve populations whose rules are very similar to TIT FOR TAT, in eleven of the forty runs, the median rule actually does substantially better than TIT FOR TAT.[5] In these eleven runs, the populations evolved strategies that manage to exploit one of the eight representatives at the cost of achieving somewhat less cooperation with two others. But the net effect is a gain in effectiveness.

This is a remarkable achievement because to be able to get this added effectiveness, a rule must be able to do three things. First, it must be able to discriminate between one representative and another based upon only the behavior the other player shows spontaneously or is provoked into showing. Second, it must be able to adjust its own behavior to exploit a representative that is identified as an exploitable player. Third, and perhaps most difficult, it must be able to achieve this discrimination and exploitation without getting into too much trouble with the other representatives. This is something that none of the rules originally submitted to the tournament were able to do.

These very effective rules evolved by breaking the most important advice developed in the computer tournament, namely, to be "nice," that is, never to be the first to defect. These highly effective rules always defect on the very first move, and sometimes on the second move as well, and use the choices of the other player to discriminate what should be done next. The highly effective rules then had responses that allowed them to "apologize" and get to mutual cooperation with most of the unexploitable representatives, and different responses that allowed them to exploit a representative that was exploitable.

Although these rules are highly effective, it would not accurate to say that they are better than TIT FOR TAT. Although they are better in the particular environment consisting of fixed proportions of the eight representatives of the second round of the computer tournament, they are probably not very robust in other environments. Moreover, in an ecological simulation, these rules would be destroying the basis of their own success as the exploited representative would become a smaller and smaller part of the environment (Axelrod 1984, 49–52, 203–5). Al-

---

[5] The criterion for being substantially better than TIT FOR TAT is a median score of 450 points, which compares to TIT FOR TAT's weighted score of 428 with these eight representatives.

though the genetic algorithm was sometimes able to evolve rules that are more effective than any entry in the tournament, the algorithm was only able to do so by trying many individuals in many generations against a fixed environment. In sum, the genetic algorithm is very good at what actual evolution does so well: developing highly specialized adaptations to specific environmental settings.

In the evolution of these highly effective strategies, the computer simulation employed sexual reproduction, where two parents contributed genetic material to each offspring. To see what would happen with asexual reproduction, forty additional runs were conducted in which only one parent contributed genetic material to each offspring. In these runs, the populations still evolved toward rules that did about as well as TIT FOR TAT in most cases. However, the asexual runs were only half as likely to evolve populations in which the median member was substantially more effective than TIT FOR TAT.[6]

So far, the simulations have dealt with populations evolving in the context of a constant environment. What would happen if the environment also changed? To examine this situation, another simulation experiment with sexual reproduction was conducted in which the environment consisted of the evolving population itself. In this experiment each individual plays the iterated Prisoner's Dilemma with each member of the population including its own twin rather than with the eight representatives. At any given time, the environment can be quite complex. For an individual to do well requires that its strategy achieve a high average effectiveness with all twenty strategies that are present in the population. Thus, as the more effective rules have more offspring, the environment itself changes. In this case, adaptation must be done in the face of a moving target. Moreover, the selection process is frequency dependent, meaning that the effectiveness of a strategy depends upon what strategies are being used by all the members of the population.

The results of the ten runs conducted in this manner display a very interesting pattern. For a typical run, see Figure 1–1. From a random start, the population evolves away from whatever cooperation was initially displayed. The less cooperative rules do better than the more cooperative rules because at first there are few other players who are responsive—and when the other player is unresponsive, the most effective thing for an individual to do is simply defect. This decreased cooperation in turn causes everyone to get lower scores as mutual defection becomes more and more common. However, after about ten or twenty

---

[6] This happened in five of the forty runs with asexual reproduction compared to eleven of the forty runs with sexual reproduction. This difference is significant at the .05 level using the one tailed chi-squared test.

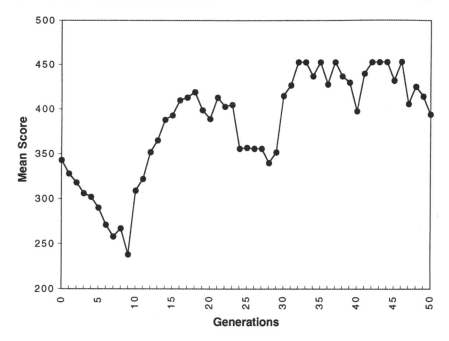

Figure 1-1. Prisoner's Dilemma in an Evolving Environment

generations the trend starts to reverse. Some players evolve a pattern of reciprocating what cooperation they find, and these reciprocating players tend to do well because they can do very well with others who reciprocate without being exploited for very long by those who just defect. The average scores of the population then start to increase as cooperation based upon reciprocity becomes better and better established. So the evolving social environment led to a pattern of decreased cooperation and decreased effectiveness, followed by a complete reversal based upon an evolved ability to discriminate between those who will reciprocate cooperation and those who will not. As the reciprocators do well, they spread in the population, resulting in more and more cooperation and greater and greater effectiveness.

Conclusions

1. The genetic algorithm is a highly effective method of searching for effective strategies in a huge space of possibilities. Following Sewall Wright (1977, 452–54), the problem for evolution can be conceptualized as a search for relatively high points in a multidimensional field of gene

combinations, where height corresponds to fitness. When the field has many local optima, the search becomes quite difficult. When the number of dimensions in the field becomes great, the search is even more difficult. What the computer simulations demonstrate is that the minimal system of the genetic algorithm is a highly efficient method for searching such a complex multidimensional space. The first experiment shows that even with a seventy-dimensional field of genes, quite effective strategies can be found within fifty generations. Sometimes the genetic algorithm found combinations of genes that violate the previously accepted mode of operation (not being the first to defect) to achieve even greater effectiveness than had been thought possible.

2. Sexual reproduction does indeed help the search process. This was demonstrated by the much increased chance of achieving highly effective populations in the sexual experiment compared to the asexual experiment.[7]

3. Some aspects of evolution are arbitrary. In natural settings, one might observe that a population has little variability in a specific gene. In other words one of the alleles for that gene has become fixed throughout the population. One might be tempted to assume from this that the allele is more adaptive than any alternative allele. However, this may not be the case. The simulation of evolution allows an exploration of this possibility by allowing repetitions of the same conditions to see just how much variability there is in the outcomes. In fact, the simulations show two reasons why convergence in a population may actually be arbitrary.

a. Genes that do not have much effect on the fitness of the individual may become fixed in a population because they "hitchhike" on other genes that do (Maynard Smith and Haigh 1974). For example, in the simulations some sequences of three moves may very rarely occur, so what the corresponding genes dictate in these situations may not matter very much. However, if the entire population are descendants of just a few individuals, then these irrelevant genes may be fixed to the values that their ancestors happened to share. Repeated runs of a simulation allow one to notice that some genes become fixed in one population but not another, or that they become fixed in different ways in different populations.

b. In some cases, some parts of the chromosome are arbitrary in

---

[7] In biology, sexual reproduction comes at the cost of reduced fecundity. Thus, if males provide little or no aid to offspring, a high (up to two-fold) average extra fitness has to emerge as a property of sexual reproduction if sex is to be stable. The advantage must presumably come from recombination but has been hard to identify in biology. A simulation model has demonstrated that the advantage may well lie in the necessity to recombine defenses to defeat numerous parasites (Hamilton et al. 1990). Unlike biology, in artificial intelligence applications, the added (computational) cost of sexuality is small.

content, but what is not arbitrary is that they be held constant. By being fixed, other parts of the chromosome can adapt to them. For example, the simulations of the individual chromosomes had six genes devoted to coding for the premises about the three moves that preceded the first move in the game. When the environment was the eight representatives, the populations in different runs of the simulation developed different premises. Within each run, however, the populations were usually very consistent about the premises: the six premise genes had become fixed. Moreover, within each population these genes usually became fixed quite early. It is interesting that different populations evolved quite different premises. What was important for the evolutionary process was to fix the premise about which history is assumed at the start, so that the other parts of the chromosome could adapt on the basis of a given premise.

4. There is a tradeoff between the gains to be made from flexibility and the gains to be made from commitment and specialization (March 1991). Flexibility might help in the long run, but in an evolutionary system, the individuals also have to survive in the short run if they are to reproduce. This feature of evolution arises at several levels.

a. As the simulations have shown, the premises became fixed quite early. This meant a commitment to which parts of the chromosome would be consulted in the first few moves, and this in turn meant giving up flexibility as more and more of the chromosome evolved on the basis of what had been fixed. This in turn meant that it would be difficult for a population to switch to a different premise. Thus, flexibility was given up so that the advantages of commitment could be reaped.

b. There is also a tradeoff between short- and long-term gains in the way selection was done in the simulation experiments. In any given generation there would typically be some individuals that did much better than the average, and some that did only a little better than the average. In the short run, the way to maximize the expected performance of the next generation would be to have virtually all of the offspring come from the very best individuals in the present generation. But this would imply a rapid reduction in the genetic variability of the population, and a consequent slowing of the evolutionary process later on. If the moderately successful were also given a chance to have some offspring, this would help the long-term prospects of the population at the cost of optimizing in the short run. Thus, there is an inherent tradeoff between exploitation and exploration, that is, between exploiting what already works best and exploring possibilities that might eventually evolve into something even better (Holland 1975, 160).

5. Evolutionary commitments can be irreversible. For example, in most of the populations facing the environment of the eight representatives, the individuals evolved strategies that are very similar to TIT FOR

TAT. Because TIT FOR TAT had done best in the computer tournament itself, I did not think that it would be possible to do much better with an evolutionary process. But as noted earlier, in about a quarter of the simulation runs with sexual reproduction, the population did indeed evolve substantially better strategies—strategies that were quite different from TIT FOR TAT. These highly effective strategies defected on the very first move, and often on the second move as well, in order to get information to determine whether the other player was the type that could be exploited or not. The more common populations of strategies cooperated from the beginning and employed reciprocity in a manner akin to TIT FOR TAT. Although these more common strategies might easily mutate to try a defection at the start of the game, such behavior would be extremely costly unless the individual already had effective ways of using the information that resulted. Moreover, once the population had evolved to be about as effective as TIT FOR TAT, such a mutation would have to be quite effective in order to survive long enough to be perfected. Thus, once the population takes a specific route (in this case, toward reciprocity) it can easily become trapped in a local maxima. Indeed, only the fact that enough simulation runs were conducted led to the discovery that in this particular environment reciprocity was only a local maxima, and that something better was in fact possible. In a field situation, such a discovery might not be possible because there might be essentially just one gene pool.

Topics Amenable to Simulation

The methodology for the genetic simulation developed in this paper can be used to explore learning processes in game-theoretic settings. Here is a list of issues that can be studied with genetic simulations, inspired by analogs to evolutionary biology:

1. *Mutation.* The simulation approach developed here suggests that there is an inherent tradeoff for a gene pool between exploration of possibilities (best done with a high mutation rate) and exploitation of the possibilities already contained in the current gene pool (best done with a low mutation rate). This in turn suggests the advantage of having mutation rates adapt to the rate of change in the environment.[8]

2. *Crossover.* In sexual reproduction, crossover serves to give each offspring genetic material from both parents. Crossover rates that are too low would frequently give whole chromosomes of genetic material from a single parent to an offspring. But crossover rates that are too high

---

[8] I owe this suggestion to Michael D. Cohen.

would frequently split up coadapted sets of alleles that are on the same chromosome. Perhaps the existence of a multiplicity of chromosomes (rather than one long chromosome) is more than a mechanical convenience, but is an adaptation to the need for low crossover rates without the disadvantage of having each offspring being likely to get genetic material from only one parent.

3. *Inversion.* Inversion changes the order of the genes in a chromosome. It can bring coadapted sets of alleles closer together on the chromosome so that they will be split apart by crossover less often. How is the ideal rate of inversion determined?

4. *Coding principles.* Biological chromosomes are known to contain material that does not directly code for proteins, but performs other roles such as marking the boundaries of genes, or perhaps serves no function at all. Genetic material may also appear in highly redundant form in the chromosome. Genetic simulation experiments might shed new light on the theoretical implications of various coding schemes and their possible role in error reduction and regulation. Or they might show how some genetic material can exist as "free riders."

5. *Dominant and recessive genes.* Mendel's famous experiments demonstrate that dominant and recessive alleles serve to overcome Darwin's concern that blending of parental characteristics would eliminate the variability of a population. Genetic simulation can be used to explore the implications of these and other genetic mechanisms for the maintenance of population variability in the face of selection pressure for local optimality. In particular, it should be possible to explore just which types of phenotypic features are best coded in terms of dominant and recessive genes, and which are best coded in other systems of genetic expression.

6. *Gradual versus punctuated evolution.* Genetic simulation experiments might also shed light on the contemporary debate about whether evolution proceeds in gradual steps or tends to move in fits and starts. This type of work might require simulations of tens of thousands of generations, but runs of such length are feasible.

7. *Population viscosity.* Obstacles to random mating may exist due to geographic or other forces tending to favor subdivisions of the population. Some computer modeling has already been done for models of this type (Boorman and Levitt 1980, 78–87; Tanese 1989), revealing clues about the qualitative features of the spread of a social trait based upon frequency-dependent selection.

8. *Speciation and ecological niches.* When distinct ecological niches exist, a single species tends to differentiate into two or more species to take advantage of the different opportunities offered by the different niches. In learning terms, differentiation into two or more species means that a new strategy is formed from ideas represented in only part of the

total population. Genetic simulation can explore this process by helping to specify the conditions under which the advantages of specialization outweigh the disadvantages of narrower mating opportunities and reduced ecological flexibility. The fundamental point is that thinking about genetics as a simulation problem gives a new perspective on the functioning of learning processes.

The genetic simulations provided in this essay are highly abstract systems. The populations are very small, and the number of generations is few. More significantly, the genetic process have only two operators, mutation and crossover. Compared to biological genetics, this is a highly simplified system. Nevertheless, the genetic algorithm displayed a remarkable ability to evolve sophisticated and effective strategies in a complex environment.

References

Axelrod, Robert. 1980a. "Effective Choice in the Prisoner's Dilemma." *Journal of Conflict Resolution* 24: 3–25.

_____. 1980b. "More Effective Choice in the Prisoner's Dilemma." *Journal of Conflict Resolution* 24: 379–403.

_____. 1984. *The Evolution of Cooperation.* New York: Basic Books.

Axelrod, Robert, and William D. Hamilton. 1981. "The Evolution of Cooperation." *Science* 211: 1390–96.

Binmore, Ken, and Larry Samuelson. 1990. "Evolutionary Stability in Repeated Games Played by Finite Automata." Center for Research on Economic and Social Theory, Working Paper 90-17, Department of Economics, University of Michigan, Ann Arbor, Mich.

Boorman, Scott A., and Paul R. Levitt. 1980. *The Genetics of Altruism.* New York: Academic Press.

Goldberg, D. E. 1983. *Computer-Aided Gas Pipeline Operation Using Genetic Algorithms and Machine Learning.* Ph.D. diss., University of Michigan (Civil Engineering).

_____. 1989. *Genetic Algorithms in Search, Optimization, and Machine Learning.* Reading, Mass.: Addison-Wesley.

Grefenstette, John J., ed. 1985. *Proceedings of an International Conference on Genetic Algorithms and Their Applications.* Pittsburgh, Penn.: The Robotics Institute of Carnegie-Mellon University.

Hamilton, William D. 1980. "Sex Versus Non-Sex Versus Parasite." *Oikos* 35: 282–90.

_____. 1982. "Heritable True Fitness and Bright Birds: A Role for Parasites." *Science* 218: 384–87.

Hamilton, William D., Robert Axelrod, and Reiko Tanese. 1990. "Sexual Reproduction as an Adaptation to Resist Parasites." *Proceedings of the National Academy of Sciences (USA)* 87: 3566–73.

Holland, John H. 1975. *Adaptation in Natural and Artificial Systems.* Ann Arbor: University of Michigan Press.

_____. 1980. "Adaptive Algorithms for Discovering and Using General Patterns in Growing Knowledge Bases." *International Journal of Policy Analysis and Information Systems* 4: 245–68.

_____. 1992. "Genetic Algorithms." *Scientific American* 267 (July): 66–72.

Lomborg, Bjorn. 1991. "An Evolution of Cooperation." Masters thesis, Institute of Political Science, University of Aarhus, Denmark.

March, James G. 1991. "Exploration and Exploitation in Organizational Learning." *Organizational Science* 2: 71–87.

Maynard Smith, J., and J. Haigh. 1974. "The Hitch-Hiking Effect of a Favorable Gene." *Genet. Res., Camb.* 23: 23–35.

Megiddo, Nimrod, and Avi Wigderson. 1986. "On Play by Means of Computing Machines." IBM Research Division, BJ 4984 (52161), Yorktown Heights, N.Y.

Miller, John. 1989. "The Coevolution of Automata in the Repeated Prisoner's Dilemma." Working Paper, 89–003, Santa Fe Institute, Santa Fe, N.M.

Riolo, Rick L. 1992. "Survival of the Fittest Bits." *Scientific American* 267 (July): 114–16.

Rubinstein, Ariel. 1986. "Finite Automata Play the Repeated Prisoner's Dilemma." *Journal of Economic Theory* 39: 83–96.

Tanese, Reiko. 1989. "Distributed Genetic Algorithms for Function Optimization." Ph.D. diss., University of Michigan (Computer Science and Engineering).

Wright, Sewall. 1977. *Evolution and the Genetics of Populations.* Vol. 4, *Experimental Results and Evolutionary Deductions.* Chicago: University of Chicago Press.

2

Coping with Noise

THE DANGER of people or nations misunderstanding each other's actions has been a long-term interest of mine. Ever since the Cuban Missile Crisis in 1962, I have been concerned that errors in perception or implementation could lead to serious conflict. As a child, I was deeply impressed with the fairy tale of a little boy who came across two dozing giants. He hit one of them on the head. This provoked a fight between the giants, and the little boy was able to use the distraction to get past them.

When I set up the computer tournaments for the Prisoner's Dilemma, I allowed for the possibility of random errors in a very simple way. I did this by informing all the entrants that one of the rules in the tournament would be a purely random strategy. Afterward, I realized that this form of randomization did not really deal with the problems of possible misunderstanding of the choice made by the other player or possible misimplementation of one's own intended choice. This was especially problematic because TIT FOR TAT is, in fact, quite sensitive to either kind of noise in the system. For example, if two players are using TIT FOR TAT and one of them makes a mistake, the echo of this mistake can go on indefinitely. In addition, if other mistakes are made, the two players eventually oscillate among all four combinations of choices and are never able to reestablish a sustained pattern of mutual cooperation (Downs et al. 1986).

In *The Evolution of Cooperation*, I suggested two ways of dealing with the echo effect. The first was to make the response to a defection somewhat less than the provocation. The second method was for the player who defected by accident to realize that the other's response need not call for yet another defection (Axelrod, 1984, 186–87). These two ideas have come to be called generosity and contrition.

In 1988, at the time of Gorbachev's very friendly overtures toward the West, I had a wonderful opportunity to see how American and Soviet defense analysts would play a Prisoner's Dilemma that included noise. At a U.S.-Soviet conference on interdependence, I invited two of the participants to play in front of the audience of social scientists. The Soviet player was Sergei Blagovolin, a specialist in nuclear strategy at the Institute of World Economy and International Relations. The American player was Catherine Kelleher, a professor and former member of the White House staff specializing in international security affairs. I told them that each of their choices would have a one-in-six chance of being misimplemented. Both players would know after the fact whether their *own* choice had been misimplemented, but they would never know whether a particular move by the other side had been the intended choice or not. The players did not know exactly how long the game would last.

The American started off with a deliberate defection, and defected a total of six times in nine moves. The Soviet player was more cooperative, defecting only four times. In the debriefing afterwards, he attributed most of the American defections to misimplementation. When asked why, the Soviet player said that he expected that Americans were fairly cooperative and that women in particular would be cooperative. The American, on the other hand, explained that she expected him to think this way. Therefore she deliberately defected, correctly expecting that she would be forgiven due to a very generous Soviet policy.[1] The story illustrates an important moral: noise calls for forgiveness, but too much forgiveness invites exploitation (Axelrod and Dion 1988).

I did not do any systematic work on how to cope with noise until I saw an article with the title "A Strategy of Win-Stay, Lose-Shift That Outperforms Tit-for-Tat in the Prisoner's Dilemma Game" (Nowak and Sigmund 1993). The article reported a simulation study that included noise and found that under the particular conditions of the study,[2] the most successful strategy is one that repeats its previous choice only when it gets one of the two highest payoffs, namely, the temptation score for exploiting the other player or the reward for mutual cooperation. Unlike TIT FOR TAT, it defects after the other player suffers an exploitation, and it cooperates after a mutual defection. My reaction to this study was to feel a little protective of TIT FOR TAT. I was therefore very curious to see how the new strategy would do in a noisy version of the variegated environment of my computer tournament.

Fortunately, at this time a postdoctoral fellow, Wu Jianzhong, was available to help. Dr. Wu is a game theorist from the Institute of Automation in

---

[1] In the game, the Soviet defected on moves 2, 3, 7, and 8. The American defected on moves 1, 3, 4, 5, 8, and 9. The second move by the Soviet was a misimplementation, and the sixth and ninth American moves were misimplementations. Using the standard payoffs, this gave the Soviet player fifteen points and the American twenty-five points. Had they both been playing TIT FOR TAT and been contrite after their own misimplementations, the Soviet player would have defected only on moves 2 and 7; the American player only on moves 3, 6, and 9. The score would have been 22 and 27 respectively. Both would have done better with contrition than either did with their combination of exploitation and excessive forgiveness.

[2] These conditions include the range of permitted strategies and manner of calculating success, as well as the presence of noise. The permitted strategies base their choice only on the outcome of the previous move. The strategies are defined in terms of the conditional probabilities to cooperate given the four possible outcomes of the previous move. The payoffs are calculated from long-term averages without discounting.

Beijing who came to work with me at Michigan. Together we reimplemented the sixty-three rules of the second round of the computer tournament on a Macintosh. When originally run in 1978, the round-robin tournament pushed the capabilities of a large mainframe computer. In 1994, the equivalent amount of computation was an easy job on a personal computer. We found that adding either generosity or contrition to TIT FOR TAT is an effective way of coping with noise. The Win-Stay, Lose-Shift strategy did not perform as well in this variegated environment.

The source code and documentation for this and most of the other programs used in this volume are available on the Internet.[3] The source code for this chapter includes all of the original tournament submissions as well as the new strategies.

After our study was published, new theoretical work by Kraines and Kraines (1995) placed the Win-Stay, Lose-Shift strategy in a broader context of learning rules. Whereas Win-Stay, Lose-Shift updates its choice based on only the preceding outcome, the broader class of learning rules called Pavlov has a parameter for how fast or slowly the rule adjusts its probabilistic behavior based on recent moves.[4] Kraines and Kraines point out that the Win-Shift, Lose-Stay strategy dates back at least to the classic book on the Prisoner's Dilemma by Rapoport and Chammah (1965), where it was called Simpleton because of its many shortcomings. The jury is still out on the question of how robust any of the broader class of Pavlov learning rules might be.

References

Axelrod, Robert. 1984. *The Evolution of Cooperation*. New York: Basic Books.
Axelrod, Robert, and Douglas Dion, 1988. "The Further Evolution of Cooperation." *Science* 242 (9 Dec.): 1385–90.
Downs, George W., David M. Rocke, and Randolph M. Siverson. 1986. "Arms Races and Cooperation." In *Cooperation Under Anarchy*, ed. Kenneth A. Oye, Princeton, N.J.: Princeton University Press.
Kraines, David, and Vivian Kraines. 1995. "Evolution of Learning Among Pavlov Strategies in a Competitive Environment with Noise," *Journal of Conflict Resolution* 39: 439–66.
Nowak, Martin, and Karl Sigmund. 1993. "A Strategy of Win-Shift, Lose-Stay That Outperforms Tit-for-Tat in the Prisoner's Dilemma Game." *Nature* 364: 56–58.
Rapoport, Anatol, and Albert W. Chammah. 1965. *Prisoner's Dilemma*. Ann Arbor, Mich.: University of Michigan Press.

[3] http://pscs.physics.lsa.umich.edu/Software/ComplexCoop.html
[4] In our article, Wu and I use Pavlov as shorthand for Win-Stay, Lose-Shift.

Coping With Noise

HOW TO COPE WITH NOISE IN THE ITERATED PRISONER'S DILEMMA

JIANZHONG WU AND ROBERT AXELROD

Reprinted from Jianzhong Wu and Robert Axelrod, "How to Cope with Noise in the Iterated Prisoner's Dilemma," *Journal of Conflict Resolution* 39, no. 1 (Mar. 1995): 183–89. Reprinted by permission of Sage Publications, Inc.

Abstract:

Noise, in the form of random errors in implementing a choice, is a common problem in real-world interactions. Recent research has identified three approaches to coping with noise: adding generosity to a reciprocating strategy; adding contrition to a reciprocating strategy; and using an entirely different strategy, Pavlov, based on switching choice whenever the previous payoff was low. Tournament studies, ecological simulation, and theoretical analysis demonstrate: (1) A generous version of TIT FOR TAT is a highly effective strategy when the players it meets have not adapted to noise; (2) If the other players *have* adapted to noise, a contrite version of TIT FOR TAT is even more effective at quickly restoring mutual cooperation without the risk of exploitation; (3) Pavlov is not robust.

An important feature of interactions in the real world is that choices cannot be implemented without error. Because the other player does not necessarily know whether a given action is an error or a deliberate choice, a single error can lead to significant complications. For example, on September 1, 1983, a South Korean airliner mistakenly flew over the Soviet Union (Hersh 1989). It was shot down by the Soviets, killing all 269 people aboard. The Americans and Soviets echoed their anger at each other in a short but sharp escalation of Cold War tensions (Goldstein 1991, 202).

The effects of error have been treated under the rubric of "noise." The best way to cope with noise has become a vital research question in game theory, especially in the context of the iterated Prisoner's Dilemma.[1] Clearly, when noise is introduced, some unintended defections will occur.

[1] Examples of recent theoretical and simulation studies of the noisy Prisoner's Dilemma and related games are Bendor et al. (1991), Bendor (1993), Boyd (1989), Fudenberg and Maskin (1990), Godfray (1992), Kollock (1993), Lindgren (1991), Nowak and Sigmund (1992, 1993), and Young and Foster (1991). For a review of earlier work, see Axelrod and Dion (1988).

This can undercut the effectiveness of simple reciprocating strategies. For example, Molander (1985) has shown that in the presence of any amount of noise, two TIT FOR TAT (TFT) players will in the long run average the same payoffs as two interacting RANDOM players.

Three different approaches to coping with noise have been proposed.

1. *Generosity.* Allowing some percentage of the other player's defections to go unpunished has been widely advocated as a good way to cope with noise (Molander 1985; May 1987; Axelrod and Dion 1988; Bendor et al. 1991; Godfray 1992; Nowak and Sigmund 1992). For example, a generous version of TFT, called GTFT, cooperates 10 percent of the time that it would otherwise defect. This prevents a single error from echoing indefinitely.

2. *Contrition.* A reciprocating strategy such as TFT can be modified to avoid responding to the other player's defection after its own unintended defection. This allows a quick way to recover from error. It is based upon the idea that one should not be provoked by the other player's response to one's own unintended defection (Sugden 1986, 110; Boyd 1989). The strategy called Contrite TFT (CTFT) has three states: "contrite," "content," and "provoked." It begins in content with cooperation and stays there unless there is a unilateral defection. If it was the victim while content, it becomes provoked and defects until a cooperation from the other player causes it to become content. If it was the defector while content, it becomes contrite and cooperates. When contrite, it becomes content only after it has successfully cooperated.

3. *Win-Stay, Lose-Shift.* A completely different strategy can be used, one based on the principle that if the most recent payoff was high, the same choice would be repeated, but otherwise the choice would be changed. This strategy emerged from a simulated evolutionary process that included noise, but allowed strategies with memory of only the preceding move (Nowak and Sigmund 1993). Called Pavlov, it cooperates unless on the previous move it was a sucker (i.e., it cooperated but the other defected) or the other player was a sucker.

For completeness, we also analyze a fourth strategy, a generous version of Pavlov, called GPavlov. This strategy acts like Pavlov, but cooperates 10 percent of the time when it would otherwise defect.

The Tournament with Noise

The basis for our analysis is the environment of the sixty-three rules of the second round of the computer tournament for the Prisoner's Dilemma (Axelrod 1984). These strategies provide a heterogeneous environment embodying a wide variety of ideas designed for doing well in the Prisoner's

Dilemma game. The lengths of interactions vary, averaging 151 moves. To this environment we add 1 percent noise, meaning that for each intended choice there is a 1 percent chance that the opposite choice will actually be implemented. Although these rules were designed without regard to noise, they can still be used to provide a useful setting for evaluating how new strategies will fare in a heterogeneous noisy environment.

The average score of each new rule when paired with the sixty-three rules of the tournament environment shows how well or poorly each does in a noisy environment.[2] The highest score is attained by GTFT, which actually does better than any of the sixty-three rules submitted. CTFT also does very well, better than all but five of the sixty-three rules. Pavlov does poorly, ranking below fifty-five of the sixty-three rules. Adding generosity to Pavlov helps only a little: GPavlov ranks below forty-eight of the sixty-three rules.

To investigate the effects of different levels of noise, the four new rules were added to the sixty-three original rules, and the expanded tournament was run at various levels of noise from 0.1 percent to 10 percent. Figure 2-1 shows the scores of the four new rules as a function of the noise level. The results show that at all levels of noise, GTFT and CTFT do well, whereas Pavlov and GPavlov do not. At the lower levels, GTFT is a little better than CTFT, but when noise is greater than 1 percent, CTFT is slightly better.

An Ecological Simulation

A more powerful test is to take into account that over time, rules that are unsuccessful in the noisy environment are less likely than are relatively successful rules to be used again. A good way to do this is with an ecological analysis (Axelrod 1984, 48ff). In an ecological analysis, the fraction of the population represented by a given rule in the next "generation" of the tournament will be proportional to that rule's tournament score in the previous generation. When this process is repeated over many generations, the proportion of the various rules changes, and the environment faced by each rule tends to emphasize those rules that have been doing relatively well in the noisy setting. The ecological simulation shows what happens when the rules that are ineffective in dealing with noise become a smaller part of the population and those that are effective at dealing with noise become a larger proportion of the population.

The process begins with equal proportions of sixty-seven rules: the sixty-three original rules and the four new ones. The noise level is set at 1

---

[2] To assure stability of these results, the scores are averaged over twenty replications of the entire tournament.

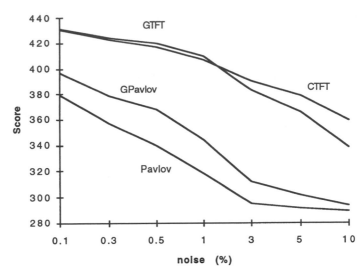

Figure 2-1. Performance as a Function of Noise

percent. The proportion of each rule is updated for 2,000 generations. Figure 2-2 shows the performance over time of the six rules that did best at the end of this process. R8, the rule that ranked eighth in the original tournament, did quite well over the first few hundred generations, but then slowly declined as the process continued to deemphasize rules that were doing poorly in the noisy environment. By generation 1,000, CTFT was the leader. It continued to grow, eventually becoming 97 percent of the population at generation 2,000. GTFT had some early success, but then faded. Both versions of Pavlov declined to less than one part in a million as early as the hundredth generation. The clear winner in this ecological simulation with noise was CTFT.

Strategic Analysis

Both Pavlov and the contrite version of TIT FOR TAT have the desirable property that when playing with their twin they can quickly recover from an isolated error. If one of two Pavlov players defects due to an isolated error, both will defect on the next move, and then both will cooperate on the following move. If one of two CTFT players defects, the defecting player will contritely cooperate on the next move and the other player will defect, and then both will be content to cooperate on the following move. Unfortunately for a player using Pavlov, its willingness to cooperate after a mutual defection can give the other player an incentive to

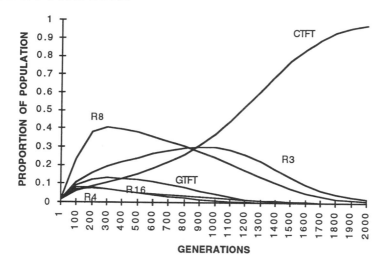

Figure 2-2. Ecological Simulation. *Note:* The strategies are the sixty-three original rules plus GTFT, CTFT, Pavlov and GPavlov. R3 is the rule that ranked third in original tournament, R4 is the rule that ranked fourth, etc. The results are shown for the top six rules in the 2,000th generation. The noise level is 1 percent.

simply defect all the time.[3] The tournament and the ecological analysis both show that although Pavlov may do well with its own twin, its success is not robust.

Generosity is effective at stopping the continuing echo of a single error, whether the error was one's own or the other player's. The level of generosity determines how quickly an error can be corrected and cooperation restored. The problem is that generosity requires a tradeoff between the speed of error correction and the risk of exploitation (Axelrod and Dion 1988).

Contrition is effective at correcting one's own error, but not the error of the other player. For example, if CTFT is playing TFT and the TFT player defects by accident, the echo will continue until another error occurs. Thus, in the original environment of sixty-three rules that were not designed to deal with noise, contrition was slightly less effective than generosity when noise was 1 percent or less. On the other hand, the ecological simulation showed that contrition is very effective as the environment becomes dominated by rules that are successful in the noisy environment. As the population becomes adapted to noise, contrition

[3] It pays to always defect when playing with Pavlov at low levels of noise if alternating T and P is better than always getting R. With standard notation, this is true when $T + wP > R + wR$ or $w < (T - R)/(R - P)$. Thus, with the standard payoffs of $T = 5, R = 3, P = 1, S = 0$, and any $w < 1$, it pays to always defect when playing with Pavlov.

becomes more and more effective. In a population adapted to noise, correcting one's own errors is sufficient because the players one meets are also likely to be good at correcting their own errors.

Conclusion

In the presence of noise, reciprocity still works, provided that it is accompanied by either generosity (some chance of cooperating when one would otherwise defect) or contrition (cooperating after the other player defects in response to one's own defection). Pavlov, a strategy based upon changing one's own choice after a poor outcome, is not robust.

Generosity can correct an error by either player, but contrition can only correct one's own error. Thus, when the population of strategies one is likely to meet has not adapted to the presence of noise, a strategy like Generous TIT FOR TAT is likely to be effective. On the other hand, if the strategies of the other players one is likely to meet have already adapted to noise, then a strategy like Contrite TIT FOR TAT is likely to be even more effective because it can correct its own errors and restore mutual cooperation almost immediately.

References

Axelrod, R. 1984. *The Evolution of Cooperation*. New York: Basic Books.

Axelrod, R., and D. Dion. 1988. "The Further Evolution of Cooperation." *Science* 242: 1385–90.

Bendor, J. 1993. "Uncertainty and the Evolution of Cooperation." *Journal of Conflict Resolution* 37: 709–34.

Bendor, J., R. M. Kramer, and S. Stout. 1991. "When in Doubt: Cooperation in a Noisy Prisoner's Dilemma." *Journal of Conflict Resolution* 35: 691–719.

Boyd, R. 1989. "Mistakes Allow Evolutionary Stability in the Repeated Prisoner's Dilemma." *Journal of Theoretical Biology* 136: 47–56.

Fudenberg, D., and E. Maskin. 1990. "Evolution and Cooperation in Noisy Repeated Games." *American Economic Review* 80: 274–79.

Godfray, H. C. J. 1992. "The Evolution of Forgiveness." *Nature* 355: 206–7.

Goldstein, Joshua. 1991. "Reciprocity in Superpower Relations: An Empirical Analysis." *International Studies Quarterly* 35: 195–209.

Hersh, Seymour M. 1986. *"The Target is Destroyed"*. New York: Random House.

Kollock, P. 1993. "An Eye for an Eye Leaves Everyone Blind: Cooperation and Accounting Systems." *American Sociological Review* 58: 768–86.

Lindgren, K. 1991. "Evolutionary Phenomena in Simple Dynamics." In *Artificial Life II: Proceedings of the Workshop on Artificial Life*, ed. C. Langton et al., 295–312. Redwood City, Calif.: Addison-Wesley.

May, R. M. 1987. "More Evolution of Cooperation." *Nature* 327: 15–17.

Milinski, M. 1993. "Cooperation Wins and Stays." *Nature* 364: 12–13.

Molander, P. 1985. "The Optimal Level of Generosity in a Selfish, Uncertain Environment." *Journal of Conflict Resolution* 29: 611–18.

Nowak, M., and K. Sigmund. 1992. "Tit for Tat in Heterogeneous Populations." *Nature* 355: 250–53.

———. 1993. "A Strategy of Win-Stay, Lose-Shift That Outperforms Tit-for-Tat in the Prisoner's Dilemma Game." *Nature* 364: 56–58.

Sugden, R. 1986. *The Economics of Rights, Co-operation, and Welfare.* Oxford: Basil Blackwell.

Young, H. P., and D. Foster. 1991. "Cooperation in the Short and in the Long Run." *Games and Economic Behavior* 3: 145–156.

3

Promoting Norms

MY LONG-STANDING interest in norms was piqued by an anecdote that I included in *The Evolution of Cooperation* (Axelrod 1984, 84–85). It was one of the many stories from the trench warfare of World War I in which the two sides showed restraint based upon reciprocity in what they called "the live and let live system." But this particular episode went further than most. It displayed an emerging ethical component. Here is the story as related by a British officer recalling his experience while facing a Saxon unit of the German Army:

> I was having tea with A Company when we heard a lot of shouting and went out to investigate. We found our men and the Germans standing on their respective parapets. Suddenly a salvo arrived but did no damage. Naturally both sides got down and our men started swearing at the Germans, when all at once a brave German got onto his parapet and shouted out: "We are very sorry about that; we hope no one was hurt. It is not our fault. It is that damned Prussian artillery." (Rutter 1934, 29)

The Saxon apology goes well beyond a merely instrumental effort to prevent retaliation. It reflects moral regret for having violated a situation of trust, and shows concern that someone might have been hurt. My theory of cooperation based on the two-person iterated Prisoner's Dilemma helped explain the restraint based upon the selfish interest of the soldiers on each side. Yet, I was troubled that the theory did not account for the moral dimension that was clearly present in this example and was probably very important for the development and maintenance of norms.

My interest in norms as a possible aid to international cooperation was also heightened by my participation in a large research project led by Kenneth Oye. The project included historical studies of how cooperation emerges in the context of international anarchy (Oye 1986). In looking for common findings in the domain of international political economy and international security, Robert Keohane and I were struck by the importance of norms in explaining when cooperation succeeded and when it failed. We were also impressed with the role of international institutions in developing shared understandings of what actually counts as adherence to international norms of conduct (Axelrod and Keohane 1986).

I also had a long-standing interest in still another approach to norms, namely, the emergence of norms as solutions to dilemmas of collective action, such as pollution and overuse of resources held in common. An obvious way to model such dilemmas was by extending the two-person Prisoner's Dilemma to the n-person Prisoner's Dilemma. This would provide a good model of problems such as overgrazing of common land or excess air pollution. In these situations everyone has an incentive to be selfish. On the other hand, if everyone is selfish, everyone is worse off than if they had all made the cooperative choice. The problem was that the policy advice based on reciprocity that works so well in the two-person Prisoner's Dilemma simply does not work for the n-person version of the game when there is more than a handful of people involved. This difficulty had been well documented in both theory and practice (Olson 1965; Hardin 1968; Schelling 1973).

My interpretation of why the n-person Prisoner's Dilemma cannot be resolved with simple reciprocity was that there was no way for the cooperating players to focus punishment on a defecting player. Given this interpretation, I thought it would be interesting to explore a new n-person game in which the players had the added option of punishing just those who do not cooperate. To avoid making the problem trivial, I also supposed that detection of "cheating" was not automatic, and that punishment was costly to the enforcer as well as the target. My hope was that the analysis of this game would lead to a deeper understanding of how and when behavioral norms emerge.

In undertaking an analysis of this norms game, I decided not to use the assumption of rationality that is standard in game theory. The empirical examples of changing norms suggested to me that when people make choices in complex settings, they are more likely to use a trial-and-error approach than a fully rational calculation. Fortunately, I had an effective tool for the study of trial-and-error learning in a strategic setting. All that I had to do was adapt the genetic algorithm I used for the two-person Prisoner's Dilemma to this new game (see Chapter 1).

The results for the norms game demonstrated that I needed another mechanism in order for norms to emerge and prove stable. I dubbed this additional mechanism "metanorms." A metanorm is based on the willingness to punish not only those who violate norms, but also anyone else who fails to punish the violators. Although this was a satisfying strategic result, I also felt a need to consider the full range of mechanisms that serve to support a norm that is partially established. Among these less formal mechanisms is the internalization of values that was exhibited in the trench warfare example. In preparing this essay, I was delighted to see that the evolutionary approach to norms could address a wide range of problems, from the demise of slavery and dueling to business reputations and the proliferation of nuclear weapons.

Although not all of my work has been well received (see the introductions to Chapters 5 and 7, for example), this essay on norms has been. An earlier version was selected as the best paper at the 1985 annual meeting of the American Political Science Association. The published version was cited along with my earlier work on the Prisoner's Dilemma when I received a five-year MacArthur Prize Fellowship in 1987. And I was asked to adapt it for a popular audience (Axelrod 1987). I think this work on norms was well received because it addressed a widely felt need to find a basis for cooperation in settings that entail many people, rather than just two.

Since then, I have wondered whether the sudden collapse of communism in Eastern Europe and the former Soviet Union could be seen in terms of the evolution of norms. The analysis of these events by Timur Kuran (1995) suggests that a key factor was a decrease in the expectation that protest would be quashed. This is an interesting interpretation that is similar to the earlier work of Mark Granovetter (1978) on tipping processes in collective behavior such as rioting. In both theories, individuals are willing to act if enough others act first. Under certain situations, a slight change in the willingness of a few people to act first can get the ball rolling. Perhaps these works will help illuminate why collective behavior sometimes evolves gradually and sometimes tips suddenly.

When I give talks about the evolution of norms I often stress the emergence of norms at the global scale, such as the norms against colonialism, racial discrimination, and torture. I have been challenged by the question of whether different societies are likely to resist the imposition of norms they consider foreign. For example, won't societies that practice female genital mutilation resist Western efforts to eliminate that practice? My response is a relatively optimistic one. I expect that as the facts become widely publicized, the practice will become so abhorrent in the West that pressure will be brought to bear. After all, when Utah applied to join the Union as a state, the Mormons discovered that polygamy was not necessary. Likewise, when the governments find that they are risking political and economic ostracism, they may discover that female genital mutilation need not be tolerated. It may take a decade or two, but I suspect that a global norm against female genital mutilation will take hold.

Although cultural uniformity is certainly not a value in itself, it seems to me that the spread of global norms has generally been a progressive process. If colonialism, dueling, and slavery have been virtually eliminated, perhaps other forms of violence and assaults on human dignity can follow.

References

Axelrod, Robert. 1984. *The Evolution of Cooperation.* New York: Basic Books.
———. 1987. "Laws of Life: How Standards of Behavior Evolve." *The Sciences* 27 (Mar./Apr.): 44–51.
Axelrod, Robert, and Robert Keohane. 1986. "Achieving Cooperation Under Anarchy." In *Cooperation Under Anarchy,* ed. 226–54. Princeton University Press.
Granovetter, Mark. 1978. "Threshold Models of Collective Behavior." *American Journal of Sociology* 83: 1420–43.
Hardin, Garrett. 1968. "The Tragedy of the Commons." *Science* 162: 1243–48.
Kuran, Timur. 1995. *Private Truths, Public Lies.* Cambridge, Mass.: Harvard University Press.
Olson, Mancur, Jr. 1965. *The Logic of Collective Action.* Cambridge, Mass.: Harvard University Press.
Oye, Kenneth, ed. 1986. *Cooperation Under Anarchy.* Princeton N.J.: Princeton University Press. The essays in this book originally appeared in the October 1985 issue of *World Politics.*
Rutter, Owen, ed. 1934. *The History of Seventh (Services) Battalion, The Royal Sussex Regiment 1914–1919.* London: Times Publishing Company.
Schelling, Thomas. 1973. "Hockey Helmets, Concealed Weapons, and Daylight Saving: A Study of Binary Choices with Externalities." *Journal of Conflict Resolution* 17: 381–428.

Promoting Norms

AN EVOLUTIONARY APPROACH TO NORMS

ROBERT AXELROD

Reprinted by permission from Robert Axelrod, "An Evolutionary Approach to Norms," *American Political Science Review* 80, no. 4 (Dec. 1986): 1095–1111.

Abstract:
Norms provide a powerful mechanism for regulating conflict in groups, even when there are more than two people and no central authority. This essay investigates the emergence and stability of behavioral norms in the context of a game played by people of limited rationality. The dynamics of this new norms game are analyzed with a computer simulation based upon the evolutionary principle that strategies shown to be relatively effective will be used more in the future than less effective strategies. The results show the conditions under which norms can evolve and prove stable. One interesting possibility is the employment of metanorms, the willingness to punish someone who did not enforce a norm. Many historical examples of domestic and international norms are used to illustrate the wide variety of mechanisms that can support norms, including metanorms, dominance, internalization, deterrence, social proof, membership in groups, law, and reputation.

An established norm can have tremendous power. This is illustrated by a historical instance of the norm of dueling. In 1804 Aaron Burr challenged Alexander Hamilton to a duel. Hamilton sat down the night before the duel was to take place and wrote down his thoughts. He gave five reasons against accepting the duel: his principles were against shedding blood in a private combat forbidden by law; he had a wife and children; he felt a sense of obligation toward his creditors; he bore no ill against Colonel Burr; and he would hazard much and could gain little. Moreover, he was

I owe a great deal to Stephanie Forrest, my research assistant, and to those who helped me think about norms: Michael Cohen, Jeffrey Coleman, John Ferejohn, Morris Fiorina, Robert Gilpin, Donald Herzog, John Holland, Melanie Manion, Ann McGuire, Robert Keohane, Robert McCalla, Amy Saldinger, Lynn Sanders, Kim Scheppele, Andrew Sobel, Charles Stein, Laura Stoker, and David Yoon. I am also pleased to thank those who helped support various aspects of this work: the Harry Frank Guggenheim Foundation, the National Science Foundation, the Sloan Foundation, and the Michigan Memorial Phoenix Project.

reluctant to set a bad example by accepting a duel. Yet he did accept, because "the ability to be useful, whether in resisting mischief or effecting good, in those crises of our public affairs which seem likely to happen, would probably be inseparable from a conformity with public prejudice in this particular" (Truman 1884, 345–48). In other words, the prospect of sanctions imposed by the general public in support of dueling caused Hamilton to risk, and ultimately to lose, his life—a powerful norm indeed, and yet one that has all but disappeared today after centuries of power over life and death.

Today, norms still govern much of our political and social lives. In politics, civil rights and civil liberties are as much protected by informal norms for what is acceptable as they are by the powers of the formal legal system. Leadership is itself subject to the power of norms, as Nixon learned when he violated political norms in trying to cover up Watergate. The operation of Congress is shaped by many norms, including those governing reciprocity (Matthews 1960) and apprenticeship (Krehbiel 1985). Across many nations, tolerance of opposition is a fragile norm that has great impact on whether a democracy can survive in a given country (Almond and Verba 1963; Dahl 1966). In international political economy, norms are essential for the understanding of the operations of many functional domains such as banking, oil, and foreign aid (Axelrod and Keohane 1985; Keohane 1984; Krasner 1983). Even in the domain of power politics, norms have virtually wiped out colonialism, inhibited the use of chemical warfare, and retarded the spread of nuclear weapons.

Not only are norms important for many central issues in political science, but they are vital to the other social sciences as well. Sociology seeks to understand how different societies work, and clearly norms are important in these processes (e.g., Opp 1979; Opp 1983). Anthropology frequently deals with the unique features of various peoples by describing in great detail their practices and values, as in the case of feuding (e.g., Black-Michaud 1975). Psychologists are concerned with how people influence each other and the manner in which an individual becomes socialized into a community (e.g., Darley and Batson 1973; Sherif 1936). Economists are becoming interested in the origin and operation of norms as they have come to realize that markets involve a great deal of behavior based on standards that no one individual can determine alone (e.g., Furubotn and Pejovich 1974; Schotter 1981).

Large numbers of individuals and even nations often display a great degree of coordinated behavior that serves to regulate conflict. When this coordinated behavior takes place without the intervention of a central authority to police the behavior, we tend to attribute the coordinated behavior and the resulting regulation of conflict to the existence of norms. To make this appeal to norms a useful explanation, we need a good theory of norms. Such a theory should help explain three things: how norms arise, how norms are maintained, and how one norm displaces another.

One of the most important features of norms is that the standing of a norm can change in a surprisingly short time. For example, after many centuries of colonialism, the intolerance of colonial dependence took hold in the relatively short period of just two decades after World War II. Before and after such a transition, the state of affairs seems very stable and perhaps even permanent. For this reason, awareness of a given norm is most intense precisely when it is being challenged. Examples of norms being challenged today include the right to smoke in public without asking permission, the use of gender-laden language, and the prohibition against the use of chemical warfare. Some of these challenges will succeed in establishing new norms, and some will fail altogether. Thus, what is needed is a theory that accounts not only for the norms existing at any point in time, but also for how norms change over time. To clarify these processes, one must first be clear about exactly what is being discussed.

In this next section the evolutionary approach to be used in this essay is explained. Following this, the results of computer simulations of the evolution of norms are presented. The computer simulations are then extended to include a specific mechanism for the enforcement of norms, called *metanorms*. After these formal models are investigated, a wide variety of processes that might help to sustain norms are discussed, along with suggestions about how they too can be modeled. The question of the origin and content of norms is considered, and finally, a summary and conclusion presents the findings of this paper in the broad context of social and political change.

The Evolutionary Approach

Norms have been defined in various ways in the different literatures and even within the same literature. The three most common types of definitions are based upon expectations, values, and behavior. That these different definitions are used for the same concept reflects how expectations, values, and behavior are often closely linked. Definitions based upon expectations or values are favored by those who study norms as they exist in a given social setting. Such definitions are convenient because interviews can elicit the beliefs and values of the participants, whereas systematically observing their actual behavior is more difficult. Because for many purposes the most important thing is actual behavior, a behavioral definition will be used in this study.

DEFINITION: *A* norm *exists in a given social setting to the extent that individuals usually act in a certain way and are often punished when seen not to be acting in this way.*

This definition makes the existence of a norm a matter of degree, rather than an all or nothing proposition, which allows one to speak of the growth or decay of a norm. According to this definition, the extent to which a given type of action is a norm depends on just how often the action is taken and just how often someone is punished for not taking it.

To investigate the growth and decay of norms, I have formulated a norms game in which players can choose to defect and to punish those they have seen defecting. The goal of the investigation is to see when cooperation based upon emerging norms will develop. Ultimately, the purpose is to learn what conditions favor the development of norms so that cooperation can be promoted where it might not otherwise exist or be secure.

To see what rational actors would do in a particular setting, a game-theory approach can be used. Game theory assumes the players are fully rational and choose the strategy that gives the highest expected utility over time, given their expectations about what the other players will do. Recent work by economists has shown great sophistication in dealing with problems of defining credible threats and of showing the consequences of requiring actors' expectations about each other to be consistent with the experience that will be generated by the resulting actions (Abreu et al. 1985; Friedman 1971; Kreps and Wilson 1982; Selten 1975).

Although deductions about what fully rational actors will do are valuable for their own sake, empirical examples of changing norms suggest that real people are more likely to use trial-and-error behavior than detailed calculations based on accurate beliefs about the future. Therefore, I have chosen not to study the dynamics of norms using an approach that depends on the assumption of rationality.

Instead, I use an evolutionary approach. This approach is based on the principle that what works well for a player is more likely to be used again, whereas what turns out poorly is more likely to be discarded (Axelrod 1984). As in game theory, the players use their strategies with each other to achieve a payoff based upon their own choice and the choices of others. In an evolutionary approach, however, there is no need to assume a rational calculation to identify the best strategy. Instead, the analysis of what is chosen at any specific time is based upon an operationalization of the idea that effective strategies are more likely to be retained than ineffective strategies. Moreover, the evolutionary approach allows the introduction of new strategies as occasional random mutations of old strategies.

The evolutionary principle itself can be thought of as the consequence of any one of three different mechanisms. It could be that the more effective individuals are more likely to survive and reproduce. This is true in biological systems and in some economic and political systems. A second interpretation is that the players learn by trial and error, keeping effective strategies and altering ones that turn out poorly. A third interpretation, and the one most congenial to the study of norms, is that the players observe each other, and those with poor performance tend to imitate the strategies of those they see doing better. In any case, there is no need to assume that the individual is rational and understands the full strategic implications of the situation.

The evolutionary approach is inherently probabilistic and involves nonlinear effects. For these reasons, it is often impossible to use deductive mathematics to determine the consequences of a given model. Fortunately, computer simulation techniques (e.g., Cyert and March 1963) provide a rigorous alternative to deductive mathematics. Moreover, simulation can reveal the dynamics of a process, as well as the equilibrium points. By simulating the choices of each member of a population of players and by seeing how the players' strategies change over time, the unfolding of a given evolutionary process can be analyzed to determine its overall implications.

The Norms Game

The norms game is described in Figure 3-1. It begins when an individual (i) has an opportunity to defect, say by cheating on an exam. This opportunity is accompanied by a known chance of being observed. The chance of being observed, or *seen,* is called S. If S is .5, each of the other players has an even chance of observing a defection if it takes place. If player i does defect, he or she gets a payoff of T (the *temptation* for defecting) equal to 3, and each of the others are *hurt* (H) slightly, getting a payoff of H equal to -1. If the player does not defect, no one gets anything.

So far the game is similar to an n-person Prisoner's Dilemma (see, e.g., G. Hardin 1968; R. Hardin 1982; Schelling 1978). The new feature comes in the next step. If player i does defect, some of the other players may see the defection, and those who do may choose to punish the defector. If the defector is *punished* (P) the payoff is a very painful $P = -9$, but because the act of punishment is typically somewhat costly, the punisher has to pay an *enforcement cost* (E) equal to -2. (See Table 3-1.)

The strategy of a player thus has two dimensions. The first dimension

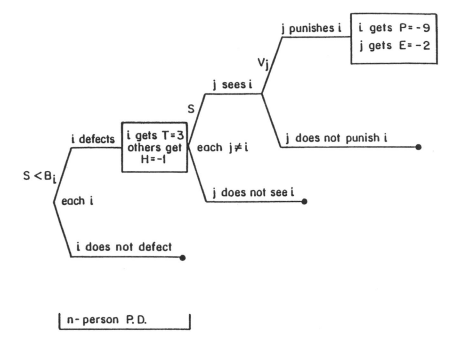

Figure 3-1. Norms Game

of player *i*'s strategy is *boldness* (B_i), which determines when the player will defect. The player will defect whenever the chance of being seen by someone is less than the player's boldness, which is to say, whenever $S < B_i$. The second dimension of a player's strategy is *vengefulness* (V_i), which is the probability that the player will punish someone who is defecting. The greater the player's vengefulness, the more likely he or she will be to punish someone who is spotted defecting.

TABLE 3-1
Example of Payoffs in the Norms Game Attained by a Player with Boldness Equal to 2/7 and Vengefulness Equal to 4/7

Event	Payoff per Event	Number of Events	Payoff
Defection	$T = 3$	1	3
Punishment	$P = -9$	1	-9
Hurt by others	$H = -1$	36	-36
Enforcement cost	$E = -2$	9	-18
SCORE			-60

Simulation of the Norms Game

The simulation of the norms game determines how the players' strategies evolve over time. The two dimensions of a strategy, boldness and vengefulness, are each allowed to take one of eight levels, from 0/7 to 7/7. Because the representation of eight levels requires three binary bits, the representation of a player's strategy requires a total of six bits, three for boldness and three for vengefulness.

The simulation itself proceeds in five steps, as follows:

(1) The strategies for the initial population of 20 players are chosen at random from the set of all possible strategies.

(2) The score of each player is determined from the player's own choices and the choices of the other players. Each individual gets four opportunities to defect. For each of these opportunities, the chance of being seen, S, is drawn from a uniform distribution between 0 and 1. To see how the scores are attained, let us focus on an arbitrary player in the initial population of one of the runs, who will be called Lee. Lee has a boldness level of 2/7 and vengefulness level of 4/7. The total payoff Lee achieved was the result of four different kinds of events, as shown in Table 3-1. Lee defected only once because only one of the four opportunities had a chance of being seen that was less than Lee's boldness of 2/7. This defection gave a temptation payoff of $T = 3$ points. Unfortunately for Lee, one of the other players observed the defection and chose to punish it, leading to a loss for Lee of $P = -9$ points. In addition the other players defected a total of 36 times, each hurting Lee $H = -1$ point. Finally, Lee observed who was responsible for about half of these defections and chose to punish each of them with a probability determined by his vengefulness of 4/7. This led to a punishment of 9 of the defections at an enforcement cost of $E = -2$ each, for a further loss of 18 points. The net result of these four types of events was a total score of −60 for Lee.

(3) When the scores of all the players are determined, individuals whose strategies were relatively successful are selected to have more offspring.[1] The method is to give an average individual one offspring and to give two offspring to an individual who is one standard deviation more effective than the average. An individual who is one standard deviation below the population average will not have his or her strategy reproduced at all. For convenience, the number of offspring is adjusted to maintain a constant population of 20. A final step is the introduction of some mutation so that new strategies can arise and be tested. This is done

---

[1] The procedure used is inspired by the genetic algorithm of computer scientist John Holland (1975; 1980).

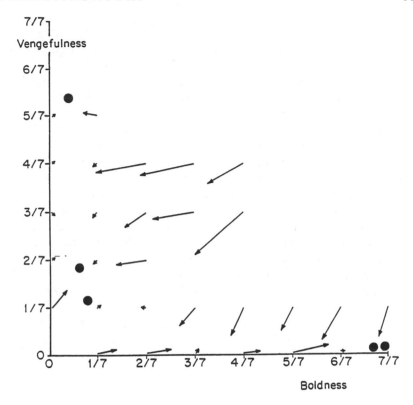

Figure 3-2. Norms Game Dynamics

by allowing a 1 percent chance that each bit of an individual's new strategy will be altered. This mutation rate gives a little more than one mutation per generation in the entire population.

(4) Steps 2 and 3 are repeated for 100 generations to determine how the population evolves.

(5) Steps 1 to 4 are repeated to give five complete runs of the simulation.

The results of the five runs are shown in Figure 3-2. The five circles indicate the average boldness and vengefulness of a population after 100 generations. Three completely different outcomes appear possible. In one of the runs, there was a moderate level of vengefulness and almost no boldness, indicating the partial establishment of a norm against defection. On two other runs there was little boldness and little vengefulness, and on the remaining two runs, there was a great deal of boldness and almost no vengefulness—the very opposite of a norm against defection. What could be happening?

The way the strategies actually evolve over time is revealed by the change that takes place in a single generation in a population's average boldness and vengefulness. To calculate his, the data are used from all 100 generations of all five runs, giving 500 populations. The populations with similar average boldness and vengefulness are then grouped together, and their average boldness and vengefulness one generation later is measured. The results are indicated by the arrows in Figure 3-2.

Now the various outcomes begin to fit into a common pattern. All five of the runs begin near the middle of the field, with average boldness and vengefulness levels near one-half. The first thing to happen is a dramatic fall in the boldness level. The reason for the decline is that when there is enough vengefulness in the population, it is very costly to be bold. Once the boldness level falls, the main trend is a lowering of vengefulness. The reason for this is that to be vengeful and punish an observed defection requires paying an enforcement cost without any direct return to the individual. Finally, once the vengefulness level has fallen nearly to zero, the players can be bold with impunity. This results in an increase in boldness, destroying whatever restraint was established in the first stage of the process—a sad but stable state in this norms game.

This result raises the question of just what it takes to get a norm established. Because the problem is that no one has any incentive to punish a defection, the next section explores one of the mechanisms that provides an incentive to be vengeful.

Metanorms

A little-lamented norm of once great strength was the practice of lynching to enforce white rule in the South. A particularly illuminating episode took place in Texas in 1930 after a black man was arrested for attacking a white woman. The mob was impatient, so they burned down the courthouse to kill the prisoner within. A witness said, "I heard a man right behind me remark of the fire, 'Now ain't that a shame?' No sooner had the words left his mouth than someone knocked him down with a pop bottle. He was hit in the mouth and had several teeth broken," (Cantril 1941, 101). This is one way to enforce a norm: punish those who do not support it. In other words, be vengeful, not only against the violators of the norm, but also against anyone who refuses to punish the defectors. This amounts to establishing a norm that one must punish those who do not punish a defection. This is what I will call a *metanorm*.

Metanorms are widely used in the systems of denunciation in communist societies. When the authorities accuse someone of doing something wrong, others are called upon to denounce the accused. Not to join in

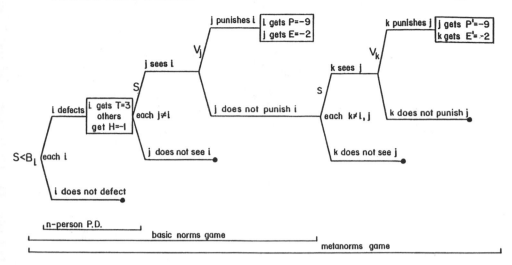

Figure 3-3. Metanorms Game

this form of punishment is itself taken as a defection against the group (Bronfenbrenner 1970; Meyers and Bradbury 1968).

As another example, when the Soviet Union supported the suppression of the Solidarity movement in Poland, the United States asked its allies to stop supplying components to the Soviet Union for its new gas pipeline. The allies, not wanting to pay the enforcement cost of this punishment, refused. The United States government then undertook the metapunishment of imposing sanctions on foreign companies that defied the sales ban (*New York Times,* Jan. 5 and June 19, 1982).

The formulation of a metanorms game can help in the exploration of the effectiveness of this mechanism. Figure 3-3 shows how the meta-norms game is based upon an extension of the norms game. If someone defects, and Lee sees but does not punish that defection, then the other players have a chance to see and punish Lee. The model makes the critical assumption that a player's vengefulness against nonpunishment is the same as the player's vengefulness against an original defection.[2] The validity of this assumption will be addressed later, but first let us see what effect it has on the evolution of the process.

A set of five runs was conducted with the metanorms game, each done as before with a population of 20 players and a duration of 100 genera-

_____

[2] For convenience, it is also assumed that the chance of being seen not punishing is the same as the chance of the original defection being seen. The payoff for metapunishment is $P' = -9$, and the metaenforcement cost is $E' = -2$.

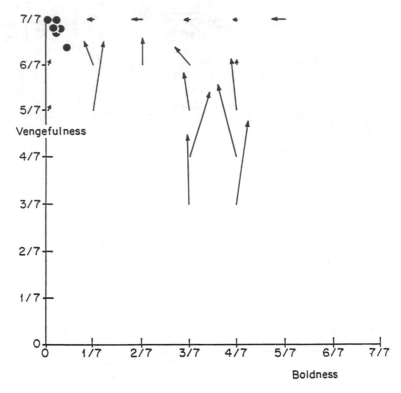

Figure 3-4. Metanorms Game Dynamics

tions. The results are shown in Figure 3-4. They are unambiguous. In all five runs a norm against defection was established. The dynamics are clear. The amount of vengefulness quickly increased to very high levels, and this in turn drove down boldness. The logic is also clear. At first there was a moderate amount of vengefulness in the population. This meant that a player had a strong incentive to be vengeful, namely, to escape punishment for not punishing an observed defection. Moreover, when each of the players is vengeful out of self-protection, it does not pay for anyone to be bold. Thus the entire system is self-policing, and the norm becomes well established.

 This result is dependent, however, on the population's starting with a sufficiently high level of vengefulness. Otherwise the norm still collapses. Thus, whereas the norms game collapses no matter what the initial conditions are, the metanorms game can prevent defections if the initial conditions are favorable enough.

Mechanisms to Support Norms

The simulations of the norms game and the metanorms game have allowed the exploration of some of the important processes in the dynamics of norms. The simulation of the norms game shows that relying on individuals to punish defections may not be enough to maintain a norm. Therefore, the question to be considered now is, What mechanisms can serve to support a norm that is only partially established? The evolutionary approach helps to develop a list of such processes, and in some cases, suggests specific methods for modeling the process by which a norm can be supported.

Metanorms

As the computer simulations show, the existence of a metanorm can be an effective way to get a norm started and to protect it once it is established. By linking vengefulness against nonpunishers with vengefulness against defectors, the metanorm provides a mechanism by which the norm against defection becomes self-policing. The trick, of course, is to link the two kinds of vengefulness. Without this link, the system could unravel. An individual might reduce the metavengeance level while still being vengeful and then later stop being vengeful when others stopped being metavengeful.

The examples cited earlier suggest that people may well punish those who do not help to enforce a valued norm. The model suggests norms can be supported if people tend to have correlated degrees of vengefulness or anger against someone who violates a particular norm and someone who tolerates such a violation. What the evolutionary approach has done is raise the possibility that metanorms are a mechanism that can help support norms, thus suggesting the interesting empirical question of whether the two types of vengefulness are indeed correlated. My guess is that there is such a correlation. The types of defection we are most angry about are likely to be the ones whose toleration also makes us angry. As of now, however, the possibility of metanorms remains speculative.

Dominance

Another mechanism for supporting a norm is the dominance of one group over another. For example, it is no coincidence that in the South, whites lynched blacks, but blacks did not lynch whites. The whites had two basic advantages: greater economic and political power, and greater numbers.

   Simulation of the effects of power and numbers can be readily done
with slight extensions of the basic model to allow for the existence of two
different groups. The competition between two groups can be modeled
by assuming that the defections of a player only hurt the members of the
other group and are therefore only punished by members of the other
group. Similarly, in the metanorms version of the model, punishments for
not punishing a defector would only occur within a group, as illustrated
by the pop bottle used by one white against another in the lynching example discussed above. Moreover, in determining strategies for the next
generation, the strategies of two groups would be allowed to adapt separately so that whites learn from whites and blacks learn from blacks.
   The two advantages of the whites are modeled separately. Their greater
economic or political power is reflected in their lessened cost of being
punished by a black. This was done by letting $P = -3$ for whites while
retaining $P = -9$ for blacks. The greater numbers of whites are reflected
directly in the relative size of the two populations, giving the whites a
greater chance to observe and punish a black defection than vice versa.
This was done by letting the population be 20 whites and 10 blacks.
   Analysis of runs based upon these conditions shows that resistance to
punishment and increased size can help a group, but only if there are
metanorms. Without metanorms, even members of the stronger group
tend to be free riders, with no private incentive to bear enforcement costs.
This in turn leads to low vengefulness and high boldness in both groups.
When metanorms are added, it becomes relatively easier for the strong
group to keep the weak group from being bold, while it is not so easy for
the weak group to keep the strong one from defecting.
   Another form of potential strength is illustrated by the case of a major
power interacting with many smaller nations. For example, the United
States may not only be in a favorable position on a given bilateral interaction but also may have many more bilateral interactions than others.
Thus, its behavior has a greater impact on the development of norms
than would the behavior of a minor power. When Libya wanted to modify the international norm of the twelve-mile limit of territorial waters to
include the entire Gulf of Sidra, the U.S. fleet deliberately sailed into the
Gulf and shot down two Libyan planes sent up to try to change the norm.
Clearly, the United States was not only stronger but had incentives to
enforce the old norm based upon its naval interests in other parts of the
world.
   Although the process of frequent interactions by a single strong player
has not yet been simulated, it is plausible that such a process would help
to establish a norm against defection because the central player would
have a greater unilateral incentive to be vengeful against defections.
   Norms can also be promoted by the interests of a few major actors,

such as the United States and the Soviet Union's both working to retard the proliferation of nuclear weapons. Their actions need not be coordinated in detail as long as together they are important enough to others to enforce a norm of the major actors' choice. The logic is somewhat analogous to Olson's "privileged group" in a collective action problem (Olson 1965, 48–50).

Internalization

Norms frequently become internalized (Scott 1971). This means that violating an established norm is psychologically painful even if the direct material benefits are positive. This is frequently observed in laboratory experiments where subjects are more equitable than they have to be and explain their behavior by saying things like "you have to live with yourself." In terms of the norms game, this type of internalization means that the temptation to defect, T, is negative rather than positive. If everyone internalizes a given norm this strongly, there is no incentive to defect and the norm remains stable. Obviously families and societies work very hard to internalize a wide variety of norms, especially in the impressionable young. They do so with greater or lesser success depending on many factors, including the degree to which the individual identifies with the group and the degree to which the norm and its sponsors are seen as legitimate.[3]

Clearly, it is rare for everyone in a group to have a norm so strongly internalized that for each the temptation to defect is actually negative. An interesting question for future modeling is, How many people have to internalize a norm in order for it to remain stable?

The logic of the norms game suggests that lowering the temptation to defect might not be enough. After all, even if most people did not defect, if no one had an incentive to punish the remaining defectors, the norm could still collapse. This point suggests that we look for internalization, not only in the reduced incentive to defect, but also in an increased incentive to punish someone else who does defect.

An increased incentive to punish, through internalization or by some other means, would lead some people to feel a gain from punishing a defector. For them, the payoff from enforcement, E, would actually be positive. Such people are often known as self-righteous busybodies and often are not very well liked by those who enjoy a defection now and then. Given enough people who enjoy enforcing the norm, the question

---

[3] Marx goes as far as to say that social norms are merely reflections of the interests of the ruling class, and the other classes are socialized into accepting these norms under "false consciousness."

of its maintenance then becomes whether the chance is high or low that
the defection will be seen.

Deterrence

In the norms game and the metanorms game the players do not look
ahead. Instead they try a particular strategy, see how it does, compare
their payoff with the payoff of others, and switch strategies if they are
doing relatively poorly. Although trial and error is a sensible way of modeling players of very limited rationality, it does not capture the idea that
players may have a great enough understanding of the situation to do
some forward-looking calculations as well as backward-looking comparisons with others. In particular, a person may realize that even if punishing a defection is costly now, it might have long-term gains by discourag-
ing other defections later.

A good example is the strong U.S. response to New Zealand's refusal
in February 1985 to allow a U.S. destroyer into Aukland harbor without
assurances that it did not carry nuclear weapons. The U.S. government
presumably did not care very much about nuclear access to New Zealand
ports, but it did care a great deal about deterring the spread of a new
norm of "nuclear allergy" among its many allies in other parts of the
world (Arkin and Fieldhouse 1985).

Social Proof

An important principle from social psychology is "social proof," which
applies especially to what people decide is correct behavior. As Cialdini
(1984, 117) explains,

> we view a behavior as more correct in a given situation to the degree that we
> see others performing it. Whether the question is what to do with an empty
> popcorn box in a movie theater, how fast to drive on a certain stretch of high-
> way, or how to eat chicken at a dinner party, the actions of those around us will
> be important in defining the answer.

The actions of those around us serve several functions. First, they provide
information about the boldness levels of others, and indirectly about the
vengefulness of the population. Hence, we can infer something about
whether it pays for us to be bold or not. Second, the actions of others
might contain clues about what is the best course of action even if there is
no vengefulness. For example, people may be driving slowly on a certain
stretch of highway, not because there is a speed trap there, but because

the road is poorly paved just ahead. Either way, the actions of others can provide information about how the population has been adapting to a particular environment. If we are new to that environment, this is valuable information about what our own behavior should be (Asch 1951; Asch 1956; Sherif 1936). The actions of others provide information about what is proper for us, even if we do not know the reasons. Finally, in many cases, by conforming to the actions of those around us, we fulfill a psychological need to be part of a group.

Our propensity to act on the principle of social proof is a major mechanism in the support of norms. The current model of norms already has a form of this mechanism built in: when a relatively unsuccessful individual seeks a new strategy, that strategy is selected from those being used by the rest of the population. This is a form of social proof, refined by giving weight to the more successful strategies being employed in the population.

In cases where other people differ in important ways, the principle of social proof tends to apply to those who are most like us. This too is easy to build into simulations with more than one group. In the simulation of blacks and whites, the blacks look only to other blacks when selecting a new strategy, and the whites look only to other whites. This makes good sense because a strategy that is very successful for a white might be disastrous if employed by a black.

Membership

Another mechanism for the support of norms is voluntary membership in a group working together for a common end.[4] Contracts, treaties, alliances, and memberships in social groups all carry with them some power to impose obligations upon individuals. The power of the membership works in three ways. First, it directly affects the individual's utility function, making a defection less attractive because to defect against a voluntarily accepted commitment would tend to lower one's self-esteem. Second, group membership allows like-minded people to interact with each other, and this self-selection tends to make it much easier for the members to enforce the norm implicit in the agreement to form or join a group. Finally, the very agreement to form a group helps define what is expected of the participants, thereby clarifying when a defection occurs and when a punishment is called for.

One might suppose it would be easy for a bold individual to join and then exploit a group that had gathered together in the expectation of mutual compliance. Actually, this does not usually happen, in part be-

---

[4] I thank David Yoon and Lynn Sanders for pointing this out to me.

cause the factors just outlined tend to isolate a defector and make it relatively easy for the others to be vengeful—especially with the help of
metanorms. Another factor is that, according to recent experimental evidence, cooperators are more likely to stay in a group than are defectors
(Orbell et al. 1984). This happens because cooperators have a stronger
ethical or group-regarding impulse than defectors, a factor that led them
to cooperate in the first place.

The metanorms game can be expanded to include the choice of
whether to join a group or not.[5] In general, the value to a person of
joining a group would depend on how many others joined. Each player
would make this choice at the start of the game. Then the interactions
concerning defections and punishments would occur as before, with the
interactions limited to those who had actually joined. As an example, an
alliance for collective security would include a group of nations that had
joined for this common purpose. Once a nation had joined, a defection
would consist of not supporting the alliance in some collective security
task. A defection would hurt the other members of the alliance, and some
of them might choose to punish the defector; they might also choose to
punish someone who did not punish the defector. Typically, the larger the
number of nations joining the group, the greater the benefits of cooperation would be for its members.

In the political sphere, voluntary membership taking the form of a
social contract has been a powerful image for the support of democratic
forms of governance. In effect, a mythical agreement is used to give legit-
imacy to a very real set of laws and institutions.

Law

Norms often precede laws but are then supported, maintained, and extended by laws. For example, social norms about smoking in public are
now changing. As more and more people turn vengeful against someone
who lights up in a confined space, fewer and fewer smokers are so bold as
to do so without asking permission. As this norm becomes firmer, there is
growing support to formalize it through the promulgation of laws defining where smoking is and is not permitted.[6]

A law supports a norm in several ways. The most obvious is that it

[5] I thank David Yoon for formulating this variant of the metanorms game and the application to alliances that follows.

[6] The same process of formalizing norms applies to private laws and regulations, as in
the case of a business that issues an internal rule about who is responsible for making
coffee.

supplements private enforcement mechanisms with the strength of the state. Because enforcement can be expensive for the individual, this can be a tremendous asset. In effect, under the law the collective goods problem of enforcement is avoided because selective incentives are given to specialized individuals (inspectors, police, judges, etc.) to find and punish violations.

The law also has a substantial power of its own, quite apart from whether it is or can be enforced. Many people are likely to take seriously the idea that a specific act is mandated by the law, whether it is a requirement to use seat belts or an income tax on capital gains. However, we all know this respect for the law has its limits, and we suspect that many people do not pay all the tax they should. Even when enforcement is possible and is attempted, the strength of the law is limited. In most cases, the law can only work as a supplement (and not a replacement) for informal enforcement of the norm. The failure of Prohibition is a classic example of an attempt to enforce a norm without sufficient social support.

In addition to enforcement and respect, a third advantage of the law is clarity. The law tends to define obligations much more clearly than does an informal norm. A social norm might say that a landlord should provide safe housing for tenants, but a housing code is more likely to define safety in terms of fire escapes. Over the domain covered by the law, the norm might become quite clear. However, this clarity is gained at the expense of suggesting that conformity with the law is the limit of one's social obligations.

Modeling the power and operation of the law is beyond the scope of this project. However, it should still be emphasized that often law is the formalization of what has already attained strength as a social or political norm. An important example is civil liberties, the very foundation of a democratic system. There are laws and constitutional provisions in support of civil liberties such as freedom of speech, but the legal system can only protect free speech if there is substantial support for it among a population willing to tolerate dissent and willing to protect those who exercise it.

In short, social norms and laws are often mutually supporting. This is true because social norms can become formalized into laws and because laws provide external validation of norms. They are also mutually supporting because they have complementary strengths and weaknesses. Social norms are often best at preventing numerous small defections where the cost of enforcement is low. Laws, on the other hand, often function best to prevent rare but large defections because substantial resources are available for enforcement.

Reputation

An important, and often dominant, reason to respect a norm is that violating it would provide a signal about the type of person you are. For example, if there is a norm dictating that people should dress formally for dinner, and you do not, then others might make some quite general inferences about you.

The importance of dressing formally when the occasion requires is not just that others will punish you for violating the norm (say, by giving you a disapproving look) but also that they will infer things about you and then act in ways you wish they would not. This is an example of the signaling principle: a violation of a norm is not only a bit of behavior having a payoff for the defector and for others; it is also a signal that contains information about the future behavior of the defector in a wide variety of situations.[7]

There are several important implications of the signaling principle for the origin and durability of a norm. A norm is likely to originate in a type of behavior that signals things about individuals that will lead others to reward them. For example, if a certain accent signals good breeding, then others may give better treatment to those who speak that way. Once this happens, more people are likely to try to speak that way. Eventually, people might be punished (e.g., despised) for not having the right accent. Thus, what starts out as a signal about one person's background can become a norm for all.[8]

The signaling principle helps explain how an "is" becomes an "ought." As more and more people use the signal to gain information about others, more and more people will adopt the behavior that leads to being treated well. Gradually the signal will change from indicating a rare person to indicating a common person. On the other hand, the absence of the signal, which originally carried little information, will come to carry substantial information when the signal becomes common. When almost everyone behaves in conformity with a signal, those who do not stand out. These people can now be regarded as violators of a norm—and dealt with accordingly.

Note that there is an important distinction between a convention, which has no direct payoffs one way or the other (such as wearing a tie for men), and a cooperative act, the violation of which leads to injury to others (e.g., queuing for service). A type of behavior with no direct payoffs can become a norm once it develops some signaling value, as is the

---

[7] For the theory of signaling, see Spence (1974). For a theory of how customs can be sustained by reputations, see Akerlof (1980).

[8] Signals can also help to differentiate groups and thereby maintain group boundaries and cohesiveness.

case when fashion leaders adopt a new style (Veblen 1899). Once this happens, a violator of this style will be looked down upon. Thus the style will become a norm; individuals will usually follow the style, and those who do not will likely be punished.

The Origin and Content of Norms

Eight mechanisms have now been identified that can serve to support a norm that is already at least partially established. What, however, are the characteristics of the behaviors that arise and then become more and more established as norms? Or to put it another way, just what is the content of behavior that might later turn into a norm?

The answer depends on what types of behavior can appear and spread in a population even when only a few people initially exhibit the behavior. This, in turn, depends on what kind of behavior is likely to be rewarded and punished for its own sake, independent of whether or not it is common behavior.

Two of the supporting mechanisms already considered can serve in this initial role: dominance and reputation. Dominance can work because if only a few very powerful actors want to promote a certain pattern of behavior, their punishments alone can often be sufficient to establish it, even if the others are not vengeful against defections. The implications for the substance of norms are obvious: it is easier to get a norm started if it serves the interests of the powerful few.

In fact, many norms obeyed and even enforced by almost everyone actually serve the powerful. This can happen in forms disguised as equalitarian or in forms that are blatantly hierarchical. An apparently equalitarian norm is that the rich and the poor are equally prohibited from sleeping under bridges at night. A blatantly hierarchical norm is that soldiers shall obey their officers. Both forms are "norms of partiality," to use the term of Ullmann-Margalit (1977).

To say that the powerful can start a norm suggests a great deal about the potential substance of such norms. Once started, the strong support the norms because the norms support the strong.

Dominance is not the only mechanism capable of starting a norm. Reputation can do so as well. Consider, for example, the idea of keeping one's promise. In a hypothetical society in which few people kept their promises, you would be happy to deal with someone who did. You would find it in your narrow self-interest to continue dealing with such a person, and this in turn would be rewarding to the promise-keeper. Conversely, you would try to avoid deals with those you knew did not keep their promises. You would, in effect, be vengeful against defectors without having to pay an enforcement cost. Indeed, your enforcement would simply be the result of your acting in your own interests, based upon the reputations of others and your calculation about what was good for yourself.

International regimes depend on just such reputational mechanisms to get norms started (Keohane 1984). In such cases, counties can be very deliberate about what promises they make and which ones they want to keep when the stakes are high (Axelrod 1979). Reputational effects can also be based upon the limited rationality of trial-and-error learning. If a person associates another's response to a particular act (say a refusal to continue dealing as a reaction to the breaking of a promise), then the violator can learn not to break promises.

This learning approach suggests the importance of being able to link the behavior with the response. Behaviors will be easier to establish as norms if the optimal response of others is prompt and rewarding. Failing a prompt response, learning can also take place if the delayed punishment is explicitly cited as a response to the earlier defection.

Summary and Conclusion

To study the development of norms, the strategic situation has been modeled as an n-person game. In the basic norms game, everyone has two types of choice: the choice to cooperate or defect, which affects everyone, and the choice of whether or not to punish a specific person seen defecting. A player's strategy is described in terms of how these choices will be made. A strategy consists of two parameters: boldness (the largest chance of being seen that will lead to a choice of defection) and vengefulness (the probability of punishing someone observed defecting). To the extent that players are vengeful but not very bold, a norm can be said to have been established.

To study the dynamics of the process, an evolutionary approach was employed. In this approach, the initial strategies are chosen at random, and the population of players is given opportunities to defect and to punish the defections they observe. The evolutionary approach dictates that strategies proving relatively effective are more likely to be employed in the future while less effective strategies are dropped. Moreover, strategies undergo some random mutation so that new ones are always being introduced into the population.

The computer simulation of this process revealed an interesting dynamic in the norms game. At first, boldness levels fell dramatically due to the vengefulness in the population. Then, gradually, the amount of vengefulness also fell because there was no direct incentive to pay the enforcement cost of punishing a defection. Once vengeance became rare, the average level of boldness rose again, and the norm completely collapsed. Moreover, the collapse was a stable outcome.

This result led to a search for mechanisms that could sustain a partially established norm. One possibility is the metanorm: the treatment of non-punishment as if it were another form of defection; that is, a player will be vengeful against someone who observed a defection but did not punish it. Simulation of the evolution of strategies in this metanorms game demonstrated that players had a strong incentive to increase their vengefulness lest they be punished by others, and this in turn led to a decline of boldness. Thus, metanorms can promote and sustain cooperation in a population.

Other mechanisms for the support of norms are also important. These include dominance, internalization, deterrence, social proof, membership, law, and reputation. In some cases, the resulting norms are hierarchical rather than equalitarian, and the cooperation exhibited is coerced rather than freely offered. A good example is the norm of black deference in the old South.

Dominance processes have been simulated by subdividing the population and letting one segment be relatively resistant to the effects of punishment by members of the other segment. Internalization can be investigated by studying the effects of making defection costly rather than rewarding for some of the defectors and by making punishment a pleasure rather than a cost for some of the observers of a defection. A more drastic change in the modeling procedures would be necessary to study some of the other mechanisms in question.

Norms are important in society and, not surprisingly, have been given a great deal of attention in the social sciences, including sociology, anthropology, political science, psychology, and economics. Although descriptions of actual norms abound, investigations of the reasons for people to obey or violate a given norm have been much less common. Even among the strategic approaches to norms, relatively little attention has been devoted to understanding the dynamics of norms: how they can get started, how a partial norm can be sustained and become well established, and how one norm can displace another. An evolutionary approach is helpful in studying these dynamics because it can help show how strategies change over time as a function of their relative success in an ever-changing environment of other players who are also changing their own strategies with experience.

A major goal of investigating how cooperative norms in societal settings have been established is a better understanding of how to promote cooperative norms in international settings. This is not as utopian as it might seem because international norms against slavery and colonialism are already strong, while international norms are partly effective against racial discrimination, chemical warfare, and the proliferation of nuclear weapons. Because norms sometimes become established surprisingly quickly, there may be some useful cooperative norms that could be hurried along with relatively modest interventions.

References

Abreu, Dilip, David Pearce, and Ennio Stacchetti. 1985. *Optimal Cartel Equilibria with Imperfect Monitoring*. Minneapolis: University of Minnesota Institute for Mathematics and Its Applications.

Akerlof, George A. 1980. "A Theory of Social Custom, of Which Unemployment May Be One Consequence." *Quarterly Journal of Economics* 94: 749–75.

Almond, Gabriel, and Sidney Verba. 1963. *The Civic Culture*. Princeton, N.J.: Princeton University Press.

Arkin, William, and Richard W. Fieldhouse. 1985. "Focus on the Nuclear Infrastructure." *Bulletin of the Atomic Scientists* 41: 11–15.

Asch, Solomon E. 1951. "Effects of Group Pressure upon the Modification and Distortion of Judgment." In *Groups, Leadership and Men*, ed. Harold Guetzkow, 177–90. Pittsburgh: Carnegie Press.

_____. 1956. "Studies of Independence and Conformity: I. A Minority of One Against a Unanimous Majority." *Psychological Monographs* 41: 258–90.

Axelrod, Robert. 1979. "The Rational Timing of Surprise." *World Politics* 31: 228–46.

_____. 1984. *The Evolution of Cooperation*. New York: Basic Books.

Axelrod, Robert, and Robert O. Keohane. 1985. "Achieving Cooperation Under Anarchy: Strategies and Institutions." *World Politics* 38: 226–54.

Black-Michaud, Jacob. 1975. *Cohesive Force: Feud in the Mediterranean and the Middle East*. Oxford: Basil Blackwell.

Bronfenbrenner, Urie. 1970. *Two Worlds of Childhood: U.S. and U.S.S.R.* New York: Russell Sage.

Cantril, Hadley. 1941. *The Psychology of Social Movements*. New York: Wiley.

Cialdini, Robert H. 1984. *Influence—How and Why People Agree to Things*. New York: Morrow.

Cyert, Richard M., and James G. March. 1963. *A Behavioral Theory of the Firm*. Englewood Cliffs, N.J.: Prentice-Hall.

Dahl, Robert A., ed. 1966. *Political Oppositions in Western Democracies*. New Haven: Yale University Press.

Darley, John M., and C. Daniel Batson. 1973. " 'From Jerusalem to Jerico': A Study of Situational and Dispositional Variables in Helping Behavior." *Journal of Personality and Social Psychology* 27: 100–108.

Friedman, James W. 1971. "A Non-Cooperative Equilibrium for Supergames." *Review of Economic Studies* 38: 1–12.

Furubotn, Eirik G., and Svetozar Pejovich, eds. 1974. *The Economics of Property Rights*. Cambridge, Mass.: Ballinger.

Hardin, Garrett. 1968. "The Tragedy of the Commons." *Science* 162: 1243–48.

Hardin, Russell. 1982. *Collective Action*. Baltimore: Johns Hopkins University Press.

Holland, John H. 1975. *Adaptation in Natural and Artificial Systems*. Ann Arbor: University of Michigan Press.

———. 1980. "Adaptive Algorithms for Discovering and Using General Patterns in Growing Knowledge Bases." *International Journal of Policy Analysis and Information Systems* 4: 245–68.

Keohane, Robert O. 1984. *After Hegemony: Cooperation and Discord in the World Political Economy*. Princeton, N.J.: Princeton University Press.

Krasner, Stephen D., ed. 1983. *International Regimes*. Ithaca, N.Y.: Cornell University Press.

Krehbiel, Keith. 1985. Unanimous Consent Agreements: Going Along in the Senate." Working paper no. 568. California Institute of Technology, Social Science Department.

Kreps, David M., and Robert Wilson. 1982. "Sequential Equilibria." *Econometrica* 50: 863–94.

Matthews, Donald R. 1960. *U.S. Senators and Their World*. Chapel Hill: University of North Carolina Press.

Meyers, Samuel M., and William C. Bradbury. 1968. "The Political Behavior of Korean and Chinese Prisoners of War in the Korean Conflict: A Historical Analysis." In *Mass Behavior in Battle and Captivity, The Communist Soldier in the Korean War,* ed. Samuel M. Meyers and Albert D. Briderman, 209–338. Chicago: University of Chicago Press.

Olson, Mancur. 1965. *The Logic of Collective Action*. Cambridge, Mass.: Harvard University Press.

Opp, Karl-Dieter. 1979. "Emergence and Effects of Social Norms—Confrontation of Some Hypotheses of Sociology and Economics." *Kylos* 32: 775–801.

———. 1983. "Evolutionary Emergence of Norms." *British Journal of Social Psychology* 21: 139–49.

Orbell, John M., Peregrine Schwartz-Shea, and Randall T. Simmons. 1984. "Do Cooperators Exit More Readily than Defectors?" *American Political Science Review* 78: 163–78.

Schelling, Thomas. 1978. *Micromotives and Macrobehavior*. New York: W. W. Norton.

Schotter, Andrew. 1981. *Economic Theory of Social Institutions*. Cambridge, Eng.: Cambridge University Press.

Scott, John F. 1971. *Internalization of Norms*. Englewood Cliffs, N.J.: Prentice-Hall.

Selten, R. 1975. "Reexamination of the Perfectness Concept for Equilibrium Points in Extensive Games." *International Journal of Game Theory* 4: 25–55.

Sherif, Muzafer. 1936. *The Psychology of Social Norms*. New York: Harper and Brothers.

Spence, A. Michael. 1974. *Market Signalling*. Cambridge, Mass.: Harvard University Press.

Truman, Ben C. 1884. *Field of Honor: A Complete and Comprehensive History of Dueling in All Countries.* New York: Fords, Howard and Hilbert.

Ullmann-Margalit, Edna. 1977. *The Emergence of Norms.* Oxford: Oxford University Press.

Veblen, Thorstein. 1899. *The Theory of the Leisure Class.* New York: Macmillan.

4

Choosing Sides

MY INTEREST in how political actors choose sides goes back at least to my days in graduate school in the 1960's. For example, my Ph.D. dissertation on conflict of interest included a chapter on coalition formation in parliamentary democracies. The basic idea was that political parties of differing ideologies might have to work together to attain a governing majority, but they seek a set of partners that will cause as little political strain as possible. In other words, politics *minimizes* the strangeness of bedfellows. This idea was contrary to the prevailing view that coalition formation is based solely upon the number of seats each party holds without regard to their politics (Riker 1962). My theory worked fairly well in predicting the membership and duration of Italian coalitions (Axelrod 1970).

The Italian case was relatively easy to analyze because there was a single left-right ideological dimension along which the parties were arrayed. Therefore I was able to predict that the actual coalitions would consist of a connected series of parties in this space, and would be no wider than necessary to form a majority in the parliament. Although the details vary, the importance of ideological affinity for coalition formation has since been confirmed across a wide range of parliamentary democracies (e.g., Lijphart 1981; Laver and Shepsle 1996).

In 1986, I first visited the Santa Fe Institute, a center of research on complexity theory. At the time, there was a great deal of talk about "spin glasses." The spin-glass model is derived from a problem in condensed matter physics. The idea is that each atom tries to align its spin to be consistent with certain of its neighbors and opposite to the others (Anderson 1989; Waldrop 1992, 138–39). This reminded me of my earlier theme that political parties try to minimize the strangeness of their bedfellows. It gave me the idea that the mathematical model of how atoms "choose" magnetic alignments (or spins) might be helpful for thinking about how political actors choose sides. In both cases, many independent actors try to reach an alignment that minimizes their frustration in terms of the actions taken by all other actors.[1] Everything depends on everything else, but a few collective outcomes are more stable than the others.

---

[1] In retrospect, I see that my study of decision-making styles also employed the idea of minimization of strain between many elements of an interacting system. In the case of decision making, the elements were causal arguments connecting policy-relevant variables. I

The spin-glass model was also interesting to me because under certain circumstances it had a geometric representation in terms of energy landscapes. Energy landscapes were very similar to the fitness landscapes that I was used to from evolutionary biology. The geometric representation of landscapes was valuable because movement in such an abstract landscape suggested a way to simulate an agent-based model of how agents choose sides.

I realized that if I could measure the affinity of each political actor to align with each of the others, I could get predictions about what alignments would actually form. I chose the case of European nations involved in World War II because there were enough independent actors to give the theory a good test. Scott Bennett, then a graduate student, and I developed a way to measure the affinity of each pair of nations in terms of characteristics that they might share. We also took account of the relative power of the nations involved. We then did what amounted to an agent-based simulation in which each of the actors kept trying to change sides if it had more affinity with the other protocoalition. Our prediction was simply that the alignment would be one of the few that was stable in the simulation. The prediction actually worked well. Even better, as we used data about propensities and power closer and closer in time to the outbreak of the war, the prediction turned out to be better and better. It even accounted for the contemporaneous pattern of realignment activities when the Warsaw Pact disintegrated.

As discussed in the introductory chapter, the main purpose of agent-based models is not prediction but a deeper understanding of how fundamental social processes operate. In this case, however, Scott and I were also able to operationalize the model and use it to make specific predictions that could be tested with historical data.

This paper has an interesting sequel in which the same theory is employed in a completely different setting, business coalitions. That story is Chapter 5.

References

Anderson, Philip W. 1989. "Spin Glass V: Real Power Brought to Bear." *Physics Today* (July): 9–10.
Axelrod, Robert. 1970. *Conflict of Interest*. Chicago, Ill.: Markham.

---

found that there was a strong tendency for an elite policy maker to present arguments that had no tradeoffs. This eliminated the inconsistencies among different causal paths (Axelrod 1976 and 1977).

———. 1977. "Argumentation in Foreign Policy Settings: Britain in 1918, Munich in 1938 and Japan in 1970." *Journal of Conflict Resolution* 21: 727–56.

———, ed. 1976. *The Structure of Decision*. Princeton, N.J.: Princeton University Press.

Laver, Michael, and Kenneth Shepsle. 1996. *Making and Breaking Governments*. New York: Cambridge University Press.

Lijphart, Arend. 1981. "Power-Sharing Versus Majority Rule: Patterns of Cabinet Formation in Twenty Democracies." *Government and Opposition* 16: 395–413.

Riker, William H. 1962. *The Theory of Political Coalitions*. New Haven: Yale University Press.

Waldrop, M. Mitchell. 1992. *Complexity: The Emerging Science at the Edge of Order and Chaos*. New York: Simon and Schuster.

Choosing Sides

A LANDSCAPE THEORY OF AGGREGATION

ROBERT AXELROD AND D. SCOTT BENNETT

Adapted from Robert Axelrod and D. Scott Bennett "A Landscape Theory of Aggregation," *British Journal of Political Science* 23 (Apr. 1993): 211–33. Reprinted by permission.

Abstract:

Aggregation means the organization of elements of a system into patterns that tend to put highly compatible elements together and less compatible elements apart. Landscape theory predicts how aggregation will lead to alignments among actors (such as nations), whose leaders are myopic in their assessments and incremental in their actions. The predicted configurations are based upon the attempts of actors to minimize their frustration based upon their pairwise propensities to align with some actors and oppose others. These attempts lead to a local minimum in the energy landscape of the entire system. The theory is supported by the results of the alignment of seventeen European nations in the Second World War. The theory has potential for application to coalitions of business firms, political parties in parliaments, social networks, social cleavages in democracies, and organizational structures.

This article presents a formal theory of aggregation, called landscape theory, and provides two tests of the theory. "Aggregation" means the organization of elements of a system in patterns that tend to put highly compatible elements together and less compatible elements apart. Landscape theory uses abstract concepts from the physical sciences and biology that have proved useful in studying the dynamics of complex systems. These concepts provide a way of thinking about the many possible ways in which elements of a system can fit together, predicting which configurations are most likely to occur, how much dissatisfaction with the outcome is inevitable and how the system will respond to changes in the relationship between the elements. As applied to political, economic, and social problems, landscape theory can be used to

For helpful suggestions the authors thank Erhard Bruderer, Michael Cohen, John Holland, Will Mitchell, David Sanders, Carl Simon, Robert Thomas, and anonymous reviewers. This work was supported by National Science Foundation grants SES 8808459 and SES 9106371.

analyze a wide variety of aggregation problems that have previously been considered in isolation:

1. international alignments,
2. alliances of business firms to set standards,
3. coalitions of political parties in parliaments,
4. social networks,
5. social cleavages in democracies, and
6. organizational structures.

In order to be useful, a theory of aggregation should have the following properties:

    a. The theory should provide a coherent explanation of why some particular aggregations (alliances, coalitions, organizational structures, etc.) form in a given system, and not others.

    b. The theory should illuminate the dynamics of aggregation to provide a deeper understanding of the actual process involved as well as the end result.

    c. The theory should be general enough to apply to many domains of politics and society.

    d. The theory should be simple enough to illuminate some fundamental aspects of aggregation.

    e. The theory should be capable of being operationalized so that its predictions can be tested.

This essay seeks to demonstrate that the landscape theory of aggregation offers excellent promise of fulfilling all five of these conditions. In particular, this article provides the first empirical test of a theory of alignment in international politics. It does so by providing a new theoretical approach to aggregation dynamics and by being practical about measurement. The significance of landscape theory is that it can provide a deeper understanding of a wide variety of important aggregation processes in politics, economics and society. How the elements of a system fit together has important implications for such vital issues as the balance of power in international politics, the way in which competing businesses can agree to set standards for their products, the construction of ruling coalitions among parties in parliamentary democracies and the ways political parties appeal to voters in a society with overlapping and cross-cutting cleavages.

By using a common set of concepts to explain a variety of distinct subjects, the current understanding of each subject can be used to help illuminate the others. Moreover, by using a common theory, such as landscape theory, one might reach a deeper understanding of how the aggregation process in each of these domains is similar to the others and how each is different from the others. In addition to purely scientific significance, landscape theory can be used as a guide to policy. For example, by providing a coherent explanation of which international alignments are likely to form, it can suggest where leverage can most efficiently be applied to move from one configuration to another. As another example, the theory could suggest which domestic political coalitions are inherently unstable and which would become stable if critical subgroups could be induced to make minor changes.

The next section formally presents landscape theory, followed by a section on how the concept of an abstract landscape has been used in the physical and natural sciences. Then the operationalization and test of the theory are provided for a case from international politics. The penultimate section shows how the theory could be applied to five other domains as well. The final section considers how the foundations of landscape theory can be made more rigorous.

Landscape Theory

This section explains the formal aspects of the theory, shows how the concepts of the approach may help to illuminate an aggregation process and enumerates the predictions that can be derived from the theory.

Landscape theory predicts how actors will form alignments. To help keep the terminology as simple as possible, the language of international alignments will be used. The theory makes two basic assumptions, both drawn from the recognition that it is difficult for a national leadership to assess the value of each potential alignment. The first assumption is that a nation is myopic in its assessments. In other words, a national leadership evaluates how well it gets along with any other nation independent of all the other members in the system. By making only pairwise evaluations, the national leadership avoids the difficult problem of assessing all combinations of nations at once.

The second basic assumption of landscape theory is that adjustments to alignments take place by incremental movement of individual nations. This rules out the possibility that a coalition will form within an alignment and then switch allegiance as a block. This strong assumption is appropriate when information regarding payoffs is uncertain, resulting in causal ambiguity between alignment actions and payoffs, and a consequent increase in negotiation costs and a reduction in the ability of nations to use side payments to arrive at an optimal solution.

Landscape theory begins with a set of n *actors* (for example, nations). The *size* of a nation, $s_i > 0$, is a reflection of the importance of that country to others. Size might be measured by demographic, industrial, or military factors, or a combination of these, depending on what is taken to be important in a particular application.

The key premise of landscape theory is that each pair of nations, i and j, has a *propensity*, p_{ij}, to work together. The propensity number is positive and large if the two nations get along well together and negative if they have many sources of potential conflict. Put another way, propensity is a measure of how willing the two nations are to be in the same coalition together. If one country has a source of conflict with another (such as a border dispute), then the second country typically has the same source of conflict with the first. Thus the theory assumes that propensity is symmetric, so that $p_{ij} = p_{ji}$.

A *configuration* is a partition of the nations, that is, a placement of each nation into one and only one grouping. An example is the postwar situation in which the nonneutral nations of Europe were divided between NATO and the Warsaw Pact. A specific configuration, X, determines the *distance*, d_{ij}, between any two countries, i and j. In the simplest version of the theory all countries are assumed to be in one of two possible groupings, so we can let distance be 0 if the two countries are in the same grouping, and 1 if the two countries are in different groupings. In other situations, other measures of distance in a configuration will be appropriate.[1]

Using distance and propensity, it is now possible to define a measure of *frustration:* how poorly or well a given configuration satisfies the propensities of a given country to be near or far from each other country. A nation, i, wants to switch sides if the frustration is less on the other side. The frustration of a country, i, in a configuration, X, is just

$$F_i(X) = \sum_{j \neq i} s_j p_{ij} d_{ij}(X) \tag{1}$$

where s_j is the size of j, p_{ij} is the propensity of i to be close to j, and $d_{ij}(X)$ is the distance from i to j in configuration X. The summation is taken over all countries except $j = i$. Note that the definition of frustration weights propensities to work with or against another country by the size of the other country. This takes account of the fact that a source of conflict with a small country is not as important for determining alignments as an equivalent source of conflict with a large country. Notice that a country's frustration will be minimized if it is:

---

[1] For example, the distance between two jobs in a hierarchical organizational structure can be regarded as the number of layers of the organization that have to be ascended to reach a common boss. See discussion of organizational structures below.

a. in the same alliance as those countries with which it has a positive propensity to align, because otherwise $p_{ij} > 0$ and $d_{ij}(X) > 0$, and

b. in a different alliance from those countries with which it has a negative propensity to align, because this would make $d_{ij}(X) > 0$ when $p_{ij} < 0$.

Note also that the myopic assumption is built into the definition of frustration, because a given country's evaluation of a configuration depends on its pairwise propensities with each of the other nations and does not take into account any higher-order interactions among groups of countries.

The next step is to define the *energy*, E, of an entire configuration, X, as the weighted sum of the frustrations of each nation in that configuration, where the weights are just the sizes of the nations. This gives the energy of a configuration as:

$$E(X) = \sum_i s_i F_i(X) \tag{2}$$

Substituting the definition of frustration into this equation allows the calculation of the energy of a configuration in terms of size of the countries, their propensities to work together, and their distances in a particular configuration:

$$E(X) = \sum_{i,j} s_i s_j p_{ij} d_{ij}(X) \tag{3}$$

The summation is over all ordered pairs of distinct countries.

The formula for the energy of a configuration captures the idea that energy is lower (and the configuration is better) when nations that want to work together are in the same grouping, and those that want to work against each other are in different groupings. Size plays a role because having a proper relationship with a large country is more important than having a proper relationship with a small country.

Once energy is defined, the abstraction begins to pay off. Given the energy of each configuration, it is possible to construct an energy *landscape*. The landscape is simply a graph that has a point for each possible configuration and a height above this point for the energy of that configuration. Figure 4-1 shows an example of a landscape where each point in the plane at the bottom of the figure indicates a specific configuration and the surface above the plane represents the energy of that configuration. Adjacent points on the landscape are those that differ in the alignment of a single nation. The landscape has a dimension for each country indicating which alignment it is in. Because it is not possible to draw a large-dimensional hypercube, in Figure 4-1 we have provided a conceptual (two-dimensional) surface instead.

The incremental assumption allows predictions to be made about the dynamics of the system. The incremental assumption provides that only

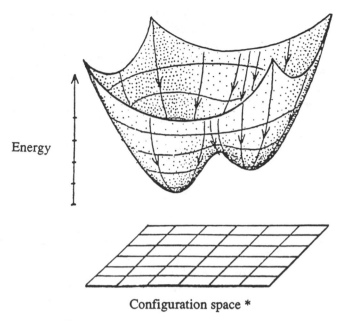

Energy

Configuration space *

Figure 4-1. A Landscape with Two Local Optima. *Source:* Adapted from Abraham and Shaw, *Dynamics—The Geometry of Behavior.* Used with permission.

* The configuration space is an *n*-dimensional binary hypercube. The hypercube has one dimension for each actor indicating which of two possible alignments that actor is in.

one nation at a time will change sides and will do so in a manner to lower its own frustration. Given that the energy of a configuration is the weighted sum of the frustrations of individual nations, when one nation lowers its frustration, the energy of the entire system is lowered.[2] The resulting reduction in energy means that wherever the system starts on the energy landscape, it will run "downhill" to an adjacent configuration that has lower energy. Thus, the changes in alignment patterns will stop only when a configuration is reached that is a local minimum. For example, in Figure 4-1 there are two local minima and thus two potentially stable configurations. Stability here means that the configuration (that is, alignment pattern) does not change any further under existing conditions.

Which stable configuration will occur depends on where the system

[2] The symmetry of propensities guarantees that if one nation reduces its frustration by switching sides, then the energy for the whole system will be reduced. For a proof, see Chapter 5, note 9.

starts. For example, in Figure 4-1 any configuration on the left-hand side of the figure tends to move to the low point on the left-hand side, which happens to be the global minimum. All the configurations that would lead to this minimum can be thought of as the *basin of attraction* of that minimum.

Specifically, the predictions of landscape theory are:

1. From a given starting configuration, the configuration will change according to the principle of downward movement to an adjacent configuration.
2. Consequently, the only stable configurations are those that are at a local minimum in the landscape.
3. With symmetric propensities there can be no cycles of configurations (such as moving from X to Y to Z and then back to X).[3]

An interesting implication of this approach is that the equilibrium reached need not be a global optimum. For example, in Figure 4-1 there are two local minima into which the system can settle. The local minimum on the right is not as good at satisfying the propensities of the countries as is the one on the left. Therefore, if the system happened to start on the far right, it would settle down to a local minimum that was not a global minimum.

Another implication is that there may not be *any* configuration that completely satisfies everyone. Even for a configuration that is the global optimum, most or even all nations may be somewhat *frustrated* in the sense that some "friends" will be in the opposite grouping and/or some "enemies" will be in the same grouping. For example, if there are three nations that mutually dislike each other (such as Israel, Syria, and Iraq), then any possible bipolar configuration will leave someone frustrated.

A further implication is that the local optimum into which the system settles can depend on the history of the system. Early history, which might be in part the consequence of small events or even chance circumstances, can determine which outcome prevails. Thus the outcome may be in part the consequence of a "frozen accident" just as the QWERTY keyboard is.[4] Once the system settles into a basin, it may be difficult to leave it. Moreover, if there is more than one local optimum, the one that the system settles into may not be the one with the lowest energy or the least total frustration.[5]

---

[3] Because every allowable change lowers the energy of the system, the system can never return to a previous configuration.

[4] Paul David, "Clio and the Economics of QWERTY," *American Economics Review Proceedings* 75 (1985): 332–37.

[5] W. Brian Arthur. "Self-Reinforcing Mechanisms in Economics," in *The Economy as an Evolving Complex System,* ed. P. W. Anderson, K. J. Arrow and D. Pines, 9–31. (Reading, Mass.: Addison-Wesley, 1988).

The theory is relevant to policy in that it illuminates where minor changes in the initial configuration can lead to major changes in the final configuration. If one begins near the boundary of two basins of attraction, then a small movement at the start can lead to large changes in the final outcome. In addition, the height of the "pass" between valleys gives the magnitude of the "energy barrier" separating one basin of attraction from another and therefore measures how difficult it would be to move the system from one local optimum to another.

To summarize: landscape theory begins with sizes and pairwise propensities that are used to calculate the energy of each possible configuration and then uses the resulting landscape to make predictions about the dynamics of the system.

Abstract Landscapes in the Physical and Natural Sciences

The idea of an abstract landscape has been widely used in the physical and natural sciences to characterize the dynamics of systems. It was originally developed to study potential energy in physical systems and had its first rigorous development in the context of Hamiltonian systems.[6] Biologists have independently developed landscapes to characterize evolutionary movement in an abstract "fitness landscape" of genes.[7] More recently, energy landscapes have been used in artificial intelligence to characterize the dynamics of complex systems such as neural networks.[8] The landscape theory of aggregation uses concepts that have been developed most thoroughly by physicists and chemists under the label of "frustrated systems" or "spin glasses."[9] A simple example is the Ising

[6] See Vladimir Igorevich Arnol'd, *Mathematical Methods of Classical Mechanics* (New York: Springer, 1978 (translated from the Russian)); Ralph Abraham and Christopher Shaw, *Dynamics—The Geometry of Behavior* (Santa Cruz, Calif.: Aerial Press, 1983); Gregoire Nicolis and Ilya Prigogine, *Exploring Complexity, An Introduction* (New York: Freeman, 1989).

[7] Sewell Wright, "The Roles of Mutation, Inbreeding, Crossbreeding and Selection in Evolution," *Proceedings of the International Congress of Genetics* 1 (1932): 356–66; Stuart A. Kauffman, "Adaptation of Rugged Fitness Landscapes," in *Lectures on the Sciences of Complexity*, ed. Daniel L. Stein (Redwood City, Calif.: Addison-Wesley, 1989), 1: 527–618.

[8] See John J. Hopfield, "Neutral Networks and Physical Systems with Emergent Computational Abilities," *Proceedings of the National Academy of Sciences (USA)* 79 (1982): 2554–58. In biology and artificial intelligence, the polarity of the landscape is reversed so that the improvement is thought of as hill-climbing rather than descent into valleys.

[9] David Pines, ed., *Emerging Synthesis in Science* (Santa Fe, N.M.: Santa Fe Institute, 1985); Debashish Chowdhury, *Spin Glasses and Other Frustrated Systems* (Princeton, N.J.: Princeton University Press, 1986); Marc Mezard, Giorgio Parisi, and Miguel Angel Virasoro, *Spin Glass Theory and Beyond* (Singapore: World Scientific, 1987).

model that studies how magnets on a plane can attain various alignments based upon their mutual attraction or repulsion.[10] Another common application is the stability of alignment of chemical bonds.[11] Landscape theory borrows four key ideas from these settings: a set of elements have pairwise propensities to align with each other in specific ways, each possible configuration has an "energy," the resulting landscape shows all possible configurations, and the dynamics of the system can be predicted from the initial conditions and the shape of the landscape. Landscape theory adds the possibility of unequal sizes of units and allows operationalizations of propensities and distances that are appropriate to specific social science applications. Unlike spin-glass theory, landscape theory does not assume that the propensities are randomly determined. Recently, landscapes have been used to explore fundamental properties of dynamic systems. In particular, catastrophe theory studies how basins of attraction can be formed or disappear due to changes in the shape of the landscape.[12]

Landscapes have not been widely used in game theory, but some of the predictions of landscape theory can be stated in game-theoretic terms. Landscape theory says that the stable configurations are exactly those that are in Nash equilibrium. What landscape theory adds to game theory is a way of characterizing all possible configurations and the dynamics among them. In particular, the idea of descent from less satisfactory patterns to more satisfactory patterns helps one characterize the entire range of possibilities in a manner that is sometimes obscure in game: theoretic treatments of n-person settings. Moreover, the idea of descent need not be justified by an appeal to farsighted rational decision making, but can easily be the result of a process in which each actor responds to the current situation in a shortsighted attempt to achieve local improvement.

Before turning to some applications of the landscape theory of aggregation, it should be pointed out that aggregation has been studied without landscapes as a descriptive problem in statistics. In the social sciences, the most commonly used descriptive technique is cluster analysis.[13] Cluster analysis has been described as "the art of finding

[10] W. Weidlick, "Statistical Description of Polarization Phenomena in Society," *British Journal of Mathematical Statistical Psychology* 24 (1971): 251–66; Daniel L. Stein, "Disordered Systems: Mostly Spin Glasses," in *Lectures on the Sciences of Complexity,*, ed. Daniel L. Stein (Redwood City, Calif.: Addison-Wesley, 1989), 1: 301–53.

[11] Nicolis and Prigogine, *Exploring Complexity.*

[12] Rene Thom, *Structural Stability and Morphogenesis* (Reading, Mass.: W. A. Benjamin, 1975 (translated from French)); E. C. Zeeman, *Catastrophe Theory* (Reading, Mass.: Addison-Wesley, 1977).

[13] Mark S. Aldenderfer and Roger K. Blashfield, *Cluster Analysis* (Beverly Hills, Calif.: Sage, 1984); Benjamin Duran and Patrick L. Odell, *Cluster Analysis* (Berlin: Springer-

groups in data,"[14] and is used "as a descriptive or exploratory tool, in contrast with statistical tests which are carried out for inferential or confirmatory purposes."[15] Unlike landscape theory, however, cluster analysis is not based on a dynamic theory of behavior and it cannot make predictions.[16]

Predicting the Alignment of the Second World War in Europe

In international relations, aggregation is usually studied in the context of alliances. The dominant approach to explaining international alliances is that states form alliances primarily to resist aggression by other powerful states.[17] Based upon the realist paradigm, this balancing behavior assumes an anarchic international system in which all states view each other as potential enemies. In landscape theory, this is equivalent to saying that all propensities are equal and negative. Given all negative propensities, landscape theory would then predict as stable any alignment where the two alliances are balanced in terms of size, as these configurations are at a local minimum of energy. If size is interpreted as power, the predictions of landscape theory under realist assumptions are precisely balance of power alliances.

Verlag, 1974); Leonard Kaufman and Peter J. Rousseeuw, *Finding Groups in Data: An Introduction to Cluster Analysis* (New York: Wiley, 1990).

[14] Kaufman and Rousseeuw, *Finding Groups in Data*, 1.

[15] Ibid., 37.

[16] Other techniques that measure how good particular configurations are according to specific static criteria based on pairwise relationships include blockmodeling, for which see Wayne Baker, "Three-Dimensional Blockmodels," *Journal of Mathematical Sociology* 12 (1986); 191–223; for simplicial decomposition, see D. W. Hearn, S. Lawphongpanich, and J. A. Ventura, "Finiteness in Restricted Simplicial Decomposition," *Operations Research Letters* 4 (1985): 125–30; for correspondence and canonical analysis, see Stanley Wasserman, Katherine Faust, and Joseph Galaskiewicz, "Correspondence and Canonical Analysis of Relational Data," *Journal of Mathematical Sociology* 11 (1989): 11–64; and for a variety of techniques based on factor analysis including smallest space analysis and nonlinear mapping, see Brian Everitt, *Graphical Techniques for Multivariate Data* (London: Heineman Educational Books, 1978). There are also econometric techniques to analyze how variables in dynamic systems aggregate from nearly decomposable subsystems: see Herbert A. Simon and Albert Ando, "Aggregation of Variables in Dynamic Systems," *Econometrica* 29 (1961): 111–38; Herbert A. Simon and Yuma Iwasaki, "Causal Ordering, Comparative Statics, and Near Decomposability," *Journal of Econometrics* 39 (1988): 149–73; Finn Kydland, "Hierarchical Decomposition in Linear Economic Models," *Management Science* 21 (1975): 1029–39.

[17] Hans J. Morgenthau, *Politics Among Nations* (New York: Alfred A. Knopf, 1956); Kenneth N. Waltz, *Theory of International Politics* (Reading, Mass.: Addison-Wesley, 1979).

Actually, when states make alignment choices they take into account more than just power. Walt develops neorealism by showing that states balance against particular threats.[18] Snyder notes that states have some interests that affect their behavior toward all other countries, such as the desire to be militarily secure, but also have specific conflicts and affinities with particular other states based upon ideological, ethnic, economic, or prestige values.[19] These "general interests" and "particular interests" establish a "tacit pattern of alignment" among states.[20] Combining these interests with the neorealist paradigm, it can be argued that Snyder's "conflicts and commonalities" contribute to the threat that states perceive from others. Liska goes so far as to suggest that ideology and historic biases may preclude "rational" alignment choices.[21] In fact, it is not unusual for scholars to note that alliance choices depend upon both power and interest.[22]

Unfortunately, particular interests and affinities have not yet been integrated into a coherent model of alignments. Landscape theory offers a way to provide this integration by representing divergent interests in the single concept of propensity, which combines with the size (power) of states to determine outcomes.

Landscape theory also provides a way of overcoming a second limitation of some leading alliance studies.[23] These studies of alliance formation focus on the decisions of individual states and hence do not predict the overall pattern of alliance aggregation. Landscape theory predicts the overall configuration by explicitly taking into account sequences of state action in reducing frustration until a local minimum is reached.

Let us now turn to the operationalization and testing of landscape the-

[18] Stephen M. Walt, *The Origins of Alliances* (Ithaca, N.Y.: Cornell University Press, 1987).

[19] Glenn H. Snyder, "The Security Dilemma in Alliance Politics," *World Politics* 36 (1984): 461–95.

[20] Ibid., 464.

[21] George Liska, *Nations in Alliance* (Baltimore, Md.: Johns Hopkins University Press, 1962): 27.

[22] See Ole R. Holsti, Terence Hopmann, and John D. Sullivan, *Unity and Disintegration in International Alliances: Comparative Studies* (New York: Wiley, 1973), 263–67 for a listing of hypotheses on alliance formation that go beyond power; also see James D. Morrow, "Social Choice and System Structure in World Politics," *World Politics* 41 (1988): 75–97.

[23] For example, Michael F. Altfeld and Bruce Bueno de Mesquita, "Choosing Sides in War," *International Studies Quarterly* 23 (1979): 87–112; Michael F. Altfeld, "The Decision to Ally: A Theory and Test," *Western Political Quarterly* 37 (1984): 523–44; James D. Morrow, "On the Theoretical Basis of a Measure of National Risk Attitudes," *International Studies Quarterly* 31 (1987): 423–38; Stephen M. Walt, "Testing Theories of Alliance Formation: The Case of Southwest Asia," *International Organization* 42 (1988): 275–316; and Walt, *Origins of Alliances*.

[handwritten margin notes: LFR in 2 aspects - "propensities" = palms of / Typology ≅ States Dyadly Quand (threat)·1 / + typology]

ory as it applies to international alignments. In any application, the operationalization and testing of landscape theory require answers to four questions:

1. Who are the actors?
2. What are their sizes?
3. What are the propensities between every pair of actors?
4. What is the actual outcome?

The answers to these questions depend on the specific domain being investigated. The operationalization and testing of the theory for international alignments can be illustrated and tested with the example of Europe in the years preceding the Second World War. This case is an appropriate test of landscape theory even given the assumption that actors are limited to membership in one of two alignments. In times when war is likely, states tend to divide into two opposing groups, for, as Waltz notes, "the game of power politics, if really played hard, presses the players into two rival camps, though so complicated is the business of making and maintaining alliances that the game may be played hard enough to produce that result only under the pressure of war."[24] The object of the test is to predict the alignment of nations that actually occurred during the war. The actors are the seventeen European nations who were involved in major diplomatic action in the 1930's.[25] The size of each nation is measured with the national capabilities index of the Correlates of War project.[26] The national capabilities index combines six components of demographic, industrial and military power.

As noted previously, power is not the only factor that states consider when making alignment choices. However, although power has been explored as it affects alignment and conflict behavior, we know of no existing typology of state interests that would allow us to create a measure of interest-based propensities. We have attempted to create such a typology here. We divide state interests vis-à-vis other states into ethnic, religious,

---

[24] Waltz, *Theory of International Politics,* 167.

[25] Specifically, the countries selected are the five major European powers (Britain, France, Germany, Italy, and the Soviet Union) and the twelve countries that had a formal defense or neutrality pact with any of them. Turkey was not considered to be in Europe. Two European countries were excluded: Albania because it was not independent of Italy, and Belgium because it withdrew from its defense agreement with France in 1936. Information about which was allied with which was not used in the analysis. The sources of alliance data are J. David Singer and Melvin Small, "Formal Alliances, 1815–1939," *Journal of Peace Research* 3 (1966): 1–31; and Melvin Small and J. David Singer, "Formal Alliances, 1815–1965: An Extension of the Basic Data," *Journal of Peace Research* 6 (1969): 257–82.

[26] David J. Singer, Stuart Bremer, and John Stuckey, "Capability Distribution, Uncertainty and Major Power War, 1920–1965," in *Peace, War, and Numbers,* ed. Bruce Russett (Beverly Hills, Calif.: Sage, 1972): 19–48.

territorial, ideological, economic and historical concerns. We believe that
this typology captures the main sources of affinities and differences between states as they might affect strategic calculations. More specifically,
in each dyad in our population we measure the presence of ethnic conflict, the similarity of the religions of the populations, the existence of a
border disagreement, the similarity of the types of governments, and the
existence of a recent history of wars between the states.[27] These five factors are combined with equal weights to provide a measure of the propensity of each pair of nations to work together.[28] Using the above
methods of measuring size and propensity, the energy was then calculated
for each of the 65,536 possible configurations.[29]

The behavior being predicted is the alignment of each country in the
Second World War. This is measured by whether a country was invaded
by another country, or had war declared against it.[30] By this criterion the
actual alignment of the Second World War in Europe was Britain, France,
the Soviet Union, Czechoslovakia, Denmark, Greece, Poland, and
Yugoslavia vs. Germany, Italy, Hungary, Estonia, Finland, Latvia,
Lithuania, and Romania. Portugal, which had a defense agreement with
Britain, was neutral.

Using the 1936 size data, the resulting landscape has two local minima,
which can be called Configuration 1 and Configuration 2. These two
configurations are shown in Table 4-1. They provide the specific predictions of what would happen when war came. The results are striking.
Configuration 1 was almost the exact alignment of the Second World

[27] Due to the limitations of available data, we have not been able to operationalize
economic issues and the level of economic interdependence in all dyads. Hence, we have
simply omitted this category when calculating propensity.

[28] With n countries, there are $n(n - 1)/2$ pairwise propensities. For $n = 17$, there are
136 pairwise propensities. Propensities are estimated as follows: ethnic conflict, a border
disagreement, or a recent history of war between two nations counted as -1 each for their
propensity. Similarity of religion was counted as $+1$ within categories (Catholic, Protestant,
Orthodox, Muslim, and Atheist), and -1 across major categories (Christian, Muslim,
Atheist), all calculated according to proportions of each religion in each country. Similarity
or difference of government type was considered for two countries with democratic, fas-
cists, or communist governments: $+1$ if they were the same type and -1 if they were of
different types. The source for ethnic conflict, border disagreement, history of war, and
government type is Hermann Kinder and Werner Hilgemann, *The Anchor Atlas of World
History*, vol. II (New York: Anchor Press, 1978). Religion is given in the Correlates of War
Project's Cultural Data Set for 1930 (version of 7/90 prepared by Phil Schaefer). Selecting
equal weights for the five propensity factors is the least arbitrary way of combining them.

[29] This is $2^{17}/2$. Each country can be in one of two possible sides, but which side is listed
first is arbitrary.

[30] For example, Britain declared war on Germany in 1939. Poland was first invaded by
Germany and hence is counted as being aligned opposite to Germany. Hungary and Romania were allied with Germany and in 1941 assisted in the invasion of the Soviet Union.

TABLE 4-1
The Two Configurations Predicted for the Second World War in Europe

CONFIGURATION 2	CONFIGURATION 1	
	Alignment 1	*Alignment 2*
Alignment 1	Britain (7.45)	Germany (11.49)
	France (5.32)	Italy (4.03)
	Czechoslovakia (1.15)	Poland (1.83)
	Denmark (0.20)	Romania (0.78)
		Hungary (0.45)
		Portugal (0.27)
		Finland (0.19)
		Latvia (0.13)
		Lithuania (0.10)
		Estonia (0.06)
Alignment 2	Soviet Union (15.01)	
	Yugoslavia (0.59)	(None)
	Greece (0.35)	
Nearest empirical match[a]	Allies (and those invaded by Germany)	Axis (and those invaded by the Soviet Union)

Note: The size is shown in parentheses, in terms of percentage of world capabilities. The predictions are based upon 1936 data.
[a]In Configuration 1, only Poland and Portugal are wrong.

War, the exceptions being Poland and Portugal which were incorrectly placed on the German side. Configuration 2 is best characterized as a pro- vs. anti-Soviet alignment consisting of the Soviet Union, Greece, and Yugoslavia against all the others.[31]

What is one to make of this? First of all, the result is statistically significant: the probability that one of only two predictions would have no more than two mistakes among the seventeen countries predicted is less than one in 200.[32] In addition, Configuration 1 had a basin of attraction that was more than twice the size of the other local minimum (47,945 configurations vs. 17,591), and hence it would be more likely to occur from a random starting initial situation.[33] Thus the configuration with

[31] In Configuration 2, Greece and Yugoslavia join the Soviet Union largely to avoid aligning with Germany, with whom both have a history of war.

[32] There are 154 configurations that are as accurate or more so than the configuration that had two mistakes among the seventeen predicted nations. Because two different predictions are made and there are $2^{17}/2 = 65,536$ configurations, the chance that one of them would be this good is $2 \times (154/65,536) = 0.0047$.

[33] Steepest descent in the energy landscape is used to calculate basin size.

the larger of the two basins of attraction was just two countries removed (Poland and Portugal) from the actual alignment of the Second World War. This configuration also had the global minimum of energy. Even more important, this configuration correctly accounted for the alignments of all the large nations and almost all of the smaller ones as well. In all, it correctly accounted for 96 percent of the total size of the countries, as measured by their national capabilities index of demographic, industrial, and military power.

As history played out, the nations did not get into the smaller basin of attraction, the one whose minimum was essentially a pro- and anti-Soviet alignment. Although such an outcome seems implausible given what we now know happened, it probably did not look quite so implausible to the participants at the time.[34] The error in placing Poland on the German side in the globally optimum configuration is not a preposterous one. Poland's foreign policy was antagonistic to both its powerful neighbors, Germany and the Soviet Union. In fact, although Germany invaded Poland first, on September 1, 1939, the Soviets invaded just sixteen days later. The error of placing Portugal on the German side (when it actually stayed neutral with pro-British sympathies) could be attributable to inadequate measures of cultural and economic affinity.[35]

Although Configuration 1 was quite close to what happened, an interesting alternative possibility is presented by Configuration 2, in which the Soviet Union aligned with Greece and Yugoslavia against everyone else (see Table 4-1). In both configurations, Greece and Yugoslavia join the Soviet Union largely to avoid aligning with Germany, with which both have a history of war. Likewise, in both configurations, Germany and the Soviet Union are on opposite sides. Almost everyone had reasons to avoid aligning with either Germany or the Soviet Union. The key difference is that the democracies and their friends aligned against one of these large antagonists in the first configuration and aligned against the other one in the second configuration.

---

[34] For example, as late as 1939 when the Soviet Union invaded Finland, there were some active voices in Britain and France calling for intervention against the Soviet Union, despite the growing consensus that Germany was the major threat. Had Germany not blocked access by invading Norway, such action against the Soviets would not have been out of the question. Incidentally, the main reason that Yugoslavia and Greece side with the Soviet Union in Configuration 2 is that they both have a war history with Germany, but no serious problems with the Soviet Union.

[35] The error of placing Poland on the German side occurred because Poland disliked the Soviet Union even more than it disliked Germany. This in turn was largely due to the Soviet Union's greater size (national capabilities) in 1936. As discussed below, this error was eliminated by 1939, as Germany mobilized its strength faster than the Soviet Union did. Portugal, which was actually neutral, was incorrectly placed on the German side because that side was more favorable for Portugal's Catholic religious propensity.

The actual alignment of the Second World War has thus been predicted quite well as early as 1936 by landscape theory using a standard power measure and the propensity measure developed above. However, it is possible that the simpler "realist" approach would do just as well. The realist approach assumes that all countries, or at least all major countries, fear each other. This can be operationalized in terms of the landscape theory by setting the pairwise propensities to be equal and negative, say -1. We tested the realist model and found that it did poorly. An analysis of the seventeen countries with all -1 propensities and the size measure from above found not two but 209 different stable configurations, none of which was as accurate as the landscape theory prediction. An analysis of the five Great Powers with -1 propensities found four possible stable configurations, of which none was the actual outcome of Britain, France, and the Soviet Union aligned against Germany and Italy. It seems that without the additional information provided by knowing what specific ethnic, religious, territorial, ideological, and historic issues existed between countries in 1936, a realist model does not have adequate information to make useful predictions. The basic problem with the realist approach is that without enough information to distinguish various types of pairwise propensities to align, large numbers of different alignments are equally plausible.

It is also possible that a cluster analysis of the propensity matrix might have revealed the Second World War alignment. Although cluster analysis normally assumes that the objects being clustered have equal weight, to approximate the landscape analysis more closely, we created a dissimilarity matrix of propensities weighted by sizes. We clustered this matrix with a standard hierarchical agglomerative technique, using the unweighted pair-group average (UPGMA) method of computing cluster dissimilarities, which we believe to be most appropriate for our purposes.[36] The two-cluster solution found Greece and the Soviet Union against everyone else, similar to the second optimum found by landscape theory, but not close to what happened historically. When we clustered Great Powers only, the analysis similarly placed the Soviet Union on the side opposite to Britain, France, Germany, and Italy.

Thus it seems that in a static analysis, landscape theory is superior to alternative methods of computing likely alignments. A further test can be provided by the observation that, as the Second World War approached, the relative sizes (that is, national capabilities) of the countries changed, due largely to the rapid growth of military expenditures, especially in Germany. An interesting exercise is to see how the landscape and the predictions change as these changes in national capabilities are entered

---

[36] Kaufman and Rousseeuw, *Finding Groups in Data*, 47–48.

into the calculations, bringing us closer to the time when war actually broke out.[37]

For 1937, the same two configurations appear as we saw for 1936, namely, Configuration 1, which is the alignment of the Second World War (except for Poland and Portugal), and Configuration 2, which is the pro- and anti-Soviet alignment. In 1938, however, there is only one local minimum and it is Configuration 1 again. Configuration 2 is no longer a local minimum. This coincides with the growing consensus in Britain that coordination with the Soviet Union might become necessary despite the repugnance of communism. In 1939, there is again only one local minimum, and it is similar to Configuration 1, only now Poland has moved from the anti-Soviet side to the anti-German side. This coincides with the growing strength of Germany, which made it much stronger than the Soviet Union by 1939.

In summary, the theory does very well in predicting the European alignment of the Second World War with data up to 1936, but does even better as later data are used. By 1938, the predictions are narrowed from two to one, and by 1939 the single prediction becomes accurate for all but one of the seventeen countries.[38] The chance that the single prediction of 1939 would be correct for sixteen of seventeen countries is less than one in three thousand.[39] Moreover, the ways in which landscape theory's predictions converged on the unique historically correct outcome seem to mirror the changes that actually took place in the late 1930s in Europe as the nations mobilized for war.

It is remarkable that such a simple theory and such a parsimonious operationalization of its concepts can come up with a prediction that is very close to what actually happened. Almost as striking is that departures from what actually happened reflect tenable alternatives to the way history played out.

We are aware of only one other theoretical prediction of the alignments in the Second World War. This is the rational-choice theory of Altfeld and Bueno de Mesquita, which predicts how nations will choose sides once a war is under way.[40] Unlike landscape theory, which uses

[37] The only change in the factors that went into the propensities from 1936 to 1939 was that Romania switched from a democratic government to an authoritarian government in 1938. Thus the changes in the landscape from 1936 to 1939 were almost entirely due to changes in the national capabilities of the various countries as they mobilized for war.

[38] Note that six of these countries were not destined to enter the war on either side for another year or two. In 1940 Hungary and Romania allied with Germany, and Denmark and Greece were invaded. In 1941, Yugoslavia and the Soviet Union were invaded.

[39] Because there are 65,536 different configurations, and only eighteen of them are off by zero or one country, the probability of a result this good happening by chance is $18/65,536 = 0.00027$.

[40] Altfeld and Bueno de Mesquita, "Choosing Sides in War."

alliance behavior only to identify active states, the Altfeld and Bueno de Mesquita model uses alliances to identify the utilities of the states and bases its predictions about alignments in war on these alliances patterns. The data used by landscape theory (such as religious and ideological differences) are much further back in the causal chain of predicting wartime alignment than are alliance data. Moreover, the Altfeld and Bueno de Mesquita model predicts events only after the outbreak of the war (for example, avoiding having to predict that Germany and Poland are on opposite sides), whereas landscape theory uses data only from before the outbreak of war, even years before. Yet another difference is that the Altfeld and Bueno de Mesquita model assesses its predictions only for countries that entered the war within two months of the outbreak, whereas the landscape theory makes predictions for all diplomatically active countries. A major limitation of the Altfeld and Bueno de Mesquita model is that it requires information about the actual wartime alignments to make any predictions because it needs this information to estimate the relative impact of the components of the expected utility equations. On the other hand, the Altfeld and Bueno de Mesquita model is superior in allowing for neutrality and in being applicable with only small modifications to wars over a long time period (1816–1965). In terms of results, the Altfeld and Bueno de Mesquita model failed to predict that Britain and France would enter the war against Germany and instead predicted that both would remain neutral. The landscape model predicted Britain and France correctly, as well as other countries that did not become involved in the conflict for several years.

Given the success of landscape theory in predicting all of the major powers, and almost all of the minor ones as well, we next applied landscape theory to the fluid situation of Europe in 1990 to see what would be predicted after the Soviet Union ceased to impose its will on eastern Europe. The analysis used the nineteen European countries that were members of NATO or the Warsaw Pact in 1989, taking account of the unification of Germany, but not the subsequent disintegration of the Soviet Union. The operationalization used the same size measure as before. There are two changes in the operationalizations of propensities, however. First, because virtually all European governments are or aspire to be market-oriented democracies, ideology was dropped as a factor contributing to propensity. Second, economic relations were included as a factor in propensity, measured by mutual membership in the Common Market.[41] Starting at the 1989 (nonoptimum) East-West alignment, land

---

[41] Thus, mutual membership in the EEC added one point to the propensities of a pair of such countries. Because of limited data availability from the former Eastern bloc countries, a more precise measure of economic interdependence is unavailable. War history was based

scape theory made the single prediction that the Soviet Union would be deserted by all of its former European allies except Bulgaria. Events prior to the collapse of the Soviet Union suggest that this was indeed what was taking place. In 1991, Poland, Czechoslovakia, and Hungary sought a formal relationship with NATO, and NATO invited them to join a new North Atlantic Cooperation Council.[42] Only Romania has failed to act in the predicted manner before the breakup of the Soviet Union. (The probability that only one error would occur by chance with this many countries is less than one in a thousand.) In terms of size, the predictions correctly accounted for 97 percent of the national capabilities of the system. In sum, the landscape theory correctly predicted that the breakup of the Warsaw Pact would result in most of the Soviet Union's allies seeking to join the Western alignment and none of the NATO members seeking to leave. Although this may not be surprising, it does show that a theory that worked for the 1930's can also work for the 1990's.

Other Potential Applications

Business Alliances

In economics, the main approach to alliance formation is to calculate and compare "coalition structure values" for each possible configuration[43] and then use a standard game-theoretic analysis to determine both the alliance configuration that is likely to emerge and the stability of each configuration. Unfortunately, the coalition structure value framework is difficult to apply to empirical data because it requires identifying and quantifying payoffs for each actor in every conceivable configuration. Unlike the reliance of landscape theory on pairwise propensities, payoffs for each firm depend in complex ways on choices made by all the other firms. For example, in the standards setting case, the size of the market will vary with the number of standards, and a given firm's market share will vary with (among other factors) how quickly the firm can bring a

---

on the Second World War; Italy was considered to have a war history with no one because it fought on both sides. An additional source for coding ethnic conflicts is Stephen F. Larrabee, "Long Memories and Short Fuses, Change and Instability in the Balkans," *International Security* 15 (1990/91): 58–91. Size data were available as of 1985. To simplify the calculations, Benelux was treated as one country and Spain/Portugal as another.

[42] *New York Times,* Nov. 11, 1991 and Jan. 11, 1992.

[43] Guillermo Owen, "Values of Games with a Priori Unions," in *Essays in Mathematical Economics and Game Theory,* ed. R. Hein and O. Moeschlin (New York: Springer-Verlag, 1977): 77–88.

product to market relative to the other firms. Not surprisingly, there has not been a single empirical test of the coalition structure values approach for the problem of standards setting.

Landscape theory, on the other hand, lends itself to empirical testing in a business setting. Chapter 5 demonstrates how landscape theory can be applied to the struggle among nine firms over the setting of a technical standard.

Coalitions of Political Parties in Parliaments

Most democracies have a parliamentary system in which political parties must form a majority coalition in order to govern. At least fourteen theories have been proposed to account for which coalitions will actually form, and empirical research on a score of countries shows that the ideological distances between the parties helps explain the results.[44] Data are available for hundreds of coalitions in all. Although most studies use only ordinal measures of ideological distance, interval level measurement is also available.[45] If the ideological distance between any two parties is regarded as inversely related to their propensity to work together, then landscape theory offers a natural way to predict parliamentary coalitions.

Social Networks

Sociologists describe social networks based upon the pairwise relationships between individuals. A classic example is the Western Electric Bank Wiring Room, with fourteen men each having six types of social ties.[46] Other examples are detailed data about the selection of a dorm head at MIT[47] and dynamic data about friendship networks.[48] Given the data

[44] Abraham DeSwaan, *Coalition Theories and Cabinet Formation* (San Francisco: Jossey-Bass, 1973).

[45] Michael-John Morgan, "The Modeling of Governmental Coalition Formation" (Ph.D. diss., Political Science Department, University of Michigan); Michael Laver and Norman Schofield, *Multiparty Government: The Politics of Europe* (Oxford: Oxford University Press, 1990); Michael Laver and W. Ben Hunt, *Policy and Party Competition* (New York: Routledge, 1992).

[46] George C. Homans, *The Human Group* (New York: Harcourt Brace, 1950); Peter Carrington and Greg H. Heil, "Coblock: A Hierarchical Method for Blocking Network Data," *Journal of Mathematical Sociology* 8 (1981): 103–31.

[47] Kathleen Carley, "An Approach for Relating Social Structure to Cognitive Structure," *Journal of Mathematical Sociology* 12 (1986): 137–89.

[48] Theodore M. Newcomb, *The Acquaintance Process* (New York: Holt, Rinehart and Winston, 1961).

about the pairwise propensities of individuals to be friends, landscape theory offers a natural way to predict how a number of people will form clusters of friendships.

Social Cleavages in Democracies

Social cleavages based upon ethnicity, race, religion, class, and so forth exist in every society, although which cleavages are most important differs from one society to another. In a democracy, political parties typically try to build electoral coalitions in part by paying close attention to the issues that appeal to those on one side or the other of these cleavages. Consequently, the structure of electoral coalitions and the stability of a political system depend in part on whether the major cleavages in a society are mutually reinforcing or are cross-cutting.[49] Cleavage theory has a wide application, from debates over redistricting in the United States to the prospects for survival of a multinational state such as the Soviet Union.

Landscape theory offers a way of formalizing cleavage theory and relating it to other coalition theories. To apply landscape theory to social cleavages, the propensities of groups to ally could be based on their pairwise conflict of interest. For example, from the 1930's to at least the 1960's, blacks and Catholics in the United States shared many political interests and therefore a political party could efficiently appeal to both. To account for an alignment such as the New Deal Coalition, landscape theory would need to be extended to allow each group to belong to a coalition to some degree rather than completely or not at all. With this extension, landscape theory could predict how changes in pairwise propensities among the groups would affect the resulting electoral coalitions. For example, it could address the question of whether in a given two-party system there is a single "natural" electoral coalition configuration at each point in time. It could also characterize conditions under which electoral coalitions would change rapidly from one local minimum to another resulting in so-called "critical elections."[50]

Landscape theory could also compare the cleavage structures of different societies to analyze the degree to which each country's cleavage pattern results in a "frustrated system."[51] An interesting feature of cleavage theory is that it proposes that democratic systems are actually more sta-

[49] Edward Alsworth Ross, *The Principles of Sociology* (New York: Century, 1920); Robert A. Dahl, *Pluralist Democracy in the United States* (Chicago: Rand McNally, 1967).
[50] Walter Dean Burnham, *Critical Elections* (New York: Norton, 1970).
[51] For example, Seymour M. Lipset and Stein Rokkan, *Party Systems and Voter Alignments: Cross-National Perspectives* (New York: The Free Press, 1967).

ble if their cleavages result in a frustrated system. The reason is that when cleavages are cross-cutting, few people will be completely dissatisfied.

Organizational Structures

An important principle in organization theory is that an efficient organization is structured so that jobs that require frequent interaction are placed near each other in the organizational structure.[52] In landscape theory, the propensity of two jobs to be near each other can be measured by their natural rate of interaction. The distance between two jobs in a given organizational structure can be regarded as the number of layers of the organization that have to be ascended to reach a common boss. Landscape theory might help account for how organizations can have two completely different stable configurations, as when the State Department can be set up along functional lines or along geographic lines.

Conclusion

Landscape theory is able to predict international alignments. It also offers promise in applications to business alliances, parliamentary coalitions, friendship networks, social cleavages, and organizational structures.

To improve the foundations of landscape theory, two activities would be helpful. First, the particular functional form that the theory takes should be justified in rigorous terms. One way to do this would be to develop a formal set of axioms about the way actors of bounded rationality behave in settings that allow aggregation. The axioms could specify how information about size and propensity is used by the actors in making their myopic choices and how the choices are made incrementally. Additional axioms would specify the allowable forms of aggregation and the symmetry of propensities. With these axioms it should be possible to demonstrate that the formula for energy of a configuration is the appropriate one, that the dynamics of the system must correspond to decreases in energy and that the only stable points of the system are the configurations that have locally minimum energy. Moreover, such a set of axioms would be useful in showing how landscape theory relates to other theories of choice and how variations in landscape theory could lead to other dynamics.

The other way in which the foundations of landscape theory could be improved is by providing guidance on how the concepts of the theory

[52] James D. Thompson, *Organizations in Action* (New York: McGraw-Hill, 1967).

should be operationalized in a particular application. Having a well-developed set of ideas about how propensity should be measured would be particularly helpful. Obviously, the details of measurement of propensity will vary from one application to another. Nevertheless, the use of a limited number of factors to determine all the pairwise propensities is likely to be widely applicable. So it would be helpful to develop some guidance on how these factors should be chosen, and how they should be coded and combined. An example of such guidance is the following: if there are complementary characteristics of actors that allow positive externalities from joint action, then such complementary characteristics should be included as one of the factors, and that factor should be coded so that actors who are dissimilar in this way have a positive propensity to work together.

To appreciate the overall orientation of landscape theory, an analogy to research on the Prisoner's Dilemma will help. The value of the Prisoner's Dilemma is not only that it gives accurate predictions, but also that it leads to a deeper understanding of political processes, such as the way in which the shadow of the future is essential for cooperation among egoists. Likewise, the intended value of landscape theory is not only in providing accurate predictions, but also in leading to a deeper understanding of aggregation processes such as the way in which an energy landscape can determine which configurations are stable. Just as the Prisoner's Dilemma helps us to see important similarities across a wide range of applications, landscape theory helps us to see how the aggregation processes in many different areas do indeed have a surprising similarity when viewed with the aid of a common theoretical framework.

5

Setting Standards

TWO PROFESSORS in the Business School at Michigan, Will Mitchell and Robert Thomas, heard me give a talk about my landscape theory with its application to wartime alignments (Chapter 4). They said that it reminded them of strategic alignments between companies. They asked if I would be interested in seeing if the theory worked in a commercial setting. So Scott Bennett and I joined Will Mitchell, Robert Thomas, and a graduate student of theirs, Erhard Bruderer, to see what would happen if we applied the same theory to a business case.

We chose the case of nine computer companies that were forming competing alliances, each seeking to establish standards for the UNIX operating system. The ability to impose technical standards on an emerging technology is often the key to its commercial success. The UNIX case was important in its own right, and was also a good illustration of the fundamental problems involved in the important area of setting technical standards. The case was also a good one for testing the landscape theory because it involved so many different companies. It worked again.

I wish I could say that these two essays using landscape theory were well received. In fact, both had trouble even getting published. A primary difficulty was that some of the reviewers did not take to the idea that an approach other than game theory could be helpful for the understanding of how actors make strategic choices. The reviewers preferred a rational-choice explanation to one that was motivated by actors with bounded rationality. It is true that the strategic choices could be put in game-theory terms using the concept of Nash equilibria. Indeed, we revised the description of the business case to highlight this fact. The point, however, is that virtually all of the power of landscape theory is in the determination of preferences (or affinities) rather than in the justification of the strategic choice. Game theory, of course, assumes preferences are given, and does not worry about where they come from. In fact, something of a paradigm shift is required to imagine that nations or business firms choose sides based upon compatibility with others rather than on the basis of forward-looking strategic calculations.

Setting Standards

COALITION FORMATION IN STANDARD-SETTING ALLIANCES

ROBERT AXELROD, WILL MITCHELL, ROBERT E. THOMAS,
D. SCOTT BENNETT, AND ERHARD BRUDERER

Reprinted from Robert Axelrod, Will Mitchell, Robert E. Thomas, D. Scott Bennett, and Erhard Bruderer, "Coalition Formation in Standard-Setting Alliances," *Management Science* 41
(Sept. 1995): 1493–1508. Reprinted by permission of the Institute of Operations Research
and the Management Sciences (INFORMS), 2 Charles Street, Suite 300, Providence, RI 02904.

Abstract:

We present a theory for predicting how business firms form alliances to develop and sponsor technical standards. Our basic assumptions are that the
utility of a firm for joining a particular standard-setting alliance increases with
the size of the alliance and decreases with the presence of rivals in the alliance,
especially close rivals. The predicted alliance configurations are simply the
Nash equilibria, that is, those sets of alliances for which no single firm has an
incentive to switch to another alliance. We illustrate our theory by estimating
the choices of nine computer companies to join one of two alliances sponsoring
competing UNIX operating system standards in 1988.

1. Introduction

Product standards have major influences on business performance and
technological development. Technologies become standards by several
different processes. A regulatory body with enforcement powers or a single dominant firm sometimes can impose a standard on a market (Besen
and Saloner 1989; Bresnahan and Chopra 1990). In the absence of a
body or firm with the power to impose a compatibility standard on a
market, standard setting may be a market outcome following head-to-
head competition among interested firms (Farrell and Saloner 1988).
However, it is increasingly common for firms to join together into one or
more standard-setting alliances in order to develop standard technology
and to sponsor adoption of a standard. The VHS alliance coordinated by
Matsushita to sponsor a video recorder standard and the technical workstation alliances created in 1988 to develop and sponsor UNIX operating
system standards are two examples of this phenomenon (Saloner 1990).
Although there is a small amount of literature on the strategies that

standard-setting coalitions employ to achieve their objectives (e.g., Weiss and Sirbu 1990), there has been little research on how a firm decides what standard-setting alliance to join. Increasing our understanding of the process by which firms choose a standard-setting alliance would provide insights into both the formation of standard-setting alliances and the standards that emerge from such alliances. Moreover, knowledge that we gain concerning standards may help us study alliance formation in other economic and social arenas where coalitions also play critical roles.

In this essay we study the formation of competing alliances to sponsor technical compatibility standards. Because standard-setting alliances must induce individual firms to join them in order to succeed, we concentrate on the incentives for firms to join such alliances. Our basic assumptions are that a firm prefers (1) to join a large standard-setting alliance in order to increase the probability of successfully developing and sponsoring a compatibility standard, and (2) to avoid allying with rivals, especially close rivals, in order to maximize its own benefits from compatibility standards that emerge from the alliance's efforts. By building on these primitives, we develop a theory and method for identifying the composition of standard-setting alliances.[1] We analyze the effectiveness of our methodology by applying it to the 1988 efforts to create and sponsor UNIX operating systems standards.

The essay proceeds as follows. In §2, we describe the economic role played by standards and introduce the rationale for our model of alliance formation in standard-setting cases. We discuss previous research concerning alliance choice and outline the theory in §3. In §4, we illustrate our approach with an analysis of the UNIX operating systems case. The illustration shows that our analysis does quite well at explaining the membership decisions of the firms involved in the technical workstation industry. We conclude by outlining avenues for further research.

2. Standards and Alliances

2.1 Reasons for Standards

Standards often develop in markets in which there are increasing returns in the number and size of firms that adopt the same core product and process design features (Arthur 1988). Network externalities are present when consumers must use complementary products or invest heavily in product-specific learning in order to use a product effectively (Katz and

---

[1] The theory is derived from the landscape theory of aggregation proposed by Axelrod and Bennett (1993), who applied the theory to international alignments of World War II.

Shapiro 1985). When complementarity and human-capital investment lock consumers into their technology choices, the users either depend on a limited selection of firms for needed support or they must provide it themselves. Hence, for products affected by network externalities, the costs to consumers of adopting such products are high and consumer interest usually is low when there are no standards. When relevant standards exist, the costs of enhancing, expanding, and using related products decrease in proportion to the relevant markets that accept the standard (David and Greenstein 1990). Thus, consumer interest in products that subscribe to accepted standards will be greater than interest in equivalent nonstandard products.

2.2 Alliances for Developing and Sponsoring Standards

The literature on standard setting indicates that standards may develop in a de jure manner when a regulatory body with the force of law sets standards, or in a de facto manner when market forces determine standards (Farrell and Saloner 1986a). De jure standards are certainly the simplest means by which standards develop. However, de facto standards are needed if there is no authoritative standard-setting body. The danger to a firm of de facto development of standards is that the standard chosen by the market may leave the firm at a competitive disadvantage because this standard may be partially or completely incompatible with the firm's technology.[2] These incompatibilities make it very costly for such a firm to provide a product that complies with the accepted standard. To avoid such competitive disadvantages, firms have incentives to sponsor de facto standards in the absence of enforceable de jure standards.

A firm sponsors de facto standards either by promoting its own proprietary methods as a standard or by entering into an alliance to develop and promote standards favored by a coalition of firms. In either case, the proposed standard must garner a large installed base of consumers to create sufficient network externalities for it to succeed (David and Greenstein 1990). Other firms may adopt the proposed technology if the installed base is large enough, and the bandwagon of adoption may lock out competing technologies (Farrell and Saloner 1986a, 1986b; Katz and Shapiro 1986).

The need for a large installed base suggests that it often will be difficult

---

[2] By technology, we mean the methods used to accomplish an end (more colloquially, ways of doing things). The definition encompasses physical products and nonphysical processes. A standard technology is a generally accepted set of key product and process design features, such that "different manufacturers provide more interchangeability than is logically necessary" (Farrell and Saloner 1985, 70).

for a single firm successfully to sponsor its own proprietary technology as a standard. Farrell and Saloner (1986a) suggest that only dominant firms, which exert substantial market power (Katz and Shapiro 1985), can successfully sponsor a standard unilaterally and create a bandwagon of adoption. Unilateral imposition of a standard is unlikely if there is no dominant firm. Brock (1975) argued that competitive rivalry among firms may impede standardization, whereas Besen and Johnson (1986) found that uncoordinated market adoption suffers when firms and users have different preferences, knowledge of others' preferences is limited, and firms pursue differential marketing strategies.

In the absence of a dominant firm and a single obvious technology, efforts to develop and sponsor standards often require the creation of implicit or explicit alliances among rivals or potential rivals (Saloner 1990). An implicit alliance may develop when a firm enters into a second-sourcing or licensing agreement with other firms to produce the sponsoring firm's technology. The sponsoring firm may offer technology licenses at a low or zero cost in order to induce other firms to adopt its technology (Farrell and Gallini 1988). Explicit alliances often develop when the technology is rapidly evolving, when there is no dominant firm, or when there are competing technologies. An explicit alliance allows members to have input and control over the developing standard, to reduce R&D costs by spreading them over multiple firms, and to combine the alliance members' variety of specialties (David and Greenstein 1990).

2.3 Incentives to Join Standard-Setting Alliances

In choosing among competing standard-setting alliances, a firm cannot determine a priori whether an alliance's standards will succeed, how profitable the standards will be, and what proportion of any profits the firm will garner. Thus, strict profit maximization is not an appropriate objective measure for firms choosing between competing alliances when alliance-specific profits are extremely prospective in nature. Instead, a firm is concerned with whether it expects to do "better" in one alliance rather than in another. In this approach, firms rank preferences over competing alliances. Therefore, we use utility maximization, based on these preferences, as an approximation to a profit maximization strategy for the alliance-selection problem.

We base our central assumptions about the incentives for firms to join standard-setting alliances on two components of the utility that a firm realizes by joining a specific alliance. First, the alliance should be as large as possible, because the probability that a technology becomes a standard increases as the aggregate size of firms offering a compatible product increases. (We discuss measures of size in §4.2.) When a firm joins an alliance and adopts the alliance's proposed standard, its size becomes part of the alliance's aggregate size.

Second, aggregate size will often conflict with competitive considerations during the process of setting standards. Therefore, we assume that a firm desires not to be allied with standard-setting rivals. Although being allied with a rival might increase the alliance's aggregate size and so increase the chance that the alliance's proposed standard will be adopted, the rival may be able to engage in effective price or product competition in the postadoption market for the standardized good. If this happens, standardization will provide little or no benefit to a firm that competes in the same market. Therefore, firms will prefer to join an alliance in which rivals have as small a presence as possible. In Weiss and Sirbu's (1990, 112) words, firms "must prevent their competitors from gaining an advantage at their expense."

The rivalry concern is heightened when an alliance serves to develop technology as well as sponsor a standard. Hamel et al. (1989), Jorde and Teece (1990), and Teece (1992) note that competitors often achieve substantial gains by cooperating in the development of new compatible technology but also must be concerned that the competitors will gain disproportionately. When the technology development activities of the alliance begin, rival firms will often possess technologies that are incompatible. Each firm has an incentive to make the alliance's standard compatible with its prealliance technologies, but it is virtually impossible for the alliance's standard to be compatible with all technologies originating from rivals. Hence, the more that rivals influence a standard-setting alliance, the less likely it is that the alliance's standard will be compatible with a given firm's prealliance technology.

The intensity of rivalry will differ among pairs of firms. All firms seek to gain advantage and so might be current or potential rivals. However, in the competition to establish technology standards, the intensity of rivalry between two firms increases with the extent to which the firms (1) offer functionally equivalent but incompatible technology, and (2) have similar market segmentation profiles.[3] Cases in which firms offer functionally equivalent but incompatible technology will lead to rivalry between them in the standard-setting process, because one or both firms would have to abandon a profitable proprietary standard by becoming partners. The intensity of rivalry will be particularly high among firms

[3] By market segmentation profile, we mean the set of product markets in which a firm operates. Firms with similar market segmentation profiles "mirror" each other, in the sense that they have a near one-to-one match between the market segments in which they operate and also between the market segments in which they do not operate.

that have similar market segmentation profiles, because the rivalry will occur throughout the firms' operations. By contrast, the intensity of rivalry will be lower among firms that have different market segmentation profiles because they do not meet head to head in all markets and because they will often possess complementary technical and market-related skills owing to their different experience.

To simplify our analysis, we define the intensity of rivalry to be either close or distant. Two firms are rivals in the standard-setting process if the adoption of a standard requires at least one of the pair to abandon a key proprietary technology. A proprietary technology is key if the firms' installed base in at least one market segment would incur substantial switching costs if the technology were no longer available due to a standard being established. Firms are also close rivals if they have similar market segmentation profiles. The firms are distant rivals if they have different market segmentation profiles and possess complementary technical and market-related skills.[4] The typology of close and distant rivals does not exhaust all possible combinations of the rivalry factors, and a more general treatment might measure the extent of rivalry between each

[4] Our assumption concerning rivalry is counter to the idea that close rivals will tend to collude or exercise mutual forbearance in order to monopolize jointly a market and then use implicit or explicit side agreements to allocate monopoly profits (Edwards 1955; Karnani and Wernerfelt 1985), especially if market concentration is high (Bernheim and Whinston 1990). The traditional reasons for allying with rivals do not apply to standard-setting situations in which each prestandards firm has its own proprietary technology that involves high switching costs of nontransferable product-specific financial and human capital investment by customers. It makes economic sense to ally with rivals in markets with low switching costs, because such alliances allow rivals to avoid price competition by restricting output and allocating market shares. In markets based on technology that requires high switching costs, the technology itself provides the restrictive function of collusive alliances because the switching costs allow firms to charge super-competitive prices without immediately losing existing customers to competitors. Instead, firms ally to establish standards in order to grow the size of the market. In such alliances, it is a disadvantage to ally with a close rival because each firm has a strong incentive to promote its own technology as a standard in order to maintain and grow its installed base. Thus, a firm is best off allying with distant rivals. Moreover, the attraction prediction assumes that the competitors can credibly control the evolution of technology and competition in their markets if they act together. Such control usually will be beyond the ability of one or a few firms in rapidly changing industrial settings, no matter what the level of current market concentration (Hartman et al. 1994). We expect that collusion among close rivals to set standards will tend to occur only when there are few firms with credible capabilities and when there is little uncertainty about the definition of the standard. In such cases, a few firms might credibly expect to be able to dominate the development of the standard and to be able to address the negotiation and defection problems that beset side agreements. Few standard-setting cases meet these conditions, and collusion and mutual forbearance are better treated as exceptions than as part of the normal process of standard-setting alliances.

pair of firms or discriminate among firms producing identical, differentiated, and complementary goods. For our purposes, a distinction between
close and distant rivals provides a useful estimation of differences in the
degree of rivalry.[5]

As a first approximation, we assume that the aggregate size and rivalry
influences are linear functions of firm size. We assume that each firm's
influence on the standard-setting process is proportional to its size, so
that a firm's desire to join an alliance is proportionally related to the size
represented by the alliances' membership. Similarly, we assume that desire to join a coalition decreases linearly in the size of each rival in the
alliance.

The linear aggregate size assumption is a plausible first approximation,
but may not be appropriate if a bandwagon for adoption develops once
the standard has garnered a large proportion of the market or installed
base (Farrell and Saloner 1986a, 1986b; Katz and Shapiro 1986). Instead, threshold effects sometimes will exist, so that moving from a market share of 50 percent to 51 percent might have more effect than moving
from, say, 90 percent to 91 percent. However, bandwagon effects will be
weaker in situations with incomplete information, especially if there is
substantial uncertainty about future technical and market development
needs. In such cases, the large size merely increases the probability of
adoption, so the outcome is not certain even when the alliance is very
large. Moreover, where technical development is an important aspect of
the coalition's purpose, then the linearity assumption may be plausible
because having more size will often add financial and technological resources needed for successful development. Differences in preferences,
technological differences, and switching costs may also prevent band-
wagons from developing (Farrell and Saloner 1988), so that a window of
opportunity for technologies to become established exists even when a
competing standard has gained a large base (Farrell and Saloner 1986a).
Technological advances, pricing strategies, and consumer lock-in can
forestall or prevent market domination by a single standard while this
window remains open. Thus, there often will be no threshold level of
aggregate size for the acceptance of a proposed standard so that, competitive considerations aside, it is always in a firm's interest to maximize the
size of its alliance. The linear size assumption will be appropriate in such
cases.

[5] The distinction between close and distant rivals is similar to the notion of strategic
groups within an industry (Caves and Porter 1977), where firms in a given industry often
compete more directly with members of their strategic group than with firms outside that
group (Fiegenbaum et al. 1996). A related idea concerning specialist and generalist firms
arises in the organizational ecology literature (e.g., Hannan and Freeman 1977).

3. Estimating Alliance Membership

3.1 Previous Theoretic Approaches to Alliance Composition

According to David and Greenstein (1990, 4), "the [economics of standards] field remains young and in a quite fluid state. Economists have hardly settled on a standard terminology, much less converged on paradigmatic modes of theoretical analysis and empirical inquiry." There is a small theoretical literature that addresses the general issue of alliance composition, including whether an alliance will form (Selten 1973; Werden and Baumann 1986) and what will be the composition of alliances formed among a given set of players (Shapley and Shubik 1969; Owen 1977; Hart and Kurz 1983; Rajan 1989). However, most attention in the standards literature has been directed to which standard will be adopted rather than which firms will join competing standard-setting alliances. The lack of attention stems from the empirical intractability of existing game-theoretic analyses of alliance composition. The most common approach to predicting alliance membership calculates and compares coalition structure values (Owen 1977) for each possible way of partitioning players into alliances (an alliance configuration). Such an analysis can suggest both the alliance configuration that will emerge and the stability of each configuration. The configuration may be a single alliance or consist of competing alliances.

Unfortunately, it is difficult to test coalition structure value predictions because of substantial information requirements. Empirical application of this approach would require identifying and quantifying payoffs for each participant in every conceivable set of alliances. This is a daunting task for managerial decision makers as well as for those who analyze the outcomes of managerial decisions. Using the conventional game-theoretic approach to carry out and analyze complex alliance composition problems is especially difficult because payoffs for each firm depend upon the choices made by all other firms. Consider the example of the standard-setting case. The size of the market will vary with the number of standards, while a given firm's market share will vary with (among other factors) how quickly the firm can bring a product to market relative to other firms. In turn, how quickly each firm develops a product depends on several factors. These include how closely other alliance members cooperate with the firm, whether one or more members has a technological advantage or head start in producing related products, and whether one or more members is powerful enough to influence the selection in favor of a proprietary standard (Katz and Shapiro 1986; Gabel 1987).

Thus, for complex alliance composition problems, it is virtually impossible to determine complete payoff functions as game theory traditionally requires. This is a problem not only for researchers but also for the firms. In contrast to the traditional approach, we develop an approach that first defines utility in terms of pairwise relations between firms and then uses the utility metric to estimate the value of an alliance configuration. Our approach provides an indirect and empirically tractable route to estimating how a firm's alliance choice may affect its profitability.

3.2   Our Theory *of Richardson*

As discussed in §2, we assume that a firm has two considerations in evaluating the value of joining a particular alliance. First, the total size of the alliance is valued because it is an indicator of the likelihood the alliance will succeed with the standard it develops. Second, the firm would prefer not to have the success of the alliance shared by its rivals, especially its close rivals. The alliance size and rivalry considerations can be combined to calculate the utility to firm i of joining alliance A, $U_i(A)$ as follows:

$$U_i(A) = \sum_{j \in A} s_j - \left[\alpha \sum_{j \in D} s_j + (\alpha + \beta) \sum_{j \in C} s_j \right], \qquad (1)$$

where s_j is the size of firm j, and C and D form a partition of alliance A into close and distant rivals of i (i.e., $A = C + D$ and $C \cap D = \varnothing$). The parameter α measures the disincentive to ally with any kind of rival. In this analysis of standard-setting alliances, we will limit α to positive values ($\alpha > 0$), ruling out cases in which two firms are drawn together by their rivalry with each other. The parameter β measures the additional disincentive to ally with close rivals. We can assume that $\beta > 0$ because competition with close rivals is more intense than with distant rivals. This specification of utility treats a firm as myopic in the sense that it bases its evaluation of an alliance only on pairwise relationships between itself and potential alliance partners.[6]

---

[6] The case with $\alpha = 0$ would arise for firms that are not rivals. Two firms are nonrivals in the current market if neither would have to abandon a key proprietary technology by becoming partners, which is most likely to occur if firms view technology standardization as an opportunity to enter new markets rather than as a change to current operations. Nonrivals will be attracted to each other because of the contribution of a nonrival's size to the aggregate size of a coalition, although even current nonrivals might view themselves as future rivals if they plan to follow similar market segmentation strategies in the future. Negative values for α and β might arise in price-setting cartels or other collusive alliances. If firms do not distinguish between close and distant rivals, then $\beta = 0$. With greater generality, rivalry could be defined for each distinct pair of firms rather than for the classes of close and distant rivals. In such a case, $p_{ij} = 1 - v_{ij}$, where v_{ij} is the degree of rivalry between firms i and j.

We can simplify Equation (1) as:

$$U_i(A) = \sum_{j \in A} s_j p_{ij}, \qquad (2)$$

where p_{ij}, the propensity of two firms to ally, is $1 - \alpha$ when i and j are distant rivals and $1 - (\alpha + \beta)$ when i and j are close rivals. Note that these propensities are symmetric, $p_{ij} = p_{ji}$.

We address the case in which there are one or two alliances. The existence of positive consumption externalities sometimes leads to the formation of a single standard-setting alliance. In other cases, the tendency to form a single standard-setting alliance will be countered, at least initially, by the desires of competing firms to influence and benefit from the standard-setting process. Such competition is often limited to two alliances rather than a larger number of coalitions because the chance of successfully creating and sponsoring a standard declines as the number of designs increases.[7] The lowered chance of successful standard creation in a multialliance world will often cause firms that are indifferent or even hostile toward each other to join together in an alliance. More than two alliances sometimes form, and the number of alliances that might form is limited only by the number of firms, but our limit is consistent with many empirical instances.

The major question for the theory is: what will be the composition of the alliances that actually form? To answer this question we need only a weak behavioral assumption, namely, that a stable alliance configuration will have to be a Nash equilibrium. This means that for a partition of the firms into at most two alliances to be stable, there will be no firm that prefers to switch sides (or, if the firms are all together, no one of them will want to go off by itself). Stated formally, let an alliance configuration, X, be a partition of the firms into two sets, A and B (where B may be empty). Then X is a Nash equilibrium if and only if for all i in A, $U_i(A) \geq U_i(B + \{i\})$.

Nash equilibrium is an inadequate solution concept in many game-theoretic settings because it may result in a very large number of possible outcomes. But, with the utility functions of the firms specified as they are in equations (1) and (2), the Nash equilibrium concept typically reduces the predicted alliance configurations to a small list. The reason is that, given symmetric propensities, the entire alliance configuration "improves" whenever a firm changes sides in an alliance configuration in order to improve its utility. The improvement can be measured by a single metric.

---

[7] The positive externality created by standardization declines as the number of standards increases and thereby reduces the principal advantage of setting standards, which is a larger post-standardization market. Hence, the costs of sharing standard technology with competitors will often exceed the benefits from standardization when there are many competing standards.

This can be seen by defining the energy of an alliance configuration, $E(X)$ as:

$$E(X) = \sum_i \sum_j s_i s_j p_{ij} d_{ij}(X),$$ (3)

where $d_{ij}(X) = 0$ if i and j are in the same alliance, and $d_{ij}(X) = 1$ if they are in different alliances.[8] Lower energy will always result if a firm improves its utility by switching alliances.[9] An alliance configuration is then a Nash equilibrium if and only if no firm can switch alliances without increasing the energy of the configuration. In fact, Nash equilibria are exactly those configurations that are local minima of the energy function evaluated over all possible configurations.

The intuitive idea behind equation (3) is that energy is lower when firms that have negative propensities to ally are in different alliances. Size plays a role because having a proper relationship with a large firm is more important than having a proper relationship with a small firm.

A corollary of this result is that there can be no cycles if firms change sides one at a time. The reason is that any movement a firm chooses to make will strictly increase its utility and thus will lower the energy of the system. But the same configuration (with the same energy) can never occur twice if the energy of the system is strictly decreasing.

4. The UNIX Case

4.1 Technical Workstations and Unix Alliances: Historical Background

The struggle over UNIX standards for technical workstations illustrates our approach.[10] Technical workstations are powerful desktop compu-

---

[8] The idea of potential energy in physical systems had its first rigorous development in the context of Hamiltonian systems (see Arnold 1978; Abraham and Shaw 1983; Nicolis and Prigogine 1989). More recently, energy has been used in artificial intelligence to characterize the dynamics of complex systems such as neural networks (Hopfield 1982).

[9] Here is the proof. Consider two configurations, X and Y, each with two alliances, differing only by the membership of a single firm, k. Without loss of generality, let $X = A'$ versus B where $A' = A \cup \{k\}$, and let $Y = A$ versus B' where $B \cup \{k\}$. To shorten the notation, let $K = \{k\}$ and $r_{ij} = s_i s_j p_{ij}$. $E(X) = \sum_{A'} \sum_B r_{ij} + \sum_B \sum_{A'} r_{ij}$, since $d_{ij}(X) = 0$ for $i \in A', j \in A'$ or $i \in B, j \in B$; and $d_{ij}(X) = 1$ for $i \in A, j \in B'$ or $i \in B, j \in A'$. Likewise, $E(Y) = \sum_A \sum_{B'} r_{ij} + \sum_{B'} \sum_A r_{ij}$. So $E(X) - E(Y) = \sum_{A'} \sum_B r_{ij} - \sum_A \sum_{B'} r_{ij} + \sum_B \sum_{A'} r_{ij} - \sum_{B'} \sum_A r_{ij} = \sum_K \sum_B r_{ij} - \sum_A \sum_K r_{ij} + \sum_B \sum_K r_{ij} - \sum_K \sum_A r_{ij}$, since $\sum_{A'} \sum_B r_{ij} = \sum_A \sum_B r_{ij} + \sum_K \sum_B r_{ij}$. But $\sum_K \sum_B r_{ij} = \sum_B \sum_K r_{ij}$ and $\sum_A \sum_K r_{ij} = \sum_K \sum_A r_{ij}$, since $p_{ij} = p_{ji}$. So $E(X) - E(Y) = 2(\sum_K \sum_B r_{ij} - \sum_K \sum_A r_{ij}) = 2(s_k \sum_B s_j p_{kj} - s_k \sum_A s_j p_{kj})$. Thus, $E(X) - E(Y) = 2s_k(U_i(B) - U_i(A))$. But $s_k > 0$. So for configurations X and Y, differing only by firm k, $E(X) > E(Y)$ if and only if $U_i(A) < U_i(B)$.

[10] The historical information in this subsection comes from public sources (e.g., Computer Technology Research Corp. 1990a, 1990b).

ters, typically used in engineering and scientific applications. The first commercial technical workstation was introduced about 1980. Worldwide sales were about \$2.5 billion in 1987 and reached \$10 billion in 1990. A key aspect of technical workstation design is the operating system, which controls the hardware and manages the flow of information and communication among the various components of the computer system. Most commercial technical workstations have used some version of the UNIX operating system, which the American Telephone and Telegraph Company (AT&T) developed at its Bell Laboratories during the 1960's. Altogether, more than 250 versions of UNIX-based operating systems have been designed by computer hardware companies and academic institutions. Applications software written for one version often does not operate on another UNIX system.

In 1984, the software incompatibility across UNIX operating systems induced several leading European, American, and Japanese computer manufacturers to form the X/Open group with the goal of encouraging the development of UNIX standards. This consensus approach to standardization failed in October 1987, however, when X/Open members AT&T and Sun Microsystems, Inc. announced that they would pursue development of a UNIX operating system based on AT&T's System V. The new system would be available to other companies under proprietary license.

A challenge to the AT&T and Sun partnership soon arose. Seven major computer manufacturers, including the Digital Equipment Corporation (DEC) and International Business Machines Corporation (IBM) responded in May 1988 by forming the Open Software Foundation (OSF). A primary purpose of the OSF was to develop a standardized UNIX operating system that did not draw on AT&T's proprietary technology. AT&T and Sun responded to the OSF by forming UNIX International, Inc. (UII) in December 1988, the members of which would advise and sponsor the development of AT&T's UNIX System V. Although some secondary participants joined both alliances, there was no overlap among the nine full sponsors of the OSF and the ten principal members of UII. Both UII and the OSF expanded after 1988 and each continued its efforts to create an operating system standard. AT&T introduced a commercial release of System V version 4 in November 1989, and the OSF released a commercial version of OSF/1 in late 1990.

This chronology extends Farrell and Saloner's (1988) argument that adoption of compatibility standards may be promoted by means of a hybrid of committee coordination and market leadership. We can view X/Open as an attempt at coordination by a single committee, the AT&T-Sun action in 1987 as a unilateral market leadership move, and the formation of the OSF and UII as subsequent attempts to create standards by competing committees. The AT&T-Sun attempt at market leadership did ıcceed because the two firms were not strong enough to exert their will on other strong firms such as DEC and Apollo, and because there was no consensus that AT&T's new UNIX operating system would succeed.[11]

4.2 Using the Theory in the UNIX Case

The first task for our analysis was to identify the relevant firms. We identified the companies that had the potential to play an important role in developing UNIX standards in 1987, the year before the OSF and UII formed. We selected nine firms: AT&T and eight companies that competed in the technical workstation market.[12] We included AT&T because it was the original developer of UNIX and held the copyright for the parent version of the operating system, possessed strong related technical experience and continued to develop UNIX in 1987, and was a potential entrant to the technical workstation industry. In addition to AT&T, we included all firms that had at least 1 percent of the worldwide technical workstation market in 1987. The eight firms satisfying this requirement together accounted for over 95 percent of technical workstation market revenue.

To calculate the Nash equilibria of potential alliance configurations among the nine firms, we required measures for individual firm size, iden-

---

[11] The UII and OSF alliances competed for acceptance by computer buyers and standardization committees for five years, until UII was disbanded in November 1993. The disbanding marked a partial victory for the OSF and some key members of UII had joined the surviving alliance by April 1994, when this description was written. At the same time, however, the OSF deemphasized its focus on centralized software development by the alliance in favor of internal development by the individual members of the alliance. This decision marks a partial return to market competition to establish a UNIX standard, perhaps because the member companies of the alliances found that they could not fully coordinate their competing interests.

[12] The technical workstation market was more important than the broader computer sector for our analysis because the UNIX standards issues arose most strongly for technical workstations. By 1987, UNIX was the dominant operating system for technical workstations. The fierce competition among technical workstation makers required firms to keep their UNIX operating systems as advanced as the hardware that they designed. As a result, the UNIX operating systems used with technical workstations were the most innovative and advanced UNIX systems available. By contrast, UNIX operating systems were used in only a tiny fraction of the mainframe and minicomputer markets, which were dominated by computers based on proprietary operating systems. Therefore, UNIX and UNIX standards were of secondary importance to mainframe and minicomputer manufacturers. Our judgment that technical workstation makers were key players is supported by the fact that each of the four firms that triggered the response to AT&T and Sun manufactured technical workstations (Apollo, DEC, Hewlett-Packard, and IBM formed the Hamilton Group, a predecessor of the OSF, early in 1988).

tification of close and distant rivals, and values for the α and β rivalry parameters. There is no one unequivocal measure of firm size in cases where uncertain expectations of market size and technological change play central roles in determining firm importance in the standard-setting process. Weiss and Sirbu (1990) identified several measures of firm size that might influence standards adoption, including sellers' and buyers' aggregate market shares in the markets most closely related to the product being standardized, net corporate assets, and aggregate installed base of products containing the technologies being standardized. Weiss and Sirbu found that buyers' market share and corporate assets had the strongest influence on acceptance for eleven cases in which standard-setting committees chose between two competing standards.

We expect the appropriate size measure to vary in different standard-setting contexts. Buyers' market share in related markets will tend to be important when the standards involve intermediate products, which are purchased and transformed by buyers before being sold to end-users. By contrast, sellers' market share will tend to be an indicator of future market power when the products are sold in a form that will be used by end-users without needing to be incorporated into more extensive systems by downstream producers. When the rate of technological change is slow, the existing installed base of products containing a firm's version of the technologies being standardized is likely to be the best measure of seller's market share, because the capabilities that contributed to a firm's past success are likely to continue to be valuable in the future. When technological change is occurring rapidly, however, many past capabilities quickly lose value, and current market share is a more appropriate predictor of future market power. Corporate assets, which may be financial size or relevant experience with the technology being standardized, will tend to matter most when relevant technologies require substantial investment of money and time.

As we discuss above, we judge sellers' current market share to be the best available empirical estimate of a firm's expected future importance when a standard-setting alliance is concerned with rapidly changing products that will be sold to end-users, as was the case with technical workstations. Therefore, for the size of the eight technical workstation manufacturers, we used each firm's 1987 share in the technical workstation market.[13] To assign a size for AT&T, which did not manufacture

[13] We used the mean of 1987 market share figures reported in 1988 by the International Data Corporation and Dataquest Inc. for the sizes of the seven largest workstation manufacturers (Sun, Apollo, DEC, HP, Intergraph, SGI, and IBM). We based the size of the eighth manufacturer (Prime) on company estimates. The analysis showed little sensitivity to differences in the size estimates and we obtained similar results for four sets of size estimates, including the mean of the Dataquest and International Data estimates, the International

technical workstations in 1987, we asked four computer industry experts to estimate the importance of AT&T with respect to its influence in establishing a UNIX standard. We assigned a size weight of 28.5 based on the median of the experts' estimates. The size places AT&T among the most important firms in establishing a UNIX standard.[14]

To operationalize the concept of close and distant rivalry, we classified each of the firms in the sample as either a specialist in the technical workstation market or a computer-products generalist. Four computer companies in the sample drew most of their revenue from the technical workstation market, including Apollo, Intergraph, Silicon Graphics (SGI), and Sun. We classed the other four computer manufacturers in the sample, which included DEC, Hewlett Packard (HP), IBM, and Prime, as generalists because they offered many lines of computer-related products. AT&T, as the creator of the UNIX operating system and primary advocate for its adoption in all computer market segments, also was a generalist because it promoted UNIX as a competitive alternative to the proprietary operating systems that the other generalists offered in several market segments. Thus, of the nine firms in this study, four were workstation specialists and five were generalists.

The firms in the study all possessed proprietary operating systems that would be affected by the emergence of a UNIX standard, so that each could be considered a rival of the others. Recall that we defined close rivals as firms that have similar market segmentation profiles, and distant rivals as firms that have different market segmentation profiles and possess complementary technical and market-related skills. Because of the head-to-head competition in the technical workstation market by specialists and in several market segments by generalists, we defined pairs of specialists and pairs of generalists as close rivals. Firms that specialized in

---

Data estimates, the Dataquest estimates reported in 1988, or slightly different estimates of 1987 market shares that were reported by Dataquest in 1989.

[14] The four anonymous experts were familiar with the technical workstation industry in 1987. One of the experts is a software firm executive. The second is an analyst with a computer software firm. The third is an industry analyst who specializes in UNIX applications. The fourth expert is also a computer industry analyst. We sent each expert a letter in which we stated that we were interested in AT&T because it owned the copyright for the parent version of UNIX, licensed UNIX to technical workstation manufacturers, continued to develop UNIX in 1987, manufactured computer hardware, and was a potential entrant to the technical workstation industry. We then asked the experts in telephone conversations to estimate the importance of AT&T, relative to the market shares of the eight other firms in our sample. The experts assigned AT&T scores of 8, 18, 39, and 50. Based on a presurvey decision, we used the median, 28.5. The two experts who assigned the lower estimates based their estimates primarily on AT&T's historically weak presence in the technical workstation market. The experts who assigned the higher estimates based their judgments on the company's 1987 potential to play a strong future role in creating a UNIX standard.

producing UNIX-based technical workstations had very intense rivalries in 1987. The specialists competed solely in one market segment and offered functionally equivalent but incompatible proprietary UNIX operating systems. Adopting a UNIX operating system standard for all UNIX workstations would require all but one firm to abandon proprietary operating systems, an act that would eliminate the switching costs for many current users to change to another system. The generalist firms also had many potential conflicts with each other, because they relied on incompatible proprietary technologies in multiple market segments. By contrast, we defined a generalist and a specialist as distant rivals because they compete less intensely than two firms of the same type and because the firms possess complementary capabilities needed for technical workstation commercialization, with the generalist providing distribution capabilities and financing and the specialist providing technical skills.[15]

The theory has two unmeasured rivalry parameters, which represent weights of the disincentive to ally with any kind of rival (α) and the additional disincentive to ally with close rivals (β). For our base case analysis, we give the parameters equal weights, $\alpha = \beta = 1$. In the UNIX case, this means that the utility lost by a firm from being allied with a distant rival equaled the utility gained from the rival's contribution to aggregate size ($\alpha = 1$), while the utility lost from being allied with a close rival substantially outweighed its size contribution ($\beta = 1$). Setting $\alpha = 1$ is reasonable because specialists and generalists were material competitors in the technical workstation market but, despite the competition, a distant rival's size would contribute to an alliance's ability to sponsor a standard successfully. Because the disincentive of having a close rival in the same alliance is greater than the disincentive of having a distant rival in the same alliance, β must be greater than 0; setting $\beta = 1$ is a reasonable first estimate of the weight. In equation (3), these parameter choices give $p_{ij} = 1 - \alpha - 0$ if i and j are distant rivals, and $p_{ij} = 1 - (\alpha + \beta) = -1$ if i and j are close rivals. The sensitivity analysis reported below shows that the estimated results are not very sensitive to small changes in these parameters.

With the chosen values for α and β, every firm would prefer to avoid an alliance with any of its close rivals. However, this might not be possible if only a limited number of alliances form. Instead, some firms will be forced to ally with some of their close rivals. For the UNIX case, we assume that there will be at most two alliances, as occurred in practice. Together, the assumptions concerning firm size, distant and close competitors, and the rivalry parameters provide a simple and plausible measure

---

[15] For example, Sun agreed to share its expertise in designing workstations and microprocessors with AT&T partly in exchange for an infusion of over $300 million.

of pairwise incentives for the firms to ally in the UNIX case. The extent to which the coalitions estimated by our approach conform to the actual membership in the OSF and UII illustrates the power of the approach.

4.3 Analysis Results

Table 5-1 displays the results of the analysis, which include a configuration that is close to the actual alliance configuration. The table also reports the size and classification of each firm. With nine firms, there are 2^8 = 256 possible alliance configurations of at most two alliances each. Two configurations of alliances were Nash equilibria. We refer to these as configurations 1 and 2. The two equilibria have quite different sets of alliances. Sun joins with AT&T, Prime, and IBM in the equilibrium of configuration 1, but is separated from them in the equilibrium of configuration 2. DEC and HP ally with Apollo, Intergraph, and SGI in configuration 1, but are separated from them in configuration 2.

To compare the estimates to the empirical outcome, we defined alliance membership in terms of the first of the OSF and UII alliances joined by each firm in the sample. We obtained information about alliance membership from the firms' 10-K reports to the Security and Exchange Commission, from articles in the business press, and through conversations with individuals at OSF, UII, and several of the companies. DEC, HP, Apollo, and IBM were founding members of the OSF in May 1988, while Intergraph and SGI joined the OSF in late 1988. Sun, AT&T, and Prime were founding members of UII in December 1988.

Table 5-1 compares the estimates with what happened. In configuration 1, eight of nine memberships are estimated correctly. Only IBM is incorrectly assigned. This is an accurate fit in terms of alliance size because the incorrect assignment (IBM) was a small part of the technical workstation market. The proportion of aggregate size that was correctly estimated was very high, namely, 97 percent, and the probability of getting this much of the aggregate size correct by chance is only 2 percent. The prediction also is reasonably accurate in terms of the number of cases, where the probability of getting eight or more of the nine cases right by chance is 6 percent when there are two equilibrium configurations.[16] The close match between empirical memberships and the pre-

---

[16] After starting with any arbitrary pair of firms, there are seven firms to be assigned for a total of 128 possible configurations (it is necessary to start with a pair of firms because there are two predicted configurations as good or better than the predicted configuration: (1) the configuration with no errors, (2) the configuration with only Prime wrong, and (3) the configuration with only IBM wrong. Therefore, the probability of predicting at least as much of the alliance size as the predicted configuration by chance is 3/128 = 0.023. In

TABLE 5-1
The Two Nash Equilibrium Configurations

	CONFIGURATION 1	
CONFIGURATION 2	*Alliance 1*	*Alliance 2*
Alliance 1	Sun (27.2, S)	DEC (18.9, G)
		HP (14.35, G)
Alliance 2	AT&T (28.5, G)	Apollo (19.9, S)
	Prime (1.0, G)	Intergraph (4.4, S)
	IBM (3.8, G)	SGI (4.15, S)
Nearest empirical match[a]	UNIX International	Open Software Foundation

Note: Size is shown in parentheses, along with whether the firm was a computer generalist (G) or technical workstation specialist (S).

[a]In Configuration 1, only the IBM prediction is wrong.

dicted alliances in this illustration provides support for the landscape approach.

We carried out sensitivity analysis concerning the rivalry parameters, finding that the results obtained with the base case rivalry assumptions ($\alpha = 1$, $\beta = 1$) are quite robust. Table 5-2 shows the configurations that occurred as α and β varied from 0.5 to 1.5 by 0.1. The number in each cell indicates how many Nash equilibria were found. The base case equilibria occurred in all cases for which $0.8 \le \alpha \le 1.5$, $0.7 \le \beta \le 1.5$, as well as for many cases outside this rectangular area. The sensitivity analysis in Table 5-2 shows that the results are not very sensitive to the precise choice of the rivalry parameters.

Table 5-3 reports the configurations that occurred as α and β varied from 0 to 5, again showing that the base case estimates are robust. The two base case configurations occurred for all calculated cases with $\alpha = 0$, $\beta \ge 4$; with $\alpha = 0.5$, $\beta \ge 2$; and with $\alpha \ge 1$, $\beta > (\alpha - 0.5)$. The sensitivity analysis in Table 5-3 provides insights concerning how the conflicting incentives of aggregate size and rivalry shape alliance formation. In general, the base case configurations occurred when firms dislike close rivals substantially more than they dislike distant rivals. Outside the ranges in which the base case configurations were found, four patterns were observed:

(1) The estimates converged to a single alliance when firms do not have strong dislike for either close or distant rivals (α and β are small, in the upper left of Table 5-3). This result shows that the attraction of aggregate-

---

terms of predicted cases when there are two equilibrium configurations, one of the 128 possible configurations is completely correct and seven are off by one firm, so that the probability of getting seven or more of the eight right by chance is $(1 + 7)/128 = 0.063$.

TABLE 5-2
Analysis of Variation in Rivalry Parameters around the Base Case

α (rivalry parameter)	β (additional rivalry parameter for close rivals)										
	0.5	0.6	0.7	0.8	0.9	1.0	1.1	1.2	1.3	1.4	1.5
0.5	1	2	4	4	8	9	8	8	6	3	3
0.6	2	4	5	9	8	7	4	3	2	2	2
0.7	5	9	8	6	3	2	2	2	2	2	2
0.8	7	3	2	2	2	2	2	2	2	2	2
0.9	2	2	2	2	2	2	2	2	2	2	2
1.0	2	2	2	2	2	2[a]	2	2	2	2	2
1.1	2	2	2	2	2	2	2	2	2	2	2
1.2	2	2	2	2	2	2	2	2	2	2	2
1.3	2	2	2	2	2	2	2	2	2	2	2
1.4	2	2	2	2	2	2	2	2	2	2	2
1.5	3	2	2	2	2	2	2	2	2	2	2

Note: The number in each cell indicates the number of Nash equilibrium configurations; cells with underlined figures include the best-fit configuration from the base case.
[a] Base case is α = 1, β = 1.

alliance size dominates when there is little rivalry, so that firms tend to settle into one universal standard-stting alliance.

(2) All 256 possible alliances are equilibrium configurations when all rivals are viewed with equal dislike (α = 1 and β = 0, which implies that $p_{ij} = 0$ for all pairs of firms).

(3) Several equilibria result when firms have strong dislike for distant rivals and relatively little additional dislike for close rivals (α > 1 and β ≤ α − 1, in the lower left of Table 5-3).

(4) Several equilibria also result when firms have little dislike for distant rivals and moderate dislike for close rivals (in the upper central part of Table 5-2, with α < 1).

We also tested the sensitivity of the results to variation in AT&T's size, because the industry's experts' estimates of AT&T's size varied substantially. The reported results, in which the best-fit estimate has an error of one firm, are found if the AT&T size is set from 19 to 29. There are either one or two errors with AT&T size from 1 to 18 and two errors with AT&T size of 30 to 34. There are no errors with AT&T size of 35 to 37. There is one error with size of 38 or more. Thus, the reported results and equivalent or better results are found for a reasonable range of sizes.

The changes in the estimates that occur as AT&T's size varies reflect plausible strategic considerations. Because AT&T is a generalist, the division of the four specialist firms does not depend on AT&T's size and is always correct. However, the division of the five generalists is sensitive to

TABLE 5-3
Extended Analysis of Variation in Rivalry Parameters

α (rivalry parameter)	β (additional rivalry parameter for close rivals)								
	0.0	0.5	1.0	1.5	2.0	2.5	3.0	4.0	5.0
0.0	1	1	1	4	9	7	3	2	2
0.5	1	1	9	3	2	2	2	2	2
1.0	256	2	2ª	2	2	2	2	2	2
1.5	9	3	2	2	2	2	2	2	2
2.0	9	7	3	2	2	2	2	2	2
2.5	9	8	6	3	2	2	2	2	2
3.0	9	8	7	4	3	2	2	2	2
4.0	9	9	8	7	6	3	3	2	2
5.0	9	10	8	8	7	6	4	3	2

Note: The number in each cell indicates the number of Nash equilibrium configurations; cells with underlined figures include the best-fit configuration of the base case. Cases with one predicted configuration are the universal alliance.
ªBase case is $\alpha = 1$, $\beta = 1$.

AT&T's size because the generalist alliances change depending on AT&T's importance. AT&T switches to progressively smaller generalist partnerships as its size grows. Finally, once AT&T becomes very large (38 or more), all the other generalists oppose it. The empirical outcome is consistent with the case in which AT&T was expected to play a large but not overwhelming role in setting the UNIX standard.

5. Conclusions and Future Research

In this essay, we have developed and illustrated an approach for predicting the membership of alliances among firms developing and sponsoring products requiring technical standardization. We started with two simple and plausible assumptions, that a firm prefers (1) to join a large standard-setting alliance in order to increase the probability of successfully sponsoring a compatibility standard, and (2) to avoid allying with rivals in order to benefit individually from compatibility standards that emerge from the alliance's efforts. We then defined the concept of utility as an approximation to profit maximization in terms of size and rivalry, and discussed the influences on incentives to ally in order to develop and sponsor standards. We showed that the Nash equilibria are the local minima of an energy function with this type of utility function.

We illustrated the effectiveness of our methodology by applying it to the 1988 efforts to create and sponsor UNIX operating systems standards. Given a plausible set of assumptions concerning firm size, rivalry, and the relative importance of rivalry and aggregate alliance size, we found a robust estimate of two alliance configurations, one of which correctly fit 97 percent of aggregate firm size and was correct in all but one firm. The success indicates that the approach provides a practical method for suggesting which firms in an industry will ally, by using only data likely to be available to managers or researchers faced with limited information.

As well as being a useful illustration of the approach, the empirical analysis provides useful insights into incentives for competing firms to ally. There may be more than one locally optimal outcome, and the specific configuration at which the system finds stability will tend to be path-dependent, in that it will be strongly influenced by the early moves in the alliance-building process.[17] For example, configuration 1 in Table 5-1 was closest to the observed outcome because AT&T and Sun allied together at the beginning of the process. Had another pair come together early in the process, say AT&T and Apollo (which, like Sun, had large market share and would have been an equally credible partner for AT&T), then a quite different outcome might well have emerged, such as that in configuration 2.

The features shared by the two potential outcomes also help us understand the empirical process of alliance formation in standard-setting cases. As can be seen in Table 5-1, the combination of specialist-generalist attribute and total subgroup size is the key factor influencing the formation of the potential alliances. Both configurations divide the specialists along the same lines into two subgroups of almost equal size (Sun versus the other three specialists). Similarly, both configurations divide the generalists along the same lines into two subgroups of almost equal size (DEC and HP versus the other three generalists). Thus, firms may balance the conflict between enjoying the benefits of standardization and incurring the problems of associating with close competitors by splitting into groups of close competitors that are as close as possible to equal size.

Our results place common arguments that the OSF alliance was formed primarily to oppose the strength of Sun and AT&T into a more general context (the OSF acronym was sometimes said to stand for "Oppose Sun Forever").[18] Although some firms undoubtedly did join the

---

[17] Arthur (1990) discusses the role of increasing returns in generating multiple optima. David (1985) and Arthur et al. (1987) discuss the role of history in influencing outcomes. Path dependence also arises in the literature on trade with external economies (e.g., Krugman 1981; Ethier 1982; Panagaryia 1986).

[18] Two "commonsense" explanations sometimes proposed for the empirical outcome are that (a) firms opposed Sun's current market power, or (b) firms other than Sun opposed AT&T's potential market power, while Sun was strong enough that it did not fear AT&T. If (a) is true, then all firms in the sample would ally against Sun, which is off by two firms; the

OSF to oppose Sun and AT&T, other firms then joined UNIX International to balance the growing size of the OSF. Because there were enough firms that could credibly expect to influence the standard-setting process, it was possible for the two alliances to achieve roughly equivalent size. The fact that the specialists and generalists could divide into nearly equal-sized subgroups, which will be common in industries with several moderately strong competitors, may help explain why the two alliances maintained a competitive standoff for five years.

The analysis also illustrates how both history and expectations may influence the determination of a stable outcome when there are multiple possible equilibria (Katz and Shapiro 1985; Krugman 1991). History can play a strong role because firms may use past and current strengths to assess each other. The rivalries and sizes used in this study are based mainly on historical positions in the technical workstation industry. However, expectations may also play an important role. In this study, AT&T's size is based on expectations of its potential importance as a standard setter, even though the company was absent from the 1987 technical workstation market.

Much important work also remains to be done to increase the scope of our approach. A more general means of operationalizing size and rivalry would be valuable. Being able to estimate the number of alliances, as well as the composition of a given number of alliances, would increase the breadth of the methodololgy. Allowing a firm to choose either neutrality or dual membership in alliances would extend the approach.[19] It would also be useful to explore nonlinear specifications of the energy function. This would allow asymmetric propensities and thereby would

---

random probability of two mistakes with nine firms and a single predicted configuration is 25 percent. If (b) is true, then there are two equilibrium configurations: all firms allied against AT&T, which is off by two firms; all firms other than Sun allied against AT&T, which is off by one firm. The best prediction in argument (b) has random probability of 6 percent, the same as our best-fit estimate. Thus, one of the commonsense ideas has less statistical power than our theory, and the other has the same power. However, taking the commonsense approach does not tell you whether to expect (a) or (b), both of which are ad hoc rationalizations. Assuming equal weights are assigned to (a) and (b), the chance of doing better than chance by believing common sense is the average of 25 percent and 6 percent, or 16 percent. Thus, our general argument has greater explanatory power than the ad hoc arguments.

[19] Two of the smaller firms in our sample eventually developed significant relationships with both UII and the OSF, and many of the other firms that joined the alliances held membership in both groups. In most cases, the dual memberships were held by relatively minor participants in the computer market. It is not surprising to find that weaker players attempt to position themselves to adapt to whichever standard emerges because the small market share players have little influence on the standard-setting process. This issue would also arise if the methodology were applied to market coordination alliances, where smaller firms often are not included in an organizing cartel.

extend the methodology to instances in which one firm wanted to join another but the second did not want to join the first. Allowing the sizes and utility components to change endogenously also would broaden the methodology. Nonetheless, this essay illustrates the power and potential value of our approach.

Starting from simple primitives, we developed a theory of coalition formation in a standard-setting situation that provides useful insights into the behavior and motivations of computer firms in our UNIX application. Using only firm sizes and the intensity of competition between firms, we estimated with a high degree of robustness the probable alliance configurations and identified motivations of individual firms that supported the predicted alliance configurations. Further development of the theory presented in this paper should enhance both our understanding of the ways standards are set by coalitions and the factors that determine coalition formation in other settings.[20]

References

Abraham, R. H., and C. D. Shaw. 1983. *Dynamics: The Geometry of Behavior.* Santa Cruz, Calif.: Ariel Press.

Arnold, V. I. 1978. *Mathematical Methods of Classical Mechanics* (translated from the Russian). New York: Springer.

Arthur, W. B. 1988. "Self-Reinforcing Mechanisms in Economics." In *The Economy as an Evolving Complex System,* ed. P. W. Anderson, K. J. Arrow, and D. Pines. SFI Studies in the Sciences of Complexity, 9–31. New York: Addison-Wesley.

———. 1990. " 'Silicon Valley' Locational Clusters: When Do Increasing Returns Imply Monopoly?" *Mathematical Social Sci.* 19: 235–51.

Arthur, W. B., Y. M. Ermoliev, and Y. M. Kaniovski. 1987. "Path Dependent Processes and the Emergence of Macro Structure." *European J. Oper. Res.* 30: 294–303.

Axelrod, R., and D. S. Bennett. 1993. "A Landscape Theory of Aggregation." *British J. Political Sci.* 23: 211–33. Included as Chapter 4 of this volume.

[20] We are indebted to John E. Jackson and Roger C. Kormendi for their help in initiating this work. We appreciate the comments of Michael D. Cohen, Douglas Dion, John H. Holland, Valerie Y. Suslow, Hal R. Varian, and Gerard Weisbuch, as well as suggestions provided by the editor and several anonymous reviewers. We were assisted by advice received from participants at the Conference on Industrial Organization, Strategic Management, and International Competitiveness, held at the University of British Columbia in June 1991. We are grateful for information provided by Jim Linck, Mark Freed, Dave Martens, and Byron Askin of the University of Michigan MBA Program, and by several computer industry experts. This work was supported in part by National Science Foundation grants SES 8808459 and SES 9106371 to Robert Axelrod.

Bernheim, B. D., and M. D. Whinston. 1990. "Multimarket Contact and Collusive Behavior." *Rand J. Economics* 21: 1–26.

Besen, S. M., and L. L. Johnson. 1986. *Compatibility Standards, Competition, and Innovation in the Broadcasting Industry.* Santa Monica, Calif.: Rand Corporation.

Besen, S. M., and G. Saloner. 1989. "The Economics of Telecommunications Standards." In *Changing the Rules: Technological Change, International Competition, and Regulation in Communication,* ed. R. W. Crandall and K. Flamm, 177–220. Washington: Brookings.

Bresnahan, T., and A. Chopra. 1990. "Users' Role in Standard Setting: The Local Area Network Industry." *Economics of Innovation and New Technology* 1: 97–110.

Brock, G. 1975. "Competition, Standards, and Self-Regulation in the Computer Industry." In *Regulating the Product Quality and Variety,* ed. Richard E. Caves and Marc J. Roberts, chap. 5. Cambridge, Mass.: Ballinger.

Caves, R. E., and M. E. Porter. 1977. "From Entry Barriers to Mobility Barriers." *Quarterly J. Economics* 91: 241–61.

Computer Technology Research Corp. 1990a (May). *Technical Workstations In-Depth.* Holtsville, N.Y.: Computer Technology Research Corp.

———. 1990b (July). *Unix in the 1990s.* Holtsville, N.Y.: Computer Technology Research Corp.

David, P. 1985. "CLIO and the Economics of QWERTY." *Papers and Proceedings of the American Economic Association* 75: 332–36.

David, P., and S. Greenstein. 1990. "Selected Bibliography on the Economics of Compatibility Standards and Standardization." *Economics of Innovation and New Technology* 1: 3–41.

Edwards, C. D. 1955. "Conglomerate Bigness As A Source of Power." In *NBER Report: Business Concentration and Price Policy,* 331–59. Princeton, N.J.: Princeton University Press.

Ethier, W. 1982. "Decreasing Costs in International Trade and Frank Graham's Argument for Protection." *Econometrica* 50: 1243–68.

Farrell, J., and N. Gallini. 1988. "Second Sourcing as a Commitment." *Quarterly J. Economics* 103: 673–94.

Farrell, J., and G. Saloner. 1985. "Standardization, Compatibility, and Innovation." *Rand J. Economics* 16: 70–83.

———. 1986a. "Installed Base and Compatibility: Innovation, Product Preannouncements, and Predation." *American Economic Review* 76: 940–55.

———. 1986b. "Standardization and Variety." *Economic Letters* 20: 71–74.

———. 1988. "Coordination Through Committees and Markets." *Rand J. Economics* 19: 235–52.

Fiegenbaum, A., S. Hart, and D. Schendel. 1996. "Strategic Reference Point Theory." *Strategic Management J.* 17: 219–35.

Gabel, H. L. 1987. "Open Standards in the European Computer Industry: The Case of X/OPEN." In *Product Standardization and Competitive Strategy,* ed. H. L. Gabel, 91–123. Amsterdam: North-Holland.

Hamel, G., Y. L. Doz, and C. K. Prahalad. 1989. "Collaborate with Your Competitors—and Win." *Harvard Business Review* 67: 133–39.

Hannan, M. T., and J. H. Freeman. 1977. "The Population Ecology of Organizations." *American J. Sociology* 82: 929–64.

Hart, S., and M. Kurz. "Endogenous Formation of Coalitions." *Econometrica* 51: 1047–64.

Hartman, R. S., D. J. Teece, W. Mitchell, and T. Jorde. 1994. "Assessing Market Power in Regimes of Rapid Technological Progress." *Industrial and Corporate Change* 2: 317–50.

Hopfield, J. J. 1982. "Neural Networks and Physical Systems with Emergent Collective Computational Abilities." *Proceedings of the National Academy of Sciences, USA* 79: 2552–58.

Jorde, T. M., and D. J. Teece. 1990. "Innovation and Cooperation: Implications for Competition and Antitrust." *J. Economic Perspectives* 4: 75–96.

Karnani, A., and B. Wernerfelt. 1985. "Multiple Point Competition." *Strategic Management J.* 6: 87–96.

Katz, M., and C. Shapiro. 1985. "Network Externalities, Competition, and Compatibility." *American Economic Review* 75: 424–40.

———. 1986. "Technology Adoption in the Presence of Network Externalities." *J. Political Economy* 94: 822–41.

Krugman, P. 1981. "Trade, Accumulation, and Uneven Development." *J. Development Economics* 8: 149–61.

———. 1991. "History Versus Expectations." *Quarterly J. Economics* 106: 651–67.

Nicolis, G., and I. Prigogine. 1989. *Exploring Complexity, An Introduction*. New York: Freeman.

Owen, G. 1977. "Values of Games with a Priori Unions." In *Essays in Mathematical Economics and Game Theory*, ed. R. Hein and O. Moeschlin, 76–88. New York: Springer-Verlag.

Panagariya, A. 1986. "Increasing Returns, Dynamic Stability, and International Trade." *J. International Economics* 20: 43–63.

Rajan, R. 1989. "Endogenous Coalition Formation in Cooperative Oligopolies." *International Economic Review* 4: 863–76.

Saloner, G. 1990. "Economic Issues in Computer Interface Standardization." *Economic Innovation and New Technology* 1: 135–56.

Selten, R. 1975. "A Simple Model of Imperfect Competition Where Four Are Few and Six Are Many." *International J. Game Theory* 2: 141–201.

Shapley, L. S., and M. Shubik. 1969. "Pure Competition, Coalitional Power and Fair Division." *International Economic Review* 10: 337–62.

Teece, D. J. 1992. "Competition, Cooperation, and Innovation: Organizational Arrangements for Regimes of Rapid Technological Progress." *J. Economic Behavior and Organization* 18: 1–25.

Weiss, M. B. H., and M. Sirbu. 1990. "Technological Choice in Voluntary Standards Committees: An Empirical Analysis." *Economics of Innovation and New Technology* 1: 111–33.

Werden, G. J., and M. G. Baumann. 1986. "A Simple Model of Imperfect Competition in Which Four Are Few but Three Are Not." *J. Industrial Economics* 34: 331–35.

6

Building New Political Actors

The immediate origin of this chapter was a concern for how nation-states form. My interest was heightened by the demise of the Soviet Union (the focus of my former policy interests) and Yugoslavia (where I took my honeymoon in 1982). Just what accounts for how large numbers of people sometimes come to live together successfully, and sometimes fail to do so? I was particularly interested in the positive process whereby independent actors sometimes cooperate so successfully that they give up some of their independence in the interests of even more effective collaboration.

Two successful examples have fascinated me at least since college. One is the example of how the thirteen American colonies gave up part of their autonomy to defeat the British, and gave up even more to construct a new nation called the United States. Over the next two centuries, the dynamic process of federal-state relations has continued to change in ways that usually favored Washington, with perhaps the largest changes associated with the outcome of the Civil War in the nineteenth century and the growth of the welfare state in the twentieth century.

The other surrender of autonomy that I found fascinating is the evolution of the multicellular organism. In a multicellular organism, such as a tree or a human, the specialization and interdependence between different kinds of cells has evolved so far that we can and do regard the entire collection of cells as a single individual (Buss 1987; Maynard Smith and Szathmary 1995).

More recently, I have followed with great interest a variety of abstract models of evolution that exhibit the emergence of heirarchical organization: new agents that are composed of collections of old agents (Fontana and Buss 1994; Kauffman 1993 and 1995; Holland 1995).

These empirical examples and abstract models led me to wonder about how to model the process by which independent actors sometimes give up part of their autonomy and create a new actor at a higher level of organization. Because my main interest has always been in political and social problems, I chose to focus on that domain. Because I enjoy developing computer models, I decided to see if I could get a computer model to construct something that looked and behaved like a new actor emerging from the self-organization of more elementary actors.

Though I can trace my interest in the emergence of new political actors back for decades, the end of the Cold War gave it new urgency. Once the Cold War was over, everyone started talking about "the new world order" with its hopes for enhanced international norms and cooperation. Like so many others, I wondered where this might all lead—and in particular, what it would take for nations to become less egotistical and more ready to give up some of their autonomy in the interest of collective action, perhaps for a global agenda. The end of the Cold War also raised new questions about the transformations of the nation-states themselves, as exemplified by the breakup of the Soviet Union and Yugoslavia. This concern was to understand the exact opposite of aggregation: the breakup of nations such as the Soviet Union and Yugoslavia. Finally, I was motivated by the question of state formation itself, both from the ruins of old multinational states and from the nations emerging from a colonial history. In sum, to understand the transformations taking place after the Cold War, it was no longer adequate to take for granted the independence or even the composition of countries.

The model I developed to study these processes employs some of the most basic processes in human history: threats and wars. The model is actually the most complicated one in this volume. For example, unlike the Prisoner's Dilemma, it takes into account the effects of unequal power and allows groups actors to gang up on each other. Despite my desire to keep things as simple as possible, it took a number of specific assumptions to get the system to generate completely new actors through the process of organizing collections of older actors. Although I make no claim that this model is either realistic or very general, it does demonstrate that it is possible to have a new level of political actor emerge from a dynamic model. In addition, the attempt to demonstrate that such emergence is possible required me to formulate a set of criteria by which one could recognize a new level of political actor if it were to form. The effort to formulate criteria for emergence of new actors may well prove to be as valuable as any particular model that exhibits such emergence.

References

Buss, Leo W. 1987. *The Evolution of Individuality.* Princeton, N.J.: Princeton University Press.

Dawkins, Richard, 1976. *The Selfish Gene.* New Edition. New York: Oxford University Press.

Fontana, Walter, and Leo W. Buss. 1994. "The Arrival of the Fittest: Toward a Theory of Biological Organization." *Bulletin of Mathematical Biology* 56: 1–64.

Holland, John H. 1995. *Hidden Order: How Adaptation Builds Complexity.* Reading, Mass.: Addison-Wesley.

Kauffman, Stuart A. 1993. *The Origins of Order: Self-Organization and Selection in Evolution.* New York: Oxford University Press.

————. 1995. *At Home in the Universe: The Search for the Laws of Self-Organization and Complexity.* New York: Oxford University Press.

Maynard Smith, John, and Eors Szathmary. 1995. *The Major Transitions in Biology.* New York: W. H. Freeman.

Building New Political Actors

A MODEL FOR THE EMERGENCE OF NEW POLITICAL ACTORS

ROBERT AXELROD

Reprinted from Robert Axelrod, "A Model of the Emergence of New Political Actors," in *Artificial Societies: The Computer Simulation of Social Life,* ed. Nigel Gilbert and Rosaria Conte (London: University College Press, 1995), 19–39. Reprinted with the permission of UCL Press.

Abstract:

The question of the aggregation and disaggregation of political actors is essential for the understanding of the future of global politics, both in terms of international security affairs and international political economy. A model based upon tribute is presented to show how new political actors can emerge from an aggregation of smaller political actors. The tribute model provides an existence proof that it is possible to use simple local rules to generate higher levels of organization from elementary actors. In particular, it shows that a dynamics of "pay or else" combined with mechanisms to increase and decrease commitments can lead to clusters of actors that behave largely according to the criteria for independent political states.

Introduction

How can new political actors emerge from an aggregation of smaller political actors? This essay presents a simulation model that provides one answer. In its broadest perspective, the work can be seen as part of the study of emergent organization through "bottom-up" processes. In such "bottom-up" process, small units interact according to locally defined rules, and the result is emergent properties of the system such as the formation of new levels of organization. Thus, the work is typical of the "Santa Fe" approach to complex adaptive systems (Stein 1989; Fontana

I thank Rob Axtell, Arthur Burks, Lars-Erik Cederman, Michael Cohen, Paul Courant, Joshua Epstein, Walter Fontana, Stephanie Forrest, Murray Gell-Mann, Nigel Gilbert, John Holland, John Miller, Melanie Mitchell, Robert Pahre, Rick Riolo, Carl Simon, and Gerard Weisbuch. For financial support I thank Project 2050 through the Santa Fe Institute, the National Science Foundation, and the LS&A Enrichment Fund of the University of Michigan.

1991; Holland 1992). The concern with increased levels of organization is also reminiscent of how biological systems managed to make the transition from single-celled organisms to multiple-celled organisms (Buss 1987), and how brains manage to function by organizing individual neurons into meaningful structures (Hebb 1949; Minsky 1985).

The task at hand involves the emergence of new political actors. This is a vital question in the post–Cold War world. We are experiencing an era in which the standard unit of politics, the nation, is no longer completely stable. We see on the one hand that some states are disintegrating, as in the former Soviet Union and Yugoslavia. We see on the other hand that larger units are being organized, such as the European Common Market and other regional associations. The question of the aggregation and disaggregation of political actors is essential for the understanding of the future of global politics, in terms of both international security affairs and international political economy.

The question of how the world can be placed on a sustainable path of development is a particularly pressing question. The emergence of new political actors is fundamental to the question of sustainability. One of the main problems of attaining sustainability is the tragedy of the commons (Hardin 1968). The tragedy of the commons arises when many independent actors (people, villages, states, or whatever) each "overgraze" because there is no mechanism to enforce the collective interests of all against the private interests of each. This leads to resource depletion, elimination of biodiversity, overpopulation, war, and other major social problems. A major route to the prevention of the tragedy of the commons is the emergence of a political actor based upon the organization of previously independent actors. Today we have political actors at the national level that can regulate resource use within their boundaries, but we do not yet have very effective political actors at the transnational level to regulate resource use at the global level.[1]

Political scientists have a variety of concepts and theories to analyze the emergence of new political actors. Unfortunately, they do not have any formal models that account for this emergence endogenously. In fact, the problem is much like biologists' interest in the emergence of multicellular organisms: research has tended to take for granted the existence of such complex units and therefore has not developed rigorous theories to explain how they might have come about in the first place (Buss 1987). For example, the major research paradigm for formal models of politics is game theory, and game theory takes as given exactly who the actors are

[1] Of course, the ability to regulate resource use does not guarantee that the ability will be wisely used. For example, the former Soviet Union had the power to control pollution from its factories, but in the interests of maximizing production it chose not to exercise that power.

in a particular setting. In contrast to the rational-choice approach of game theory, the model of this essay uses techniques of complex adaptive systems. It takes as given the existence of the lower-level actors, and generates higher-level actors from the interactions among them.

Given that the goal is to account for the emergence of new political actors, it is important to have a set of criteria that can be used to identify a new actor when one emerges. Here are my criteria for identifying a new political actor as an emergent set of relationships among previously existing units:

1. Effective control over subordinates
   a. little rebellion
   b. no independent "foreign policy"
2. Collective action ("all for one and one for all")
   a. paternalism (protection of the weak by the strong)
   b. joint foreign policy
3. Recognition by others as an actor

This list is largely inspired by historical and contemporary international law and practice concerning the recognition of new states in the world community of nations. For example, the thirteen colonies became a new nation called the United States when the central government was established that had:

1. Effective control over the individual states:
   a. with only low levels of rebellion (at least until the Civil War), and
   b. with a prohibition on treaties between the individual states and other nations;
2. Collective control over some important resources:
   a. that allowed federal interests to dominant state interests at least in certain important domains, and
   b. that allowed for a common foreign policy in matters of war and peace; and
3. Recognition of its independence by other nations such as France and Britain.

Although the emergence of the United States is hardly typical, it does illustrate the essential properties of how a new political actor can result from the aggregation of smaller political actors. In the American case, the aggregation was of colonies whose own autonomy was short-lived and precarious during the revolutionary period. The more typical case, and the one modeled here, is that in which the emergent actor is essentially an empire in which a core unit dominates its neighbors. A good example of this process is the growth of the Russian (and later Soviet) empire from a small core around Moscow. Other examples include the growth by accretion of neighboring lands by Rome and China.

Coercion in general and extortion in particular have played a central role in the formation of states over the centuries (Tilly 1985 and 1990). For this reason, at the heart of the present model is the simple dynamic of "pay or else." An elementary actor can make a demand of a neighbor for payment of resources, with the threat that if payment is not forthcoming there will be a war.

In the tribute model, wars result in changes in wealth (and thus power), but not in outright territorial conquest.[2] This allows each territory to maintain itself as a separate actor, thereby allowing for the possible emergence of sets of territorial actors who might form new aggregate actors. Although no territory changes hands, war results in costs to both sides, but especially to the weaker side. Thus, the heart of the model is a tribute system in which an actor can extract resources from others through tribute payments and use these resources to extract still more resources. Alliances are also allowed, so that actors can work together. Whether a set of elementary actors actually emerges as a stable aggregate actor will then depend on the dynamics of the tribute system: whether groups of actors actually emerge that function as a single aggregate, and whether alliance patterns emerge that lead to stable coordinated actions.

Unlike my earlier work on the Prisoner's Dilemma (e.g., Axelrod 1984), the tribute model is based upon extortion rather than cooperation. Also unlike the earlier work, it does not assume that the actors are equal in power, but instead takes power differences as vital and as resulting directly from the dynamics of the model. Nor does it assume that the actors interact only two at a time. Like my earlier work, it is not a rational model. The tribute model assumes that actors develop more or less strong commitments to each other based upon their prior actions. These commitments can be thought of as the result of psychological processes (e.g., to stand by those who have helped you in the past), or the result of political rules of thumb (e.g., to support those who may later help you in your time of need). Actions are based upon simple decision rules rather than game-theoretic calculations of optimal choice, because rational calculations would be virtually impossible to make in such a complex setting. An important and novel feature is that the behavior of the actors changes over time as the actors apply simple decision rules to data about the historical experience they have gathered through prior interactions.

The project will be successful to the extent that it can account for

---

[2] This contrasts with Cusack and Stoll (1990), whose simulation model uses conquest of territory as the major dynamic.

important phenomena that cannot be accounted for by existing formal theories, and can do so with only a few assumptions. The main result to be generated is the emergence of new political actors at a higher level of organization, and the main assumptions have to do with how elementary actors interact with each other. As we shall see, the model spontaneously generates not only emergent actors, but also other interesting phenomena that exist in the world of international politics.

The Tribute Model

The basic units of the model are ten actors arranged on a line. The actors can be thought of as independent political units, such as nations. The reason for having so few actors and having such a simple geography as a line (rather than a two-dimensional space) is to keep the data analysis as simple as possible. As long as no vital conceptual features are lost, simplicity is the best modeling strategy. To avoid introducing arbitrary distinctions between actors on the ends of the line and those in the interior, the line is wrapped around into a circle. This gives each of the ten actors exactly two neighbors.

There is one resource in the model, called wealth. Each actor is given some initial wealth. The initial wealths are chosen from a uniform distribution between 300 and 500. These parameters, like all the others in the model are somewhat arbitrary and are selected for convenience.

The basic cycle of the model is called a year. In each year, three actors are chosen one after another at random to become active. An active actor, A, may demand tribute from one of the other actors, B. Initially, the target, B, must be a neighbor, but later this restriction will be relaxed when alliances are considered. The model is based upon a dynamic of "pay or else." The target, B, then has a choice of paying tribute to the demander, or fighting.

The selection of actors to be active is based upon the notion that ambitious leaders and potential disputes arise at random. But once given an opportunity to make a demand, the activated actor need not actually make a demand if it finds that the current situation is not favorable.

If A does make a demand, the target B has a choice:

If B pays, wealth is transferred directly from B to A. The amount of wealth transferred is 250 if B has that much. Otherwise, the amount transferred to A is whatever B has. This transfer represents tribute that B pays to A to avoid a fight.[3]

_____

[3] Having a fixed maximum demand is arbitrary, but avoids the need for the actors to calculate what demand they will make.

If B fights rather than pays, each side loses 25 percent of the *other* side's wealth (or both lose proportionally less if either side does not have that much wealth).[4] This is a simple Lanchester attrition dynamic (Lanchester 1916; Epstein 1985). The idea is that in a fight both sides suffer, but the stronger side imposes more damage than the weaker side does.[5]

After the three activations, the yearly cycle ends with a "harvest" that increases each actors' wealth by 20. This feeds some new wealth into the system. A typical run is 1,000 years.

The next question to consider is decision rules used by the actors for making and responding to demands. It would be virtually impossible for actors to develop fully rational rules in the tribute game because of its complexity over time and space. Therefore the model uses heuristic decision rules that capture some of the key short-term considerations facing the players:

> The active actor needs to decide whom, if anyone, to make a demand of. The ideal target of a demand is weak enough so that it might choose to pay rather than fight, and so that it will not cause much damage if it does choose to fight. On the other hand, the ideal target should be strong enough to be able to afford to pay as much as possible. A suitable decision rule combining both of these considerations is to choose among the potential targets the one that maximizes the product of the target's vulnerability times its possible payment. The target's vulnerability is $(W_A - W_T)/W_A$ where W_A and W_T are the wealths of the active actor and the target, respectively. The target's payment is how much the other side can pay, which is the lesser of its wealth and the full tribute of 250. If no potential target has positive vulnerability (i.e., no potential target is weaker than the demander), then no demand is made.
>
> The decision rule used for the target is simpler: fight if and only if it would cost less than paying would.

So far, the model has considered only pairwise interactions. But in order to study the development of emergent actors, there has to be a way for the basic actors to work together. The key idea is that actors develop degrees of commitment to each other. These commitments are caused by

---

[4] For example, if A has 400 and B has 300, A loses $0.25 * 300 = 75$, and B loses $0.25 * 400 = 100$. The wealths after the fight would then be $400 - 75 = 325$ for A, and $300 - 100 = 200$ for B. Note that the disparity in wealth increases from 100 to 125. If B began the fight with only 50, then B would lose all 50 (which is half the damage A is capable of doing), and A would lose half of the maximum damage B is capable of causing, that is, $0.25 * 0.50 * 50 = 12.5$.

[5] The demander is assumed to carry out its implicit threat to fight if the demand is not met. This assumes, in effect, that the demander's need to maintain its reputation is strong enough to maintain the credibility of the threat.

their choices to pay or fight, and in turn have consequences for how they will pay or fight in the future. The basic idea is that if two elementary actors fight, another adjacent actor will join the side to which it has greater commitment. If it has equal commitment to the demander and the target, it stays neutral. If it does join one side or the other, it contributes forces (i.e., wealth) in proportion to its commitment to that side.

Initially, no one has any commitments to others, and each actor is fully committed to itself. Commitment of i to j increases when:

   a. i pays tribute to j (subservience),
   b. i receives tribute from j (protection), or
   c. i fights on the same side as j (friendship).

Similarly, commitment decreases whenever:

   d. i fights on the opposite side as j (hostility).

The motivation for these rules of commitment dynamics are simple. When one actor pays tribute to another, it is also likely to be partially under its political domination and therefore compelled to assist it next time. A state typically becomes committed to helping the patron whether by choice or necessity, as illustrated by the participation of many Latin American states in World War II after Pearl Harbor. Conversely, the protection of states that have provided benefits is also commonplace, so as to protect future sources of revenue. The next point is that if two sides have fought together in the past, they tend to be partially committed to each other in the future, as in the case of the United States and South Korea after the Korean War. On the other hand, two states that have fought each other are less likely to support each other in the future, as in the case of Germany and France after World War I.[6]

The model assumes that increases and decreases of commitment are in constant amounts, namely, increments of 10 percent. In addition, one actor's commitment to another can never be more than 100 percent nor less than 0 percent. The commitment processes described above maintain the symmetry of commitment. This is because two actors start with no commitment to each other and their commitments to each other always grow and decline in unison. For example, if two actors fight on the same side in a war, then their commitment to each other will increase by 10 percent.

The final part of the model deals with coordination of actors. To keep interactions similar to land combat, coordinated action is assumed to require contiguity. Thus, an actor is an eligible target for a demander only if everyone between them joins the demander. Others may then join the

---

[6] For evidence on the friendship and hostility aspects, see Axelrod and Bennett (1993).

demander or the target if everyone closer to that side also joins that side. For example, the actor in position 5 may make a demand on actor 8 only if actors 6 and 7 join actor 5. This requires that actors 6 and 7 are both more committed to 5 than to 8. Then, if 5 does make a demand on 8, actor 10 may join the defense of 8 only if 9 joins too.

Commitments and wealths are common knowledge.[7] Thus, when an active actor is evaluating the vulnerability of an eligible target, it can take into account the commitments and wealth of all actors who would join either side. Likewise, the target of a demand can determine the cost to itself of fighting by calculating the damage that the attacking alliance could do, and the proportion of that damage that the target would suffer, which is the proportion of the defending alliance's wealth contributed by the defender.

The Dynamics of the Tribute System

Like any stochastic simulation, the tribute model needs to be run many times to explore the type of histories it generates. In the case of the tribute model there are two sources of random variation: the initial wealths of the actors, and the selection of three actors each year to become active. A good way to begin to appreciate the dynamics of the model is to look at history from the perspective of a single actor, say actor 5. This reveals the sequence of events (demands, payments, and fights) that it takes part in. The history also illustrates how alliances are built up from the events that cause commitments.

For example, here is the first few years of history for actor 5 in the first run. In year 9, 5 was active and made its first demand, a demand on a neighbor, actor 4. Finding payment would be more costly than fighting, 4 chose to fight. In the resulting fight each lost wealth, but the defender was weaker and thus lost more than the attacker. In the next year, 5 was again active, and again made a demand on 4. Having been weakened by the previous fight, this time 4 found it cheaper to pay tribute. The payment not only helped 5 at the expense of 4, but led to a mutual commitment of subservience and protection between 4 and 5 at the 10 percent level. The next time that 5 became active (year 11), it was able to make a demand of 3 (with 4's support). Target 3 chose to pay, making it, too, partially committed to 5. In year 14, 5 became active again and targeted 2. However, 2 refused to pay, so 5 fought with the help of 3 and 4, both of whom were

[7] In international politics, wealth can usually be estimated with rough accuracy, but commitments are harder to predict. There is a rich empirical and theoretical literature on commitment. See, for example, Schelling (1960), Huth (1988), Powell (1990), Bueno de Mesquita and Lalman (1992), and Axelrod and Bennett (1993).

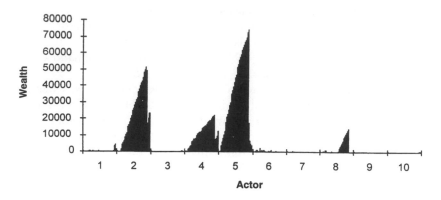

Figure 6-1. Wealth of Each Actor over 1,000 Years (Population 1)

partially committed to 5. Because 3, 4, and 5 all fought on the same side, they each became 10 percent more committed to the others. And because they each fought on the opposite side of 2, they would have become 10 percent less committed to 2 had they had any commitment to 2.

Having looked at some event-by-event history, let us examine the big picture. Figure 6-1 shows the wealth of each of the ten actors over the long time span of 1,000 years. The figure clearly shows that three actors were wealthier than the others over most of the history, with actor 5 reaching the highest wealth. A close examination of the figure also shows that something dramatic happened near the end of the 1,000 years: a sudden decline in all three of the wealthy actors, especially in the biggest one. Figure 6-2 shows the number of fights in every twenty-five-year period, and also shows the total wealth of the entire population over time. There were many fights at the start but then fewer, with a resurgence of fights in the last 100 years. The resurgence of fights corresponds to the collapse of the population's wealth at around year 900. This kind of major collapse happened only once in five runs of the model.

Quite different histories were generated for new populations simulated under the same conditions. For example, Figures 6-3 and 6-4 show that the second population had four successful actors (rather than three), no fights at all after year 200 (rather than continuing fighting and a late resurgence), and a steady growth of global wealth (rather than a collapse). Figures 6-5 and 6-6 show the third population had two wealthy actors, an uneven pattern of fights, and several moderate declines in global wealth. The fourth and fifth populations showed still other combinations of number of wealthy actors, frequency of fights, and trends in population wealth. Thus, five runs of the same model with the same

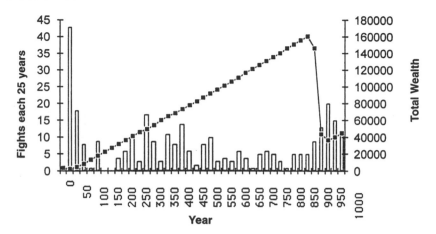

Figure 6-2. Fights (bars) and Population Wealth (line) in Population 1

parameters give quite different histories.[8] Different combinations of initial wealth and the order in which actors become active can evidently make a large difference in the development of the history of the system.

Still another way of looking at the dynamics of the model is to examine the development of patterns of commitment. Typically the first pattern to emerge was a set of proximity relationships in which actors developed low levels of commitment to neighbors, and sometimes to neighbors of neighbors. This pattern is illustrated with the pattern of commitments in year 25 of population 2 (see Table 6-1). The other common pattern of commitments develops after this, and consists of two clusters of actors. A *cluster* can be defined as a set of actors all of whom are highly committed to each other (say, at the 50 percent level). Table 6-2 shows the same population twenty-five years later, divided neatly into two clusters, with no commitments at all between members of different clusters.[9]

To see how this population can become divided so quickly into two distinct clusters, look at the sequence of payments and fights involving a single illustrative actor, actor 5. Table 6-3 shows the fights and payments involving actor 5 from year 25, when it had only one partial commitment, through year 50, when it was fully integrated into a cluster of four actors. The events of year 35 can serve to illustrate the dynamics of commitments that lead to the development of distinct clusters. In that year, 3 and 4 fought 5, 6, and 7. This led 5 to increase its commitment to 6 and 7

---

[8] A run takes only twenty-three seconds on a Macintosh Quadra 700 using Pascal. Of course, the analysis can take days or weeks.

[9] In many cases, there were two large clusters with one or two actors participating in both of the clusters.

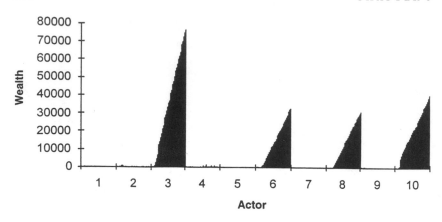

Figure 6-3. Wealth of Each Actor over 1,000 Years (Population 2)

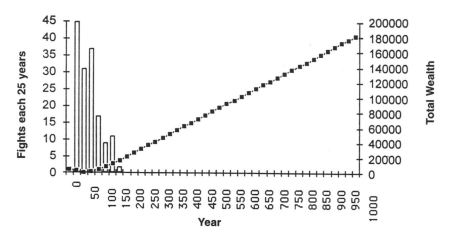

Figure 6-4. Fights (bars) and Population Wealth (line) in Population 2.

while decreasing its commitment (if any) to 3 and 4. In general, as fights take place, they increase the commitments of those fighting on the same side, and decrease the commitments of those fighting on opposite sides. Thus, as clusters begin to form, they tend to get ever more distinct. This is because pairs of actors who fought together became even more committed to each other, and pairs on opposite sides lost whatever partial commitment they may have had to each other. By year 45, fights were taking place that involved all ten actors, leading to the pattern of two strong and distinct clusters that was shown in Table 6-2.

Having seen how commitments can lead to clusters in an illustration from population 2, let us now return to the unusual case of population 1,

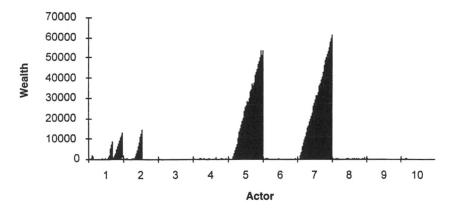

Figure 6-5. Wealth of Each Actor over 1,000 Years (Population 3)

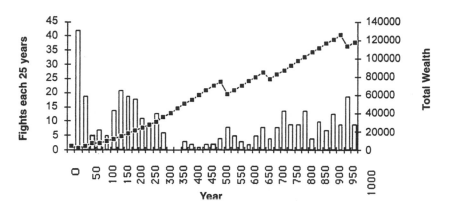

Figure 6-6. Fights (bars) and Population Wealth (line) in Population 3

where the strongest actor collapsed. The dynamics over the full 1,000 years was shown in Figures 6-1 and 6-2. Now we can look in detail at the period of collapse that took place between years 890 and 950. This is shown in Figure 6-7. In year 911, actor 10 targeted actor 9, resulting in a "world war" involving actors 5–9 versus all the others. Actor 5, the strongest actor, joined in even though it had minimal commitment to 9 because it had none at all to actor 10. Because 5's commitment to 9 was only at the 10 percent level, it contributed only 10 percent of its forces to the fight and suffered only slightly. But later that same year, 9 again attacked 10, and this time when 5 joined in, it contributed 20 percent of its forces (having become a little more committed to 9 as well as all the others in that alliance), and suffered a little more. Now 5 was even more

TABLE 6-1

Commitments Forming a Proximity Pattern (from Population 2, Year 25)

					j					
i	1	2	3	4	5	6	7	8	9	10
1	100	30	0	0	0	0	0	0	10	40
2	30	100	0	0	0	0	0	0	20	20
3	0	0	100	20	0	0	0	0	0	0
4	0	0	20	100	30	0	0	0	0	0
5	0	0	0	30	100	0	0	0	0	0
6	0	0	0	0	0	100	0	0	0	0
7	0	0	0	0	0	0	100	0	0	0
8	0	0	0	0	0	0	0	100	50	0
9	10	20	0	0	0	0	0	50	100	10
10	40	20	0	0	0	0	0	0	10	100

Note: Actors 1 and 10 are adjacent.

TABLE 6-2

Commitments Forming Pattern of Two Clusters (from Population 2, Year 50)

					j					
i	1	2	3	4	5	6	7	8	9	10
1	100	100	70	0	0	0	0	100	100	100
2	100	100	100	0	0	0	0	100	100	100
3	70	100	100	0	0	0	0	100	90	70
4	0	0	0	100	100	60	100	0	0	0
5	0	0	0	100	100	100	100	0	0	0
6	0	0	0	60	100	100	100	0	0	0
7	0	0	0	100	100	100	100	0	0	0
8	100	100	100	0	0	0	0	100	100	100
9	100	100	90	0	0	0	0	100	100	100
10	100	100	70	0	0	0	0	100	100	100

Note: Actors 1 and 10 are adjacent.

committed to everyone in its emerging cluster of 5–9. In years 915–918 there were five more "world wars" with the same alignments (although different demanders and targets). As both sides became more committed to the members of their own emerging clusters, more and more forces were committed and more and more damage was done. The result was a sharp decline in the wealths of the largest actors (5 on one side and 2 and 4 on the other).

This dramatic decline of the strongest actor is due to its being dragged into fights involving weak actors to whom it had developed commit-

TABLE 6-3
Development of Cluster of Commitments
(Fights and payments involving individual 5 of population 2
between years 25 and 50)

Year	Active Actor	Target Actor	Roles	Commitment with Actor 5 Increases[a]	Commitment with Actor 5 Decreases[b]
30	4	5	- - a A D - - - - -		3, 4
30	6	5	- - - - P R - - - -	6	
32	3	4	- - A D d - - - - -	4	3
32	4	5	- - a A D d - - - -	6	3, 4
33	4	3	- d D A a - - - - -	4	2, 3
34	5	7	- - - - R - P - - -	7	
35	5	4	- - d D A a a - - -	6, 7	3, 4
36	3	4	- a A D d - - - - -	7	2, 3
36	8	7	a a - - d d D A a a	6, 7	1, 2, 8–10
37	6	5	- - - - P R - - - -	6	
38	8	7	a a a - d d D A a a	6, 7	1–3, 8–10
38	2	7	a A a - d d D a a a	6, 7	1–3, 8–10
41	8	7	a a a - d d D A a a	6, 7	1–3, 8–10
42	6	5	- - - - P R - - - -	6	
42	5	4	- - - P R - - - - -	4	
44	5	7	- - - - R - P - - -	7	
46	7	8	d d d a a a A D d d	4, 6, 7	1–3, 8–10
47	7	8	d d d a a a A D d d	4, 6, 7	1–3, 8–10
48	7	3	d d D a a a A d d d	4, 6, 7	1–3, 8–10
48	5	3	d d D a A a a d d d	4, 6, 7	1–3, 8–10

Key to roles:
A = attacker,   a = attacker's ally,
D = defender,   d = defender's ally,
P = payer,   R = receiver of tribute.
[a]Increases by 10 percent, up to 100 percent.
[b]Decreases by 10 percent, down to 0 percent.

ments. This is reminiscent of what happened to two dominant powers, the Hapsburgs in the seventeenth century and Britain in the nineteenth to twentieth centuries. Paul Kennedy has an apt term for the dangers of the excess commitments that strong powers tend to take on. It is "imperial overstretch" (Kennedy 1987). This is just what is illustrated in Figure 6-7. It is striking that a simple model developed to generate new political actors produced behavior that has been the subject of a major policy debate in contemporary international affairs (e.g., Nye 1990).

Clusters are not only settings for mutual commitment; they are also settings for extraction of tribute. The strongest actor in a cluster typically

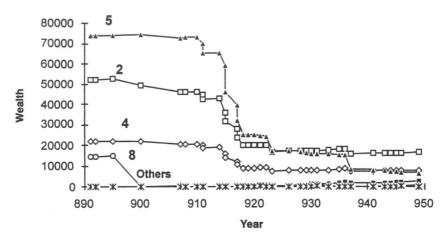

Figure 6-7. Late Collapse of a Powerful Actor. Payments and Fights Involving Actor 5 (Population 1, Years 890–950)

stays strong and grows by making demands on and collecting tribute from the other members of its cluster. As actors slowly grow due to their annual "harvest," the strong member makes demands upon the weak and reduces their wealth. In fact, as the strong member selects lucrative targets, its demands automatically tend to be rotated among members of the cluster. This rotation has the unplanned consequence of preventing any target from growing very strong. But sometimes a weak member of a cluster escapes demands just long enough to grow sufficiently strong to make its own demands on still weaker members. If luck lets it be active often enough at this critical stage, it can collect sufficient tribute so that the strongest member no longer finds it advantageous to challenge the newly wealthy actor. An example of this process occurred after year 100 in population 3 (see Figure 6-8). In this example, actor 5 has managed to grow in the shadow of the strongest actor of its cluster, actor 7.

Demands within clusters do not always get resolved by payments of tribute. In fact, civil wars can occur, that is, fighting among members of the same cluster. The strongest member of a cluster is typically strong enough to prevent such a fight from taking place if it took sides. If, however, the strongest member is equally committed to the attacker and the defender (perhaps by being totally committed to both), then it would stay neutral. This allows civil wars to occur if the active actor finds a lucrative target within the same cluster, and the target finds it more costly to pay tribute than to fight. The attacker and defender may even find allies among the others if the others are not equally committed to the two sides.

Surprisingly, initial differences in wealth do not matter for wealth in

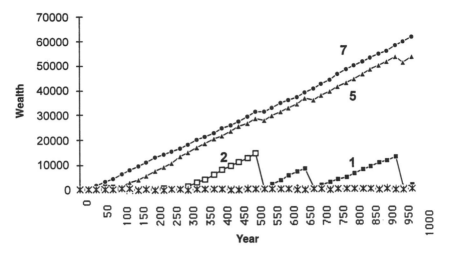

Figure 6-8. Internal conflict. Growth of a Second Strong Actor in a Cluster of Actors 4–8 (Population 3)

the long run. In five populations of the model there were fifty actors in all, fourteen of whom were quite successful, using a criterion of wealth of over 10,000 after 1,000 years. Of these fourteen successful actors, half had less than average initial wealth and half had more than average initial wealth. One might expect that initial wealth would be a great advantage because it would allow an actor to make successful demands on its neighbors at first, and thereby build up a dominant position in a cluster. But having substantial initial wealth can also make an actor a lucrative target for other strong actors. In addition, having substantial initial wealth can make one overconfident, given the limited rationality of the decision rules in effect.[10]

The results of the model's performance can now be summarized in terms of six characteristics:

1. *Things usually do not settle down.* Instead, the history of the model shows considerable complexity. For example, as late as year 900, one of the populations suffered a series of fights that destroyed more than three-fourths of the global wealth (see Figure 6-2).

2. *Histories show considerable variability.* The combinations of

[10] For example, suppose an actor with wealth of 500 makes a demand on a neighbor with 400. The neighbor will fight rather than pay (losing 0.25 * 500 = 125, which is less than payment of the standard demand of 250). Because the target fought, the demander loses 0.25 * 400 = 100, and is worse off for having made the demand. Had the initial wealths been greater than 1,000, this would not happen because the cost of fighting would be greater than the standard demand of 250.

wealthy actors, frequency of fights, and trends in population wealth differ considerably from one population to another. Even though each actor is using the same decision rules, the results differ greatly due to random differences in initial wealth and in the order in which actors become active.

3. *"Imperial overstretch" can bring down even the strongest actor.* As an actor becomes committed to others due to tribute relationships and fighting together, it becomes exposed to the risks of whatever fights the others get into. Because actors decide on demands and responses based upon their own calculations, even a weak actor can choose to make or resist a demand for its own reasons, and thereby drag into the struggle a strong actor who is committed to it.

4. *Civil wars can occur among the smaller members of a cluster.* Although the strongest member of a cluster can typically prevent a fight among members of the same cluster by taking sides, it would not do so if it had equal commitment to the two sides. Therefore, smaller members a cluster may fight each other while the strongest member stands aside.

5. *A cluster can have more than one powerful member.* Clusters are often like empires, with one powerful actor and many weaker ones who pay tribute to it. But as we have seen in the case of Figure 6-8, it is also possible for a second actor to grow strong in the shadow of the first.

6. *Initial endowment does not guarantee or even predict success.* Before clusters of commitments are established, wealth can be as much a handicap as an asset. The reason is that wealth makes an actor a lucrative target for other strong actors, and can make one overconfident in making demands.

Have New Actors Emerged?

Returning to the original goal of the project, we can now assess the extent to which the emergent clusters of mutually committed actors are really new actors at a higher level of organization. Recall that a cluster is defined as a set of actors who are each committed to the others at a level of at least 50 percent. This definition provides a set of candidates who may or may not be emergent political actors. To see if clusters actually behave as newly emergent political actors, we return to the original set of criteria:

   1. Effective control over subordinates
        a. In the simulation, clusters exhibit no rebellion. There were no fights in a cluster against the strongest member. Note that this result is not built into the model's assumptions. After all, it would certainly be possible for several

members of a cluster to join in attacking the strongest member. (There were, however, some fights among the secondary actors within a cluster, tolerated by the strongest.)

　　b. Independent "foreign policy" occurred on only rare occasions. On these rare occasions, the strongest member *was* dragged into trouble by commitment to a client ("imperial overstretch").

　　2. Collective action ("all for one and one for all")

　　　　a. The strong did protect the weak.

　　　　b. Members of a cluster did act together with respect to outsiders, both in attack and defense.

　　3. Recognition by others as an actor did occur, since joint action of clusters was foreseen and taken into account by outsiders. Note that the model assumes that everyone can anticipate the effect of current alliances. The fact that clusters were stable means that the short-term calculation based on alliances was tantamount to long-term recognition of emergent actors based upon stable clusters.

In sum, the tribute model did produce clusters of mutual commitment, and these clusters did exhibit to a high degree all the attributes of an emergent new political actor. In fact, even the exceptions reflected the kind of exceptions present in international affairs, as illustrated by imperial overstretch.

Variations of the Model

One of the advantages of a simulation model is that it is relatively easy to answer "what if" questions about the effect of varying the parameters or the premises of the model. Here is a very brief sample of some of these questions, with answers based on further simulation runs:

　　1. *Does the model settle down after 1,000 years?* No. Even in runs up to 10,000 years there are repeated large wars, and strong actors continue to rise and fall.

　　2. *Are there better decision rules?* Yes. An example is adding a constraint so that a demand will not be made of a target who would find it cheaper to fight than to pay. An individual using this revised rule does much better than the others. Moreover, if everyone is using the revised rule, any single individual who uses the old rule does worse than the others.

　　3. *Does it pay to give and receive commitments?* Yes. An actor who neither gives nor receives commitment does very poorly. Moreover, if just one actor gives and receives commitments (and the others do not, except with that actor), then that actor does very well.

　　4. *What happens if everyone can reach everyone else (as in sea power)?*

In this extreme case, a single powerful actor tends to dominate, and there are relatively dense patterns of commitment. Presumably, in a two-dimensional space, where everyone has more neighbors than in a one-dimensional space but fewer than in the "sea power" case, there might be an intermediate level of dominance and density of commitment.

5. *What if wealth does not enter into anyone's calculations?* If the demands are made without regard to wealth, and if everyone always fights, then the result is two clear clusters, one of which has virtually all the wealth.

6. *Do "islands of commitment" grow?* Yes. If two adjacent actors initially have just 10 percent commitment to each other (and all other commitments are zero), then these two actors develop complete commitment to each other, and both tend to prosper.

Conclusion: Building Stepping Stones to Theory

The tribute model provides an existence proof that it is possible to use simple local rules to generate higher levels of organization from elementary actors. In particular, it shows that a dynamics of "pay or else" combined with mechanisms to increase and decrease commitments can lead to clusters of actors that behave largely according to the criteria for independent political states.

Like most simulation models, the tribute model generates huge amounts of historically rich data. Indeed, a major challenge in any simulation study is to find ways of analyzing and presenting data that help us see the forest for the trees. The present essay illustrates four different kinds of historical analysis. In effect, these are four different ways of looking at history.

   a. history from the point of view of a single actor: plots of relative wealth of individual actors over time,

   b. history from a global point of view: joint plots of wealth and number of fights over time,

   c. history from the point of view of the emergence of new actors: commitment matrixes revealing emerging clusters of actors, and

   d. history as "news": event data, including chronologies of tribute payments and wars fought between alliances.

Perhaps the most useful outcome of a simulation model is to provide new ways of thinking about old problems. In the present case, the need to determine whether or not the model was successful in generating new political actors forced the specification of explicit criteria for recognizing a new political actor should one arise. This in itself is a useful exercise. In addition, the same need led to the development of different ways of viewing history, and especially ways of analyzing the interaction among emerging clusters of actors.

In the future it would be good to use these conceptual and statistical developments to answer some new questions suggested by the model. For example, the dynamics we have seen in the tribute model suggest the following interesting questions:

a. What are the minimal conditions for a new actor to emerge?
b. What tends to promote such emergence?
c. How are the dynamics affected by the number of elementary actors?
d. What can lead to collapse of an aggregate actor?
e. How can new actors grow in the shadow of established actors?

Although no one would believe that the answers to these questions given by the model itself would necessarily be accurate for the real world, a realistic hope is that the concepts developed in generating the answers for the model would be useful in providing new ways of thinking about comparable questions in the real world. Indeed, understanding the dynamics of the tribute model might also suggest specific hypotheses that could be tested with data from the real world. In addition, the study of one model, such as the tribute model, can provide the basis for insights into how even simpler models can be developed that might allow deeper insights into issues of emergent political organization.

Finally, a simulation model like the tribute model can lead to insights into where there might be policy leverage in the real world. For example, one might be able to identify situations in which slight changes in the system could lead to substantially improved outcomes—in terms of fewer destructive wars or greater coordination of political action. If we knew when minor inputs could lead to major gains, we would have valuable clues to consider for policy leverage in the real world—the world where avoiding war and achieving sustainability really matter.

References

Axelrod, R. 1984. *The Evolution of Cooperation*. New York: Basic Books.

Axelrod, R., and D. S. Bennett. 1993. "A Landscape Theory of Aggregation." *British Journal of Political Science* 23: 211–33. Included as Chapter 4 of this volume.

Bueno de Mesquita, B., and D. Lalman. 1992. *War and Reason: Domestic and International Imperatives*. New Haven: Yale University Press.

Buss, L. W. 1987. *The Evolution of Individuality*. Princeton, N.J.: Princeton University Press.

Cusack, T. R., and R. J. Stoll. 1990. *Exploring Realpolitik: Probing International Relations Theory with Computer Simulation.* Boulder, Colo.: Lynne Rienner.

Epstein, J. M. 1985. *The Calculus of Conventional War: Dynamic Analysis Without Lanchester Theory.* Washington, D.C.: Brookings.

Fontana, W. 1991. "Functional Self-Organization in Complex Systems." In *1990 Lectures in Complex Systems,* SFI Studies in the Sciences of Complexity, vol. 3, ed. L. Nadel and D. Stein, 407–26. Redwood City, Calif.: Addison-Wesley.

Hardin, G. 1968. "The Tragedy of the Commons." *Science* 162: 1243–48.

Holland, J. H. 1992. "Complex Adaptive Systems." *Daedalus* 121: 17–30.

Hebb, D. O. 1949. *The Organization of Behavior.* New York: Wiley.

Huth, P. 1988. *Extended Deterrence and the Prevention of War.* New Haven: Yale University Press.

Kennedy, P. 1987. *The Rise and Fall of the Great Powers.* New York: Random House.

Lanchester, F. W. 1916. *Aircraft in Warfare: The Dawn of the First Arm.* London: Constable. Key chapters reprinted as "Mathematics in Warfare." In *The World of Mathematics,* ed. J. Newman. 1956. New York: Simon and Schuster.

Minsky, M. 1985. *Society of the Mind.* New York: Simon and Schuster.

Nye, J. S., Jr. 1990. *Bound to Lead, The Changing Nature of American Power.* New York: Basic Books.

Powell, R. 1990. *Nuclear Deterrence Theory: The Search for Credibility.* Cambridge, Eng.: Cambridge University Press.

Schelling, T. 1960. *The Strategy of Conflict.* New York: Oxford University Press.

Stein, D. L., ed. 1989. *Lectures in the Sciences of Complexity.* Redwood City, Calif.: Addison-Wesley.

Tilly, C. 1985. "War Making and State Making as Organized Crime." In *Bringing the State Back In,* ed. P. B. Evans, D. H. Rueschemeyer, and T. A. Skocpol, 169–91. Cambridge, Eng.: Cambridge University Press.

———. 1990. *Coercion, Capital, and European States, AD 990–1990.* Oxford: Basil Blackwell.

7

Disseminating Culture

THIS CHAPTER deals with the fundamental question of how we become who we are through our interactions with others. The immediate origin of this chapter is similar to the motivation of the previous chapter: a desire to understand how nations emerge. In the previous chapter, I focused on threats and wars as mechanisms for the development of new political actors from the competition and collaboration of more elementary political actors. This time I wanted to study the even more fundamental process of how communities evolve in the first place. It seemed to me that a key part of the process was the development of enough shared culture so that a group of people could work well together. I recognized that in modern times, governments themselves promote culture through powerful mechanisms such as universal schooling and the regulation of mass media. But I was primarily interested in how the dissemination of culture works below and indeed before the activities of powerful governments.[1] How do people come to share enough in the way of language, habits, beliefs, and values that they can build the basis of common institutions such as effective government?

The approach I took was to model social influence: the way people tend to change each other in the very process of interaction. My academic interest in social influence dates back twenty years to my concern with how people try to persuade each other, especially in foreign policy argumentation. In that context I compared and contrasted styles of British, German, and Japanese leaders in terms of the pattern of causal beliefs they espoused while trying to persuade others to adapt their own preferred policies (Axelrod 1976 and 1977a). I also had a long-standing interest in how the separate parts of a person's belief and value system more or less fit together. This was an interest that goes back to my very first publication, which was on the structure of public opinion on policy issues (Axelrod 1967; see also Axelrod 1973 and 1977b).

In fact, my interest in social influence dates back even further than the beginning of my academic career. I distinctly remember an assignment I got when I was fourteen years old. The city council of our town, Evans-

---

[1] I do not use the more common term *diffusion of culture* because in anthropology that term has taken on connotations about the spread of supposedly "superior" (or at least attractive) Western culture.

ton, Illinois, was considering a proposal to cross-train the police officers and firefighters. My teacher asked us to write about whether it was a good idea or not. The plan certainly seemed like a good idea to me because the police would learn some additional first aid skills to use if they were the first on the scene of a fire, and the firefighters would learn some crowd control techniques to use if *they* happened to be the first on the scene. I called the local fire station to see what the people there thought. The man who answered the phone told me, "I don't know much about it, but we're all against it down here." I was not sure just why they were all against it (probably job security), but the response made a deep impression on me: it was possible to have an opinion based upon social influence rather than independent analysis. Moreover, one could be quite comfortable with this method of arriving at opinions. As I thought about it, I realized the firefighter I had talked to was perhaps more sensible than I first thought. In many circumstances, reliance on social influence could be a quite sensible way to reach an opinion.

The present model of social influence is the simplest model in this volume, and perhaps the most ambitious. It is the simplest in the sense that its basic mechanism follows a simple rule that leaves no room for strategic choice. It is strictly adaptive in style. It is also the simplest in that the entire description of the context and the dynamics of the model can be stated in two or three sentences. It is the most ambitious model in this volume in that it deals with how our very identities are shaped: who we are affects whom we interact with, and whom we interact with shapes who we become.

Besides being the simplest and most ambitious model in the volume, it is also the most surprising and the most controversial. It is the most surprising in that when I simulated a population with my model, my expectations were wrong as often as they were right, even though I was the one who designed the model. In addition, one of the key results was so counterintuitive that at first I thought it must have been due to a programming error. But it was not.[2] The model is the most controversial in that I have had the most trouble getting it published. I first sent it to the *American Political Science Review*, where one reviewer said about the model, "It is one that political scientists were educated to hate. No one makes choices. No one seeks to influence anyone else. Change has no costs, politically or economically. Cultural change occurs all-together in a community, with no leaders or laggards. In sum, politics are absent."

Nevertheless, that reviewer was "enchanted" by the manuscript and urged its publication. The other two reviewers thought the manuscript

---

[2] Appendix A provides an independent replication of this model and confirms its key results.

needed more politics, and urged either substantial revisions or submission to a journal in another field. I chose the latter course. I made a variety of corrections and clarifications suggested by the reviewers, and sent it to the *American Sociological Review.*

The *American Sociological Review* had no trouble seeing the paper as proper sociology. The deputy editor who was assigned the manuscript wrote, "This is one of the more interesting simulation papers I have read," but "I am not very enthusiastic overall about these types of papers." The reviewers all thought the paper had real promise (each with his or her own set of proposed revisions), and the deputy editor's summary was "I suggest we should honor the reviewers' advice: to invite a revise and resubmit."

Because the deputy editor was not enthusiastic about simulation in general, I decided that it would be difficult to convince her to accept the paper as long as the reviewers retained any qualms at all. Therefore I decided to send it elsewhere.

My third try was the *Journal of Conflict Resolution,* known for its interdisciplinary range. This time, one reviewer was completely positive and the other asked only that I expand the model to include cultural drift. With the editor's encouragement, I gave this a try but found that the results were so complicated that I felt unable to give a coherent account of them. Therefore I proposed including a brief description of the difficulties of dealing with cultural drift, and leaving their solution for future research. The editor agreed, and accepted the paper with this addition to the section on "Extensions of the Model." The moral of the story, I suppose, is that persistence pays.

References

Axelrod, Robert. 1967. "The Structure of Public Opinion on Policy Issues." *Public Opinion Quarterly* 31: 51–60.

———. 1973. "Schema Theory: An Information Processing Model of Perception and Cognition." *American Political Science Review* 67: 1248–66.

———. 1976. *The Structure of Decision: The Cognitive Maps of Political Elites.* Princeton, N.J.: Princeton University Press.

———. 1977a. "Argumentation in Foreign Policy Settings: Britain in 1918, Munich in 1938, and Japan in 1970." *Journal of Conflict Resolution* 21: 727–56.

———. 1977b. "How a Schema Is Used to Interpret Information." In *Thought and Action in Foreign Policy,* ed. G. Matthew Bonham and Michael J. Shapiro, 226–41. Basel: Berkhauser Verlag.

Disseminating Culture

THE DISSEMINATION OF CULTURE: A MODEL WITH LOCAL CONVERGENCE AND GLOBAL POLARIZATION

ROBERT AXELROD

Reprinted from Robert Axelrod, "The Dissemination of Culture: A Model with Local Convergence and Global Polarization," *Journal of Conflict Resolution* 41 (1997): 203–26. Reprinted by permission of Sage Publications, Inc.

Abstract:

Despite tendencies toward convergence, differences between individuals and groups continue to exist in beliefs, attitudes, and behavior. An agent-based adaptive model reveals the effects of a mechanism of convergent social influence. The actors are placed at fixed sites. The basic premise is that the more similar an actor is to a neighbor, the more likely that that actor will adopt one of the neighbor's traits. Unlike previous models of social influence or cultural change that treat features one at a time, the proposed model takes into account the interaction between different features. The model illustrates how local convergence can generate global polarization. Simulations show that the number of stable homogeneous regions decreases with the number of features, increases with the number of alternative traits per feature, decreases with the range of interaction, and (most surprisingly) decreases when the geographic territory grows beyond a certain size.

Maintenance of Differences

If people tend to become more alike in their beliefs, attitudes, and behavior when they interact, why do not all such differences eventually disappear? Social scientists have proposed many mechanisms to answer this question. The purpose of the present essay is to explore one more mechanism. The mechanism proposed here deals with how people do indeed become more similar as they interact, but also provides an explanation of why the tendency to converge stops before it reaches completion. It there-

I thank Chris Achen, David Axelrod, Rob Axtell, Scott Bennett, Arthur Burks, Lars-Erik Cederman, Michael Cohen, Paul Courant, Joshua Epstein, Jay Harrington, Larry Hirschfeld, John Holland, David Lazer, Robert Pahre, Rick Riolo, Carl Simon, and Dan Sperber. For financial support I thank Project 2050 through the Santa Fe Institute, and the LS&A Enrichment Fund of the University of Michigan.

fore provides a new type of explanation of why we do not all become alike. Because the proposed mechanism can exist alongside other mechanisms, it can be regarded as complementary with older explanations, rather than necessarily competing with them.

Unfortunately, there is no good term to describe the range of things about which people can influence each other. Although beliefs, attitudes, and behavior cover a wide range indeed, there are even more things over which interpersonal influence extends, such as language, art, technical standards, and social norms. The most generic term for the things over which people influence each other is *culture*. Therefore, the term *culture* will be used to indicate the set of individual attributes that are subject to social influence. It should be emphasized that there is no connotation that within a single society there is a uniform culture. In addition, the meaning or significance of the elements of culture is not specified. Instead, the question being investigated is how people influence each other on a given set of features, and why this influence does not lead to homogeneity.

The process by which people become similar to each other or retain their differences is central to a variety of important topics, including the following:

1. *State formation.* The formation of a national state is facilitated when its people have shared meanings and interlocking habits of communication (Deutsch 1953 and 1969). Giddens (1979) and Anderson (1991) show how nationalism is needed by the state, and the sense of imagined community is central to the attainment of nationalism. Thus, the process of at least partial convergence is critical for the formation of states.

2. *Succession conflicts.* Although states, once formed, typically seek to reduce internal cleavages, such cleavages often persist. Civil wars, especially wars of succession, tend to occur around unresolved conflicts in societies, especially when the conflicts have a clear territorial basis. Indeed, even expert observers were surprised by the extent to which lines of fracture in the Soviet Union survived decades of state efforts to ameliorate them. The process by which people become similar to each other or retain their differences is clearly vital to our understanding of how states survive or disintegrate.

3. *Transnational integration.* On a larger scale, the same processes are central to the prospects for further development of transnational institutions such as the European Community, GATT, and the United Nations. The development of international and especially transnational institutions depends in large part on the extent to which norms and ease of understanding come to be shared over territories more extensive than boundaries of current states.

4. *Domestic cleavages.* It has long been recognized that the everyday domestic politics of democracies is largely shaped by the nature of the

societal cleavages (e.g., Lipset et al. 1956; Campbell et al. 1960; Key 1961). An important question is whether such cleavages will be ameliorated or reinforced through local interactions (e.g., Coleman 1957; Putnam 1966). America's current debate over multiculturalism is just one example of our concern with the dynamics of cultural difference.

In addition to these specific topics, the effects of cultural change in the broadest sense have long been central questions. Understanding how a culture can get established, how it can spread, and how it can be sustained has growing importance in today's world. We wonder whether English will become a quasi-universal language, whether standards for new technologies can be established, and whether popular songs and dress will become universal. We applaud the spread of a common culture when it favors efficient communication, prevents unnecessary conflict, and fosters action for global needs such as sustainable growth. On the other hand, with the spread of common culture, we abhor the harm done to peoples whose cultures are destroyed, the loss to the rest of us of the wisdom embodied in these vanishing cultures, and the loss to everyone of the adaptive potential made possible by cultural diversity.

Existing explanations for why differences are durable employ a wide variety of mechanisms. They are all valid explanations under specific conditions.

1. *Social differentiation.* Groups actively differentiate themselves from each other (Simmel [1908] 1955). People who identify with one group often emphasize and even promote differences with members of other groups. In the case of ethnic groups, this differentiation can lead to sharpening of cultural and geographic boundaries between groups (Barth 1969; Hannan 1979).

2. *Fads and fashions.* When people want to be different from others, fads will come and go. When some want to be different but others want to copy them, the result is fashion: a never-ending chase of followers running after leaders.

3. *Preference for extreme views.* Tendencies toward homogeneity of opinion can be counteracted if people tend to prefer extreme positions on issues. This idea was first proposed by Abelson and Bernstein (1963). Recent simulation models have shown how this mechanism can lead to polarization and clustering (Nowak et al. 1990; Latane et al. 1994).

4. *Drift.* There may be random changes in individual traits. This can lead to differentiation among subgroups. For example, languages slowly evolve and differentiate.

5. *Geographic isolation.* If people move to be near others who are similar to themselves, the result can be clustering of similar people (e.g., Schelling 1978). If carried to extremes, geographic or other forms of voluntary or imposed segregation can sustain differences by reducing interactions between members of different groups.

6. *Specialization.* People may have interests that are at least partially resistant to social influence. This resistance has been modeled as factors that have a persistent effect on an individual despite social influence (Friedkin and Johnsen 1990; Marsden and Friedkin 1993).

7. *Changing environment or technology.* When the environment is constantly changing, the response may be constantly changing as well. If the environment is changing faster than people can respond to it, then differences may persist as different people or groups change in different ways in response to their ever-changing environment.

Despite the existence of so many mechanisms for the maintenance of differences, none of them takes into account the fundamental principle of human communication that "the transfer of ideas occurs most frequently between individuals . . . who are similar in certain attributes such as beliefs, education, social status, and the like" (Rogers 1983, 274; see also Homans 1950). The model of social influence offered here abstracts this fundamental principle to say that communication is most effective between similar people. Put another way, the likelihood that a given cultural feature will spread from one individual (or group) to another depends on how many other features they may already have in common. Similarity leads to interaction, and interaction leads to still more similarity. For reasons that will be explored below, this process need not lead to complete convergence. Indeed, the most interesting thing about the model is the way it can generate few or many distinct cultural regions depending on the scope of cultural possibilities, the range of the interactions, and the size of the geographic territory.

The present model offers a new way of looking at the dynamic process of social influence. The model is not intended to predict any particular historical events. Instead, it is meant to show the consequences of a few simple assumptions about how people (or groups) are influenced by those around them.

Approaches to Social Influence

Although over a hundred definitions of "culture" have been proposed (Kroeber and Kluckhorn 1952), everyone agrees that culture is something people learn from each other. For the present purposes, culture is assumed to satisfy two simple premises: people are more likely to interact with others who share many of their cultural attributes, and interactions between two people tend to increase the number of attributes they share. For example, a person is more likely to talk to someone who speaks a similar language than one who speaks a dissimilar language, and the very act of communication tends to make their future patterns of speech even more similar. The process of social influence applies not only to language, but also to beliefs, attitudes, and behaviors. It applies to everything from style of dress to fundamental values, and from the adoption of Arabic numerals to the adoption of computer standards.

Anthropologists have taken two distinct approaches to the study of cultural change. The diffusionists treated a given culture as a set of distinct traits, each of which could be passed along (or diffused) to another culture (for a review, see Voget 1975). More recently, most anthropologists have emphasized the interconnections between the many traits that make up a culture, viewing culture as a system of symbols by which people confer significance on their own experience (e.g., Geertz 1973). This holistic approach stresses that the meaning of any given trait is embedded in the whole set of relationships with other traits, and consequently that a given culture tends to be a more or less integrated package. Unfortunately, neither approach has done much to formalize its ideas of cultural change in formal models whose implications can be systematically explored. (For exceptions see Renfrew 1973; Renfrew and Cooke 1979; Sabloff 1981.)

Other social scientists have provided models of how social influence works within a given society. These models of change within a single society also help illuminate how one group might influence another, and hence how one culture might influence another. An early example is Coleman's sociological model of the spread of smoking among teenage boys in which friendship affects behavior and behavior affects friendship (1965). Psychologists and sociologists have also proposed models of social influence (Nowak et al. 1990; Friedkin and Johnsen 1990; Carley 1991; Marsden and Friedkin 1993). Political scientists have built models of attitude change in political campaigns (Putnam 1966; Huckfeldt and Sprague 1991; Brown and McBurnett 1993). Organization theorists have modeled social influence in formal organizations (March 1991; Harrison and Carroll 1991). Theories about changes in beliefs, attitudes, and behavior have also been developed for the spread of social norms (e.g., Lewis 1967; Ullmann-Margalit 1977; Axelrod 1986), the spread of knowledge (Carley 1991), the diffusion of innovations (see Rogers 1983; Nelson and Winter 1982), and the establishment of technical standards (Saloner and Farrell 1986; Axelrod et al. 1995).

Finally, biologists have modeled the joint contribution of genetics and learning in social influence (Cavalli-Sforza and Feldman 1981; Lumsden and Wilson 1981; Boyd and Richerson 1985: see also Durham 1991).

A striking fact about these models is that they treat each feature of a culture independently of the other features.[1]

---

[1] One exception is Carley's (1991) model of the spread of knowledge. In this model, group differences disappear unless members of different groups initially share no knowledge in common. The only other exception is the "indirect bias" model of Boyd and Richerson (1985), which allows the attractiveness of a cultural trait to be affected by a control trait. But even in this model, only one cultural trait is considered.

The model of social influence given in this essay is new in two regards. First, it explicitly takes into account that the effect of one cultural feature depends on the presence or absence of other cultural features. Second, it takes into account that similar individuals are more likely to influence each other than dissimilar individuals. The only other formal model that treats culture as multidimensional does not take into account the degree of cultural similarity in its mechanism for social influence (Epstein and Axtell, 1996).[2]

The methodology of the present study is based on three principles:

1. *Agent-based modeling.* Mechanisms of change are specified for local actors, and then the consequences of these mechanisms are examined to discover the emergent properties of the system when many actors interact.[3] Computer simulation is especially helpful for this bottom-up approach, but its use predates the availability of personal computers (e.g., Schelling 1978).

2. *No central authority.* Consistent with the agent-based approach is the lack of any central coordinating agent in the model. It is certainly true that important aspects of cultures sometimes come to be standardized, canonized, and disseminated by powerful authorities such as church fathers, Webster, and Napoleon. The present model, however, deals with the process of social influence before (or alongside of) the actions of such authorities. It seeks to understand just how much of cultural emergence and stability can be explained without resort to the coordinating influence of centralized authority.

3. *Adaptive rather than rational agents.* The individuals are assumed to follow simple rules about giving and receiving influence. These rules are not necessarily derivable from any principles of rational calculation based upon costs and benefits, or forward-looking strategic analysis typical of game theory. Instead, the agents simply adapt to their environment.

The Model

Culture is taken to be what social influence influences. For present purposes, the emphasis is not on the content of a specific culture, but rather

[2] The Epstein and Axtell "Sugarscape" model is very rich, incorporating trade, migration, combat, disease, and mating. For example, actors of similar culture are allowed to mate, and actors of dissimilar culture are allowed to fight.

[3] Agent-based models in political science have usually focused on conflict processes (such as war and military alliances) rather than social influence. Examples are Bremer and Mihalka (1977), Schrodt (1981), Cusack and Stoll (1990), Axelrod (1995), and Cederman (forthcoming). Agent-based models dealing with social influence are Huckfeldt and Sprague (1991) and Brown and McBurnett (1993). A wide-ranging agent model is Epstein and Axtell (1996).

on the way in which any culture is likely to emerge and spread. Thus, the model assumes that an individual's culture can be described in terms of his or her attributes, such as language, religion, technology, style of dress, and so forth.

Because the model can be abstract about the specific content of an individual's culture, it describes a culture as a list of *features* or dimensions of culture. For each feature there is a set of *traits,* which are the alternative values the feature may have. For example, one feature of a culture could be the color of belt that is worn, and the traits would be the various alternative colors that might be worn in a society. To be concrete, suppose that there are five features and each feature can take on any one of ten traits. Then a culture can be described as a list of five digits such as 8, 7, 2, 5, and 4. In this case, the first cultural feature has the eighth of its possible values. This abstract formulation means that two individuals have the same culture if they have the same traits for each of the five features. The formulation allows one to define the degree of cultural similarity between two individuals as the percentage of their features that have the identical trait.

The model includes a geographic distribution of individual agents. A simple example would be a set of 100 sites, arrayed on a ten by ten grid. Because there is no movement in the model, the sites themselves can be thought of as homogeneous villages. These sites are the basic actors of the model. Each site can interact only with its immediate neighbors. A typical site has four neighbors (north, east, south, and west). Sites on the edge of the map have only three neighbors, and sites in the corners have only two neighbors.

Table 7-1 shows a typical starting situation with randomly assigned cultures. As expected, most of the sites share no more than one feature with any of its neighbors. The underlined site, however, happens to share two features (the fourth and the fifth features) with its neighbor to the south. Because these two sites share two of the five attributes, their cultural similarity is 40 percent.

The process of social influence in the model can be described as a series of events. The basic idea is that agents who are similar to each other are likely to interact and then become even more similar. This is implemented by assuming that the chance of interaction is proportional to the cultural similarity two neighbors already have. Here, then, is the formal statement of the entire dynamics of the model:

Repeat the following steps for as many events as desired.

Step 1. At random, pick a site to be active, and pick one of its neighbors.

Step 2. With probability equal to their cultural similarity, these two sites interact. An interaction consists of selecting at random a feature on which the active site and its neighbor differ (if there is one), and

TABLE 7-1
A Typical Initial Set of Cultures

74741	87254	82330	17993	22978	82762	87476	26757	99313	32009
01948	09234	67730	89130	34210	85403	69411	81677	06789	24042
49447	46012	42628	86636	27405	39747	97450	71833	07192	87426
22781	85541	51585	84468	18122	60094	71819	51912	32095	11318
09581	89800	72031	19856	08071	97744	42533	33723	24659	03847
56352	34490	48416	55455	88600	78295	69896	96775	86714	02932
46238	38032	34235	45602	39891	84866	38456	78008	27136	50153
88136	21593	77404	17043	39238	81454	29464	74576	41924	43987
35682	19232	80173	81447	22884	58260	53436	13623	05729	43378
57816	55285	66329	30462	36729	13341	43986	45578	64585	47330

Note: The underlined site and the site to its south share traits for two of the five cultural features, making a cultural similarity of 40 percent.

changing the active site's trait on this feature to the neighbor's trait on this feature.[4]

This process can be illustrated using Table 7-1. In step 1, suppose the underlined site is selected, along with its neighbor to the south. In step 2, the active site and its neighbor have a 40 percent chance of interacting because they share traits for two of their five features. If they do interact, then the culture of the underlined site would take on the trait of one of the three features that was different in the culture of its neighbor to the south. For example, if the first feature was the one to change, then the value of 6 from the neighbor's first feature would become the value of the first feature of the underlined site, changing its culture from 82330 to 62330. This change will increase the cultural similarity of these two sites from 40 percent to 60 percent, making it even easier for them to converge still further.[5]

Note that the activated site, rather than its neighbor, is the one that may undergo change. This is done to guarantee that each site has an equal chance of being a candidate for social influence, even though the sites on the edge of the map have fewer neighbors than sites in the interior.

[4] For those who prefer symbolic statements, here is a complete description of how the culture, c, at a site can change. Select a random site (s), a random neighbor of that site (n), and a random feature (f). Let $G(s,n)$ be the set of features, g, such that the cultural traits are unequal, i.e. $c(s,g) \neq c(n,g)$. If $c(s,f) = c(n,f)$ and G is not empty, then select a random feature, g, in $G(s,n)$, and set $c(s,g)$ to $c(n,g)$. This implementation of the model takes advantage of the fact that the probability that a random feature, f, will have the same trait at two sites equals the cultural similarity between those two sites.

[5] The simulation is done one event at a time to avoid any artifacts of synchronous activation of the sites. See Huberman and Glance (1993).

The Emergence of Regions of Shared Culture

How do cultural regions develop? Does everyone come to share the same culture, or do distinct cultural regions develop? Does the system settle down, and if so, how long does it take?

To begin to answer questions like these, it pays to start with a single run of the model over time.[6] To make the development of cultural regions more apparent, we can shift our attention from the details of the culture at each site to the cultural similarities between adjacent sites. These cultural similarities can be represented in a map, such as the one in Figure 7-1(a). This shows the (cultural) distances between adjacent sites at the start. Notice that most of the boundaries are drawn in black, indicating that at most one of the five features is shared. The site marked "A" in Figure 7-1(a) corresponds to the underlined site in Table 7-1. Notice that the boundary between this site and the one to its south is drawn in dark gray, indicating that the cultural similarity between them is 40 percent at the start of the run.

The other panels of Figure 7-1 show what happens over time.[7] Time is measured in events, representing the activation of a site. For example, Figure 7-1(b) shows the start of the emergence of distinct cultural regions after 20,000 events. For our purposes, a *cultural region* can be defined as a set of contiguous sites with the identical culture. Notice that already at this stage, many cultural boundaries have disappeared as some cultural regions have grown to include four or five sites.

By 40,000 events the cultural regions have gotten bigger. In addition, even many of the boundaries between regions are now light gray, indicating that there is only a single feature on which they differ. By 80,000 events, there are only four regions left. In fact, by 81,000 events, the region surrounded by light gray gets completely absorbed into the largest region, leaving only three regions. Not only that, but the remaining three regions are completely stable because members of adjacent regions have absolutely no features in common and hence cannot interact.

Some of the questions can now be answered about the effects of social influence over time and space in this model.

[6] The model can be regarded as a Markov process with absorbing states. Unfortunately, the mathematical tools for analyzing Markov processes, such as eigenvalue analysis, are not very helpful in this case because the dynamics are so complex. For example, the number of possible states for the situation given in Table 7-1 is 10^{500}, which is far more than the number of atoms in the universe. Other agent-based models that can be regarded as Markov processes have also had to resort to computer simulation (e.g., Bremer and Mihalka 1977; Schrodt 1981; and Cusack and Stoll 1990).

[7] The model is coded in Pascal. Running on a Macintosh Quadra 700, the run shown in Figure 7-1 took eleven seconds. See fn. 12 for source code availability.

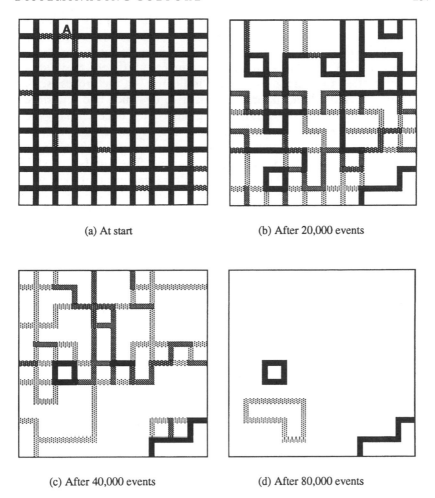

(a) At start   (b) After 20,000 events

(c) After 40,000 events   (d) After 80,000 events

Figure 7-1. Map of Cultural Similarities. *Note:* Cultural similarity between adjacent sites is coded as: Black ≤ 20%, Dark Gray = 40%, Gray = 60, Light Gray = 80%, White = 100%. This run was conducted using five cultural features and ten traits per feature, using the initial conditions shown in Table 7-1. Each interior site has four neighbors.

1. Initially, most neighboring sites have little in common with each other, and hence are unlikely to interact. However, when two sites *do* interact they become more similar, and hence are more likely to interact in the future.

2. Over time, specific cultural features tend to be shared over a larger and larger area. Indeed, regions start to form in which *all* the features are exactly the same.

3. Eventually, no further change is possible. This happens when every pair of neighboring sites have cultures that are either identical or completely different. If a pair are identical, they can interact but the interaction will not cause either to change. If they are completely different, they will not even interact. In the sample run shown in Figure 7-1, the process settled down with exactly three cultural regions, two of which had few sites.

4. Initially, there are almost as many regions as sites, but eventually there are only a few regions. An indication of the extent to which the process of social influence resists complete homogenization is the number of regions that remain when no further change is possible. The number of *stable regions* can be defined as the number of cultural regions that exist when each cultural region has nothing in common with any of the regions it is adjacent to. In the sample run, shortly after the time shown in Figure 7-1(d), exactly three stable regions survived, two of which had few sites.

5. In retrospect, the origins of the stable cultural regions can be seen far back in history.[8] For example, the cultural region of four sites in the southeast corner of Figure 7-1(d) can be clearly discerned as far back in time as Figure 7-1(b). However, looking just at the map of cultural similarities at that early time would not allow one to know which of the many cultural regions that existed then would survive.

The Number of Stable Regions

For society, an important question is how many cultural regions will survive. Although all social influence in the model involves convergence between neighbors, the process of convergence can stop with several surviving cultural regions, each of which is completely different from the adjacent cultural regions.

In the sample run, three cultural regions survived. This is fairly typical of runs done under identical conditions but with different random choices. In a set of 100 runs of this type, the median number of stable regions was three. But there was also quite a bit of variation. In 14 percent of the runs there was only one stable region, while in 10 percent of the runs there were more than six.

Scope of Cultural Possibilities

The model can be used to explore how the number of stable regions depends on various factors such as the scope of cultural possibilities, the range of the interactions, and the size of the geographic territory. First

---

[8] This is an example of what is called path dependence (e.g., Arthur 1988).

consider the scope of cultural possibilities. In the model, cultural complexity depends on two things: the number of cultural features and the number of possible traits that each feature can have. For example, in the sample run there were five features, each with ten possible traits. A plausible hypothesis is that the more variety that is possible among cultures, the greater the number of stable regions there will be. This hypothesis would be based on the idea that the more features and the more traits per feature, the more cultural regions there would be at the end.

Table 7-2 shows the average number of regions that resulted from all combinations of five, ten, or fifteen features as well as five, ten, or fifteen traits per feature. For each combination of parameters, ten runs were conducted. Table 7-2 shows that the original culture of five features of ten traits each gave an average of 3.2 stable regions.

When the number of traits per feature was held at ten, but the number of features was increased from five to ten or fifteen cultural features, the process converged to a single stable region. Thus, as the number of features grows, so does the likelihood of complete cultural convergence. This seems counterintuitive at first, because one might suppose that more features would make convergence more difficult. In fact, just the opposite is true. The reason is that with more features, there is a greater chance that two sites will have the same trait on at least one feature, and therefore will be able to interact. With interaction comes the sharing of the trait on an additional cultural feature. So with more features in the culture there is a greater chance neighbors will have something in common, and thus they will have a greater chance to attain complete cultural convergence with each other.

The effect of differing the number of traits on each feature is also shown in Table 7-2. Again there is a curious result: increasing the number of traits per feature has the opposite effect of increasing the number of features. For example, moving from ten to fifteen traits when there are five features actually increases the average number of stable regions from 3.2 to 20.0. When there are few features and many traits then there is a good chance that two neighbors will share no features, and thus be unable to interact. This in turn makes it easier for many distinct regions to form, each of which has no features in common with any adjacent region.

In sum, the complexity of the culture needs to be differentiated to account for the number of stable regions. Having more features (i.e., dimensions) in the culture actually makes for fewer stable regions, but having more alternatives on each feature makes for more stable regions.

Range of Interaction

The next question is how the process of cultural formation is influenced by the number of neighbors with which a site can interact. So far, each

TABLE 7-2
Average Number of Stable Regions

NUMBER OF	TRAITS PER FEATURE		
CULTURAL FEATURES	5	10	15
5	1.0	3.2	20.0
10	1.0	1.0	1.4
15	1.0	1.0	1.2

Note: These runs were done with a territory of 10 × 10 sites, and each interior site had four neighbors. Each condition was run ten times.

interior site was allowed to interact with four adjacent sites. It is plausible that if interactions could occur over somewhat greater distances, the process of cultural convergence would be made easier. The expected result would be fewer distinct regions when the process settled down.

To test this hypothesis, additional runs were conducted in which each site could interact with other sites using larger neighborhoods, encompassing eight and twelve neighbors for interior sites. The neighborhoods with eight sites consisted of the four adjacent sites plus the four diagonal sites, making a square neighborhood. The neighborhoods of twelve sites consisted of those eight sites plus the four sites that were two units in each of the cardinal directions, making a diamond shaped neighborhood. To study the effect of neighborhood size, the entire set of ten replications of each of the nine kinds of culture was run for the neighborhood of sizes of four, eight, and twelve.

As expected, larger neighborhoods result in fewer stable regions. Averaged over the nine types of culture, small neighborhoods have 3.4 stable regions, medium-sized neighborhoods give 2.5 stable regions, and large neighborhoods generate only 1.5 stable regions. Thus when interactions can occur at greater distances, cultural convergence is easier.

Size of the Territory

The final statistical question is how the outcome of social influence process is affected by the size of the territory. In all the runs so far, the size of the territory was 10 × 10 sites. Over the nine different kinds of culture and three different sizes of neighborhoods, there was an average of 2.5 stable regions. One would suppose that the more sites there are, the more cultural regions result.

To test this hypothesis, additional territories were examined that were

5×5 sites, and 15×15 sites. A complete factorial design was done for each of the eighty-one conditions: three sizes of territory, nine types of culture, and three types of neighborhood. Each condition was replicated ten times, giving 810 runs in all. The results are very surprising. In these runs, the size of the territory had no substantial effect on the number of cultural regions formed. Here are the averages: with small (5×5) territories there were 2.4 stable regions, with medium (10×10) territories there were 2.5 stable regions, and with larger territories (15×15) there were 2.2 stable regions.

Clearly, a more detailed analysis of the effect of size is needed. The best way to do this is to hold the other parameters constant. For convenience, the other parameters can be fixed at the levels that gave the largest number of stable regions. This means few cultural features (five), many traits per feature (fifteen), and small neighborhoods (four neighbors for interior sites). With these parameters held constant, the number of stable regions can be determined as a function of the size of the territory.

The results are shown in Figure 7-2, which summarizes forty runs each for territories from 2×2 sites up to 35×35 sites, and ten runs each for territories of 50×50 and 100×100 sites. Consistent with the earlier runs shown in Table 7-2 (with few features and many traits per feature), there were about twenty stable regions in a territory of 10×10 sites. The overall result shown in Figure 7-2 is that the number of stable regions increases until it reaches a maximum of about twenty-three when the territory has 12×12 sites. The number of stable regions then declines to about six for a territory of 50×50 sites and about two for a territory of 100×100 sites.

The earlier result suggesting that territorial size did not have a substantial effect on the number of stable regions can now be seen as misleading. The earlier analysis averaged nine kinds of culture and three ranges of interaction, leading to about the same number of stable regions no matter whether the territory was 5×5, 10×10, or 15×15. The results shown in Figure 7-2, however, demonstrate that when the type of culture and the range of interaction is held constant, the number of stable regions is very sensitive to the size of the territory: both small and large territories have few stable regions, whereas moderate-sized territories have the largest number of stable territories.

Why do moderate-sized territories have the largest number of stable territories? It is no surprise that smallest territories have the fewest stable regions. After all, small territories simply do not have enough sites to contain many different cultures. So it is not surprising that as the size of the territory increases from, say, 2×2 sites to 12×12 sites, the number of stable regions increases. What is really surprising is that as the size of the territory increases further, the number of stable regions actually de-

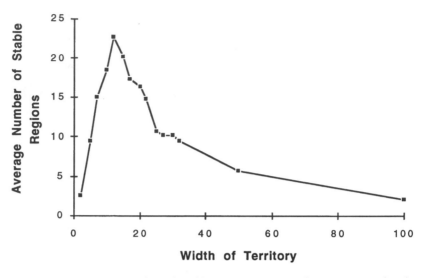

Figure 7-2. Average Number of Stable Regions. *Note:* The parameters for these runs are five cultural features, fifteen traits per feature, and four neighbors for interior sites. Each territory size was replicated forty times, except the territories with 50×50 sites and 100×100 sites, which were replicated ten times.

creases. So the interesting question is: why do large territories have fewer stable regions than moderate-sized territories?

The result is so surprising that one might wonder whether it is due to a programming error. Fortunately, this explanation can be ruled out. The present simulation model has been independently implemented by another team in what is apparently the first systematic effort to align two related agent-based simulation systems (Axtell et al. 1996). The key results of the present model were confirmed.

One might also wonder whether the phenomenon of large territories having fewer stable regions has something to do with the existence of boundaries on the territories. Boundaries can be eliminated by wrapping around the northern and southern edges, and the eastern and western edges. Simulations with this neighborhood topology show the same pattern as before: the number of stable regions increases for a while as the size of the territory increases, but then declines. Although the peak occurs earlier (i.e., with somewhat smaller territories) and is not as high (i.e., with somewhat fewer stable regions), the shape of the curve is similar to the one in Figure 7-2. So the existence of territorial boundaries is not the cause of large territories having fewer stable regions than moderate-sized territories.

To see why larger territories have fewer stable regions, it is useful to examine what happens over time in runs of various sizes.

Analysis of Histories

Dialects

To understand the historical development of social influence in this model, it pays to examine an artificially constructed illustration where there are just two cultural regions, differing in a single feature. I use the term "dialects" to describe two such similar cultures. To keep things really elementary, suppose there are just six sites on a line from west to east, and the neighbors of each site are the adjacent sites. (See Table 7-3.)Suppose, further, that the four on the west have the same culture, namely 11111, whereas the two sites on the east have culture 11112. If the activated site and its selected neighbor are both within the same region, no change would occur, because there would be no cultural difference to transmit. Thus, the only possibility for change would be if the active site was in one region and its selected neighbor was in the other. The consequence would be that the boundary between the two regions would move by one site, either to the east or to the west. Moreover, these two possibilities are equally likely. The next time a social influence takes place, the regional boundary will move again, and once again there is an equal chance the boundary will move to the east as to the west. The movement of the regional boundary follows a process known as a random walk with absorbing barriers (e.g., Kemeny et al. 1966, 283). In this illustration, stability will be reached when the boundary between the regions moves all the way to the east or to the west, that is, when one dialect has completely "eaten" the other dialect.

An interesting thing about this illustration is that the larger region is more likely to "eat" the smaller region than the other way around. The reason is that the random walk of the boundary is more likely to reach the nearer edge of the map before it reaches the further edge. Thus, the majority culture is more likely to survive than the minority culture, even though there is absolutely no bias in the process of social influence. This brings to mind the effort at universities and elsewhere to protect the diversity of a multicultural society.

This result that large regions tend to "eat" small regions can help explain what happened toward the end of the run shown in Figure 7-1. Recall that after 80,000 events there were four regions, one of which differed from the largest region in a single cultural feature (see Figure 7-1(d)). Once history got to this stage, the small dialect with just four

TABLE 7-3
An Illustration of Social Influence between Dialects

---

a. Suppose there are two regions in a territory of 6x1 sites. Suppose the regions are dialects, differing in a single feature. Suppose one region has four sites while the other region has two sites:

$$11111 \quad 11111 \quad 11111 \quad 11111 \quad 11112 \quad 11112$$

b. Since most sites are identical to all of their neighbors, there are only two possibilities for social influence. These two possibilities are equally likely:

i. The fourth site is activated and borrows from the fifth site, moving the regional boundary to the west.

$$11111 \quad 11111 \quad 11111 \quad 11112 \quad 11112 \quad 11112$$

ii. The fifth site is activated and borrows from the fourth site, moving the regional boundary to the east.

$$11111 \quad 11111 \quad 11111 \quad 11111 \quad 11111 \quad 11112$$

c. Eventually, the process will stop when one dialect or the other is eliminated. More likely, the 11111 dialect will eliminate the 11112 dialect because it started with more sites.

---

sites was much more likely to become extinct than the large dialect, which has ninety-one sites. Notice that as long as the sites in the other two small regions had nothing in common with any of their neighbors, they would not change. The possibility for social influence ended when the larger dialect "ate" the smaller dialect, resulting in just three stable regions.

The idea of dialects of similar cultures leads to the idea of cultural zones of similar regions. This in turn can help unravel the puzzle of why large territories have few stable regions.

Cultural Zones

Recall that a cultural region is a set of contiguous sites with identical cultures. A related idea is a *cultural zone:* a set of contiguous sites each of which has a neighbor with a "compatible" culture. Cultures are compatible if they have at least one feature in common. This means that neighboring sites with compatible cultures can interact. Thus, although the sites in a single cultural zone may include many different regions, each of the regions in a zone is able to interact with adjacent regions in the same zone.[9]

To see how zonal and regional boundaries develop over time in a relatively small territory, let us return to the run illustrated in Figure 7-1. In Figure 7-1(d) there are four regions. However, there are only three zones, as indicated by the black boundaries between adjacent sites, that have no features in common. The run ends when no further change is possible, and this happens when each zone has exactly one region, since that implies that sites in different regions can no longer interact. In the run shown in Figure 7-1, stability was reached when the small dialect was "eaten" by the largest region. The resulting three regions correspond exactly to the three zones of Figure 7-1(d). Going back in history to Figure 7-1(c), there were dozens of regions but exactly the same three zones. In fact, this is a common historical pattern, with the zones developing before the regions. Thus the number of zones provides an early indication of just how many stable regions there will be.

Figure 7-3 shows how the number of regions and zones develop over time in a single run with a very large (100 × 100) territory with 10,000 sites.[10] Initially, the number of regions is virtually the same as the number of sites because it is very unlikely that two adjacent sites will have each of their five features be equal when there are fifteen possible traits for each feature. However, even at the start there are fewer zones than regions because many sites will have at least one feature in common with at least one neighbor. As Figure 7-3 shows, the number of regions declines gradually until there are about a thousand regions, and then declines in stages until there are only two regions. On the other hand, the number of zones declines quickly to just two. As mentioned above, when the number of regions equals the number of zones, no further change is possible. It is striking that it takes more than four times as long for the stable regions to be determined than for the final number of zones to form. So most of the history of the run was spent with many compatible cultures "struggling for survival" within just two cultural zones, until finally only a single culture survived in each zone. Because one of the final two zones has only one site, all of this "struggle" took place over the 9,999 sites of the other final zone.

---

[9] Technically, two sites are in the same zone if there is a path of adjacent sites from one to the other such that each site has at least one feature in common with the next one on the path.

[10] Note that for Figure 7-3, the parameters were chosen to generate relatively large numbers of stable regions. With these parameters, the average number of stable regions in 10 × 10 territories was about 18.6, whereas in 100 × 100 territories, the average was only 2.1. (See Figure 2. The slight discrepancy for the number of stable regions in the 10 × 10 territory in Figure 7-2 compared to the corresponding cell in Table 7-1 is due to averaging over different runs.)

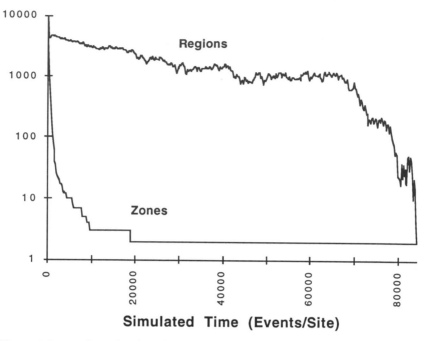

Figure 7-3. Number of Cultural Regions and Cultural Zones over Time in a Run with a Large Territory. *Note:* The territory is 100 × 100 sites. The other parameters are as in Figure 7-2. Note logarithmic scale.

Dissolution of Cultural Boundaries

Over time, boundaries between regions in the same cultural zone tend to dissolve. For example, if two adjacent sites share three of their five cultural features, there is a good chance that they will interact and then share four features. Then they may interact again and come to share all five of their features. Of course, things are more complex than this because either of the two sites might also interact with others, and this might actually decrease the cultural similarity between them. But on average, cultural similarity between adjacent sites in the same cultural zone tends to increase.

On the other hand, adjacent sites in different cultural zones cannot interact because they have no cultural features in common. This is why boundaries within cultural zones tend to dissolve, but boundaries between cultural zones tend to be stable. Nevertheless, even boundaries between cultural zones can dissolve. A boundary between two cultural zones can dissolve if a site on the zonal boundary adopts a trait for a feature from another region in its zone. If this newly adopted trait happens to match the corresponding feature of a neighboring site from the other zone, then the zonal boundary will begin to dissolve. This accounts for how the number of cultural zones decreases over time, as shown in Figure 7-3.

Another way of looking at the dynamic process is to consider how alternative traits for a cultural feature move around in a zone as neighboring sites interact. As long as there are many regions within each zone, there are different cultural traits for at least some of the features in the zone. As these traits move around in the zone through interactions, they have a chance of dissolving boundaries, both regional and zonal. The net effect is that the more time it takes for a territory to settle down, the more chance there is that zonal as well as regional boundaries will be dissolved.

Large territories take much longer to reach stability than smaller territories, and this gives the regional and even zonal boundaries in large territories more opportunities to dissolve. This is true even though in comparing territories of different sizes, simulated time should be measured in events per site rather than simply events. The reason why time is measured in events per site is that in reality various sites might be active at virtually the same time.

Just how does time to stability vary as a function of territorial size? Over a great range of territories, from four to 10,000 sites, the time to stability is almost exactly proportional to the number of sites in the territory. For example, with 1,024 sites (in a 32×32 territory), each site needs an average of 10,036 events to reach stability. When there are about 2.5 times as many sites (in a 50×50 territory), about 2.5 times as many events per site are needed to reach stability (or 25,900 events). As the number of sites doubles, each site has twice as many chances to be active before stability. Therefore, doubling the number of sites in a territory allows four times as many activations in all. This in turn provides many more opportunities for boundaries to dissolve, eventually reducing the number of regions that will still exist when no further change is possible. (By the way, to do a run of a 100×100 territory, each site needs a little over 100,000 events before stability is reached. Because there are 10,000 sites, a single run of this size requires simulating a billion events.)

In sum, combining an analysis of dialects, cultural zones, and the dissolution of cultural boundaries helps explain how territorial size determine the number of stable regions. In small territories there is not much room for many stable regions. In moderate-sized territories there is enough room. In large territories, there is even more room, but the process of social influence and the consequent movement of cultural alternatives goes on so long that virtually all of the cultural boundaries eventually dissolve.

Discussion

Perhaps the most important lesson of the social influence model is that intuition is not a very good guide to predicting what even a very simple dynamic model will produce. The social influence model is very simple indeed. Its mechanism can be stated in a single sentence: with probability equal to their cultural similarity, a randomly chosen site will adopt one of the cultural features of a randomly chosen neighbor. That's it. Yet, it turns out to be very difficult to anticipate how the number of stable cultural regions varies as a function of the four parameters in the model. Two of the results were intuitively obvious, but two were not. The two results that were intuitive were that the number of stable regions increases with the number of possible traits that each cultural feature could take, and decreases with the range of interaction. The two counterintuitive results are that the number of stable regions decreases with more cultural features, and with large territories. The computer runs of the social influence model demonstrate that unaided intuition about how dynamic processes develop over time is not necessarily very reliable.

The social influence model also illustrates how new distinctions are suggested by a formal model. The model demonstrates that two different aspects of cultural complexity work in opposite directions. More cultural features lead to fewer stable regions, but more traits on each feature lead to more stable regions. Thus, in considering the complexity of a cultural system, one should distinguish between the number of different features and the number of traits that each feature can take.

The social influence model also suggests that functionalist explanations for common observations need not be the only or even the simplest ones. For example, suppose there are two equally attractive variants of a cultural practice, and the less common one vanishes over time. A functionalist explanation would be that those practicing the less common variant switched to the more common variant because there was some advantage in doing things the way most other people do. This makes good sense for problems of coordination, such as which side of the street to drive on, or which technical standard to employ (Lewis 1967; Saloner and Farrell 1986; Axelrod 1995). But, as we have seen, the social influence model demonstrates that even if there is no advantage to adopting the majority practice, the majority practice may still tend to drive the minority practice to extinction. The reason is that if neighbors following different practices are equally likely to switch to the other practice, the practice with the fewest followers is the one most likely to become extinct first. Thus the mere observation that a practice followed by few people was lost does not necessarily mean either that the practice had less intrinsic merit or that there was some advantage in following a more common practice. As in the social influence model, it could be that even unbiased changes in adherence lead to a less common practice disappearing simply because it is more vulnerable to random fluctuations in numbers of adherents.

The results of the social influence model suggest two other warnings about potentially false conclusions from empirical observations. Polarization occurs in the model even though the only mechanism for change is one of convergence toward a neighbor. Thus, when polarization is seen, it need not be due to any divergent process. Likewise, when cultural traits are highly correlated in geographic regions, one should not assume that there is some natural way in which those particular traits go together. The social influence model shows how homogeneous cultural regions can arise without any intrinsic relationship between the separate dimensions that become correlated.

The social influence model suggests new empirical questions and hypotheses. For example, the model predicts that large territories will actually have fewer stable regions than moderate-sized territories. I have been able to find only one relevant empirical study. This was a study of the number of languages on the various Solomon Islands (Terrell 1977). It found that islands with less than 100 square miles had a single language. Above that size, the number of languages increases about one for every 190-square-mile increment in island area. This is clearly a different result than predicted by the social influence model. Two reasons for the discrepancy are suggested by the empirical study itself: languages tend to diverge in large islands, and there is greater ecological diversity in large islands. The social influence model ignores both of these effects. Thus, a remaining unanswered question is what would happen to the number of distinct cultures as a function of territory when there is no systematic divergence, and when the territory is uniform.

Extensions of the Model

One advantage of a very simple model is that new things can be added without cluttering it up very much. The following are examples of potentially interesting extensions to the present model of social influence: cultural drift (modeled as spontaneous change in a trait), terrain effects (some pairs of adjacent sites less likely to interact than others), early geographic differences (nonrandom initial traits), status (some sites less likely to change than others), cultural attractiveness (some traits less likely to change than others), technological change (continuing introduction of new and more attractive traits), material basis for culture (interaction between trait attractiveness and terrain), public education and broadcasting (some interactions come from widely disseminated messages), mobility,[11] organizational culture (substituting hierarchical for geographic neighborhoods), sociology of science (interaction among semi-isolated disciplines with drift, technological change, and organizational culture), and cultural divergence (interaction between dissimilar sites causing increasing cultural distance).

Perhaps the most interesting extension and, at the same time, the most difficult one to analyze is cultural drift. Cultural drift is involved in phenomena such as linguistic shifts and religious fragmentation. It could also be used to take account of the fact that there is always some chance that neighbors will affect each other no matter how different their cultures.

Although it is easy to introduce cultural drift, analyzing its full implications is challenging. In the original version of the model, the cultures in any given run eventually stop changing. This happens when every pair of neighboring sites have cultures that are either identical or completely different. When this occurs, the resulting cultural regions are stable, and the number of stable regions can be used as a measure of the heterogeneity of the population.

When cultural drift is introduced, however, social influence continues indefinitely and thus any regions that do form are not stable. This raises two questions about how to analyze the effects of cultural drift. The first question is: what is the best measure of the heterogeneity of the population when a simple count of stable regions cannot be used? The second question is: how long should a given run be allowed to go before the measurements are taken?

In answer to the first question, there are at least four plausible measures of heterogeneity of the population at any given time. Taking a local view, one could consider differences between all pairs of neighboring sites. Then one could either measure how many features differed between neighbors or count the number of neighboring pairs that had any differences. Alternatively, one could take a more global view and count the number of cultural regions or zones that existed at a given time, even though they were not stable.

In answer to the second question, there are two plausible ways to decide when the measurements should be taken. One way is to use a given amount of "historical" time, regardless of the number of sites in the territory. This would entail using a given number of expected activations per site. The other method would be to run the model until a selected mea-

---

[11] The fact that larger neighborhoods result in fewer stable regions suggests that mobility will also result in fewer stable regions. This is confirmed in simulations using the present model reported by Axtell et al. (1996).

sure of heterogeneity no longer changed very much over time. This would allow the necessary time for each territory to achieve an equilibrium between the forces of social convergence and the forces of cultural drift. This method would presumably require more "historical time" for large territories than small territories.

After a measure of heterogeneity and a duration method are selected, the model can be run with cultural drift. In particular, the effects of all the parameters can be studied and compared to their effects in the original model. These parameters include the number of cultural features, the traits per feature, the number of neighbors for each interior site, and the size of the territory. Preliminary analysis suggests the effects of changes in the parameters are quite complicated. For example, at a given rate of cultural drift, the effects of some of the parameters seem to depend on just which measure of heterogeneity is being used. Moreover, there are statistical interactions among the effects of the various parameters. Finally, a complete analysis would also require varying the rate of cultural drift as well as the parameters of the original model. In sum, it is not trivial to determine how the introduction of cultural drift affects cultural change in the present model of social influence.[12]

Conclusion

The proposed model shows how individual or group differences can be durable despite tendencies toward convergence. It treats culture as the attributes that social influence can influence. Unlike previous models of cultural change or social influence, this one is based on the interplay between different dimensions or features that characterize people. The basic assumption is that the opportunity for interaction and convergence is proportional to the number of features that two neighbors already share. Stable cultural differences emerge as regions develop in which everyone shares the same culture, but have nothing in common with the culture of neighboring regions.

The degree of polarization is measured by the number of different cultural regions that exist when no further change is possible. Theoretical and statistical analysis shows that polarization increases when there are few dimensions to the culture, when there are many alternative traits on each dimension, and when interactions are only with adjacent sites. Moreover, polarization is highest when the size of the territory is big

---

[12] For those wishing to explore this and other extensions of the model, the source code and documentation are available on the Internet at http://pscs.physics.lsa.umich.edu/Software/ComplexCoop.html. At that site, use the link to "Disseminating Culture."

enough to allow for many cultures, but small enough for the change process to settle down before all cultural boundaries are dissolved by the spread of cultural traits.

The proposed model is unique not only in considering the interplay between different features of culture, but also in regarding each feature as having a whole set of alternatives. Previous models of social influence treat culture as either a continuous dimension or a single pair of alternatives. If culture is seen as a continuous dimension, then convergence tends to lead to homogeneity unless some other mechanism is introduced to prevent it. If culture is seen as one variable with a single pair of alternatives, only two possibilities are open. Even if a set of binary alternatives is allowed (e.g., Epstein and Axtell 1996), then the present model would yield no more than two different cultures among its stable regions.[13] Thus, to sustain cultural variety in the proposed model, there must be several dimensions to the culture, and each dimension must have more than two alternative traits.

The social influence model illustrates three fundamental points:

    1. Local convergence can lead to global polarization.

    2. The interplay between different features of culture can shape the process of social influence.

    3. Even simple mechanisms of change can give counterintuitive results, as shown by the present model, in which large territories generate surprisingly little polarization.

The model suggests some interesting interpretations for the four topics mentioned at the start of the paper. Of course, a simple model can only be suggestive and can never be definitive.

1. *State formation.* Because the formation of a national state is facilitated by social convergence over a territory (Deutsch 1953 and 1969; Cederman forthcoming), the results of the model demonstrate how arbitrary the actual boundaries can be. For example, if the political process took hold at the historical era represented by the third panel of Figure 7-1, a state would be more likely to form in the relatively homogeneous southern part of the map than in the relatively heterogeneous northern part, even though there was initially nothing to distinguish north from south. In technical terms, the outcome is highly path dependent (e.g., Arthur 1988).

2. *Succession conflict.* Cultural assimilation of multinational states has turned out to be much harder than most observers had predicted before

---

[13] With two traits per feature, the only stable outcome would be for every site to have either the same culture or the complementary culture of each of its neighbors. Because the complement of a complement is the original culture, at most two different cultures would be possible among all the stable regions.

the breakup of the Soviet Union and Yugoslavia. The model of social influence offered here suggests how local interaction can lead to cohesive communities without actually leading to homogenization over large distances. The model helps explain how terrain that discourages long-distance interaction (as in the physically rugged territory of the Caucasus or of the former Yugoslavia) promotes small-scale homogeneity along with large-scale diversity.

3. *Transnational integration.*

a. The model throws an interesting light on the effect of centuries-long European expansion to dominate much of the globe. It is not surprising that increasing a cultural area homogenizes the newer additions to the old. It is more surprising that the old regions should homogenize internally. In other words, the model suggests that the expansion of European influence from the fifteenth century could help homogenize Europe itself.

b. With recent advances in transportation, mass media, and information technology, many interactions are now largely independent of geographical distance. With random long-distance interactions, the heterogeneity sustained by local interaction cannot be sustained.[14] An interesting corollary is that leaders of states can try to slow or eliminate the homogenization by cutting their citizens off from interactions with outsiders. Recently, however, the regimes of both Burma and North Korea have had second thoughts about the price to be paid for such isolation.

c. The model also throws light on the controversial thesis of Huntington (1993) that conflict in the future will largely be along the boundaries of very large cultural regions rather than between nations within the same cultural region. The results of the present model demonstrate that as the relevant political territory gets larger, the number of distinct cultural regions can be expected to decline, even in the absence of conquest.

4. *Social cleavages.*

a. Different levels of government performance in different regions of Italy have been traced to differences in civic traditions that date back 700 years (Putnam 1993, 121–62). The interesting addition to the model that these results suggest is that some stable civic cultures are more effective than others in promoting good government. This in turn suggests that the role of informal organizations as the basis of social capital and trust (Putnam 1995; Fukuyama 1995) can be analyzed in terms of how the processes of social influence can lead to uniformity over large areas without necessarily leading to complete homogenization.

b. The model gives the largest number of stable regions when there

---

[14] This result was confirmed with the present model by allowing every agent to interact with every other agent (Axtell et al. 1996).

are few cultural features and many traits per feature. This suggests that the hardest differences to resolve through social influence are those with few issues, but with many distinct possibilities for each issue. The surprising part of this conclusion is that having fewer issues causes such rapid local convergence that large-scale convergence may not occur.

c. In the near future, electronic communications will allow us to develop patterns of interaction that are chosen rather than imposed by geography. If individuals are linked together at random, one could expect substantial convergence over time. In the more likely case that the interactions will be based on self-selection, people will tend to interact with others who are already quite similar to them on relevant dimensions (Resnick et al. 1994; Abramson et al. 1988). An implication of the model is that such self-selection could result in an even stronger tendency toward both "local" convergence and global polarization. Only then the "local" convergence will be based not on geography, but on emergent patterns of more or less like-minded communication. The implications for resolving the tensions inherent in a multicultural society are problematic.

References

Abelson, Robert, and A. Bernstein. 1963. "A Computer Simulation Model of Community Referendum Controversies." *Public Opinion Quarterly* 27: 93–122.

Abramson, Jeffrey, F. Christopher Arterton, and Gary R. Orren. 1988. *The Electronic Commonwealth*. New York: Basic Books.

Anderson, Benedict. 1991. *Imagined Communities: Reflections on the Origin and Spread of Nationalism*. 2d ed. London: Verso.

Arthur, W. Brian. 1988. "Urban Systems and Historical Path Dependence." In *Cities and Their Vital Systems,* ed. J. Ausubel and R. Herman, 85–97. Washington D.C.: National Academy Press.

Axelrod, Robert. 1986. "An Evolutionary Approach to Norms." *American Political Science Review* 80: 1095–1111. Included as Chapter 3 of this volume.

———. 1995. "A Model of the Emergence of New Political Actors." In *Artificial Societies: The Computer Simulation of Social Life,* ed. N. Gilbert and R. Conte, 19–39. London: University College Press. Included as Chapter 6 of this volume.

Axelrod, Robert, Will Mitchell, Robert E. Thomas, D. Scott Bennett, and Erhard Bruderer. 1995. "Coalition Formation in Standard-Setting Alliances." *Management Science* 41: 1493–1508. Included as Chapter 5 of this volume.

Axtell, Robert, Robert Axelrod, Joshua Epstein, and Michael D. Cohen. 1996. "Aligning Simulation Models: A Case Study and Results." *Computational and Mathematical Organization Theory* 1: 123–41. Included as Appendix A of this volume.

Barth, Fredrik. 1969. *Ethnic Groups and Boundaries*. Boston: Little, Brown.

Boyd, Robert, and Peter J. Richerson. 1985. *Culture and the Evolutionary Process*. Chicago: University of Chicago Press.

Bremer, Stuart A., and Michael Mihalka. 1977. "Machiavelli in Machina: Or Politics Among Hexagons." In *Problems of World Modeling*, ed. Karl Deutsch et al., 303–37. Cambridge, Mass.: Ballinger.

Brown, Thad A., and Michael McBurnett. 1993. "Emergence of Political Elites." Paper presented at European Conference on Artificial Life, Brussels, May 19–21.

Campbell, Angus, Philip E. Converse, Warren E. Miller, and Donald E. Stokes. 1960. *The American Voter*. New York: Wiley.

Carley, Kathleen. 1991. "A Theory of Group Stability." *American Sociological Review* 56: 331–54.

Cavalli-Sforza, L. L., and M. W. Feldman. 1981. *Cultural Transmission and Evolution: A Quantitative Approach*. Princeton, N.J.: Princeton University Press.

Cederman, Lars-Erik. Forthcoming. *Emergent Actors in World Politics: How States and Nations Develop and Dissolve*. Princeton, N.J.: Princeton University Press.

Coleman, James S. 1957. *Community Conflict*. New York: Free Press.

———. 1965. "The Use of Electronic Computers in the Study of Social Organization." *European Journal of Sociology* 6: 89–107.

Cusack, Thomas R., and Richard Stoll. 1990. *Exploring Realpolitik: Probing International Relations Theory with Computer Simulation*. Boulder, Colo.: Lynne Rienner.

Deutsch, Karl W. 1953. *Nationalism and Social Communication: An Inquiry in the Foundations of Nationality*. Cambridge, Mass.: Technology Press; New York· Wiley.

———. 1969. *Nationalism and Its Alternatives*. New York: Knopf.

Durham, William H. 1991. *Coevolution: Genes, Culture, and Human Diversity*. Stanford, Calif.: Stanford University Press.

Epstein, Joshua M., and Robert Axtell. 1996. *Growing Artificial Societies: Social Science from the Bottom Up*. Washington, D.C.: Brookings Institution Press; and Cambridge, Mass.: MIT Press.

Friedkin, Noah E., and Eugene C. Johnsen 1990. "Social Influence and Opinions." *Journal of Mathematical Sociology* 15: 193–205.

Fukuyama, Francis. 1995. *Trust*. New York: Free Press.

Geertz, Clifford. 1973. *The Interpretation of Cultures*. New York: Basic Books.

Giddens, Anthony. 1979. *The Constitution of Society*. Berkeley: University of California Press.

Hannan, Michael T. 1979. "The Dynamics of Ethnic Boundaries in Modern States." In *National Development and the World System*, ed. J. Meyer and M. Hannan, 253–327. Chicago: University of Chicago Press.

Harrison, J. Richard, and Glenn R. Carroll. 1991. "Keeping the Faith: A Model of Cultural Transmission in Formal Organizations." *Administrative Science Quarterly* 36: 552–82.

Homans, George C. 1950. *The Human Group*. New York: Harcourt, Brace.

Huberman, Bernardo A., and Natalie S. Glance. 1993. "Evolutionary Games and Computer Simulations." *Proceedings of the National Academy of Sciences (USA)* 90: 7716–18.

Huckfeldt, Robert, and John Sprague. 1991. "Discussant Effects on Vote Choice: Intimacy, Structure, and Interdependence." *Journal of Politics* 53: 122–58.

Huntington, Samuel P. 1993. "The Clash of Civilizations?" *Foreign Affairs* 72: 22–49.

Kemeny, John G., J. Laurie Snell, and Gerald L. Thompson. 1966. *Introduction to Finite Mathematics*. 2d ed. Englewood Cliffs, N.J.: Prentice-Hall.

Key, V. O. 1961. *Public Opinion and American Democracy*. New York: Knopf.

Kroeber, Alfred L., and Clyde Kluckhorn. 1952. "Culture: A Critical Review of Concepts and Definitions." *Papers of the Peabody Museum* 47: 643–44, 656.

Latane, Bibb, Andrzej Nowak, and James H. Liu. 1994. "Measuring Emergent Social Phenomena: Dynamism, Polarization and Clustering as Order Parameters of Social Systems." *Behavioral Science* 39: 1–24.

Lewis, David K. 1967. *Convention: A Philosophical Study*. Cambridge, Mass.: Harvard University Press.

Lipset, Seymour Martin, Martin A. Trow, and James S. Coleman. 1956. *Union Democracy*. Glencoe, Ill.: Free Press.

Lumsden, Charles J., and Edward O. Wilson. 1981. *Genes, Mind, and Culture: The Coevolutionary Process*. Cambridge, Mass.: Harvard University Press.

March, James G. 1991. "Exploration and Exploitation in Organizational Learning." *Organization Science* 2: 71–87.

Marsden, Peter V., and Noah E. Friedkin. 1993. "Network Studies of Social Influence." *Sociological Methods and Research* 22: 127–51.

Nelson, Richard R., and Sidney G. Winter. 1982. *An Evolutionary Theory of Economic Change*. Cambridge, Mass.: Harvard University Press.

Nowak, Andrzej, Jacek Szamrej, and Bibb Latane. 1990. "From Private Attitude to Public Opinion: A Dynamic Theory of Social Impact." *Psychological Review* 97: 362–76.

Putnam, Robert D. 1966. "Political Attitudes and the Local Community." *American Political Science Review* 60: 640–54.

———. 1993. *Making Democracy Work: Civic Traditions in Modern Italy*. Princeton, N.J.: Princeton University Press.

———. 1995. "Bowling Alone." *Democracy* 6: 66–78.

Renfrew, Colin. 1973. *The Explanation of Social Influence: Models in Prehistory*. Pittsburgh: University of Pittsburgh Press.

Renfrew, Colin, and Kenneth L. Cooke. 1979. *Transformations: Mathematical Approaches to Social Influence*. New York: Academic Press.

Resnick, Paul, Neophytos Iacovou, Mitesh Suchak, Peter Bergstrom, and John Riedl. 1994. "GroupLens: An Open Architecture for Collaborative Filtering of Netnews." In *Proceedings of the ACM 1994 Conference on Computer-Supported Cooperative Work: Chapel Hill, N.C.*, 175–86. New York: Association for Computing Machinery.

Rogers, Everett M. 1983. *Diffusion of Innovations*. 3d ed. New York: Free Press.

Sabloff, Jeremy A. 1981. *Simulations in Archeology.* Albuquerque: University of New Mexico Press.

Saloner, G., and J. Farrell. 1986. "Installed Base and Compatibility: Innovation, Product Preannouncements, and Predation." *American Economic Review* 76: 940–55.

Schelling, Thomas. 1978. *Micromotives and Macrobehavior.* New York: Norton.

Schrodt, Philip A. 1981. "Conflict as a Determinant of Territory." *Behavioral Science* 26: 37–50.

Simmel, Georg. [1908] 1955. *Conflict and the Web of Group-Affiliations.* New York: Free Press.

Terrell, John. 1977. "Human Biogeography in the Solomon Islands." *Fieldiana: Anthropology* 68: 1–47.

Ullmann-Margalit, Edna. 1977. *The Emergence of Norms.* Oxford: Clarendon Press.

Voget, Fred W. 1975. *A History of Ethnology.* New York: Holt, Reinhart and Winston.

APPENDIXES

A

Replication of Agent-Based Models

THIS APPENDIX originated in an observation and suggestion by Michael Cohen. The observation was that in order for agent-based modeling to become a widely used tool in social science research, it will be necessary to develop the tools for a close comparison of comparable models. This process of close comparison or "alignment" is needed to determine whether two modeling systems can produce the same results, which in turn is the basis for critical experiments and for tests of whether one model can subsume another. The suggestion was that my model of social influence (see Chapter 7) was simple enough to serve as a good target model for an alignment exercise, and that the Sugarscape modeling environment of Joshua Epstein and Robert Axtell would be a good environment in which to try a "docking" experiment on alignment. I thought Mike's idea was a good one, so we invited Josh and Rob to join us in performing this replication study.

This project seemed very straightforward when the four of us began, but we found two surprising things along the way. The first was that comparing two versions of the same model required us to develop a new set of concepts. The second surprise was that even apparently trivial differences in how time is handled in the model can lead to noticeable differences in outcomes, suggesting that care needs to be taken in making and reporting these choices.

This replication study had no trouble getting published. In fact, it has engendered substantial interest among people doing agent-based modeling in the social sciences because of a felt need to develop clearer standards for the emerging field.

The publication of the paper was especially useful for me. When my social influence model was first submitted for publication, a reviewer said that one of the reported results was so counterintuitive that additional effort would be needed to verify that the outcome was the result of the model rather than an error in the programming. I was happy to be able to report back that the model had become the subject of the very first effort to reimplement an agent-based model in a different modeling environment. Moreover, I could report that the suspicious result was confirmed and the replication had been accepted for publication in another journal.

This methodological paper was quite effective in putting to rest one of the objections to the substantive report of the model.

The "docking" exercise is offered as an aid to those who want to help make agent-based modeling become part of a cumulative scientific enterprise. (Those who would like tips on how to undertake agent-based modeling may also consult Appendix B.)

Replication of Agent-Based Models

ALIGNING SIMULATION MODELS: A CASE STUDY AND RESULTS

ROBERT AXTELL, ROBERT AXELROD, JOSHUA M. EPSTEIN, AND MICHAEL D. COHEN

Adapted from Robert Axtell, Robert Axelrod, Joshua Epstein, and Michael D. Cohen, "Aligning Simulation Models: A Case Study and Results," *Computational and Mathematical Organization Theory* 1 (1996): 123–41. Reprinted by permission of *CMOT.*

Abstract:

This essay develops the concepts and methods of a process we will call "alignment of computational models," or "docking" for short. Alignment is needed to determine whether two models can produce the same results, which in turn is the basis for critical experiments and for tests of whether one model can subsume another. We illustrate our concepts and methods using as a target a model of cultural transmission built by Axelrod. For comparison we use the Sugarscape model developed by Epstein and Axtell.

The two models differ in many ways and, to date, have been employed with quite different aims. The Axelrod model has been used principally for intensive experimentation with parameter variation, and includes only one mechanism. In contrast, the Sugarscape model has been used primarily to generate rich "artificial histories," scenarios that display stylized facts of interest, such as cultural differentiation driven by many different mechanisms including resource availability, migration, trade, and combat.

The Sugarscape model was modified so as to reproduce the results of the Axelrod cultural model. Among the questions we address are: what does it mean for two models to be equivalent, how can different standards of equivalence be statistically evaluated, and how do subtle differences in model design affect the results? After attaining a "docking" of the two models, the richer set of mechanisms of the Sugarscape model is used to provide two experiments in sensitivity analysis for the cultural rule of Axelrod's model.

Our generally positive experience in this enterprise has suggested that it could be beneficial if alignment and equivalence testing were more widely practiced among computational modelers.

The authors gratefully acknowledge financial assistance from the Brookings Institution, World Resources Institute, John D. and Catherine T. MacArthur Foundation, the Santa Fe Institute, the Program for the Study of Complex Systems, the LS&A Enrichment Fund of the University of Michigan, and the U.S. Advanced Research Projects Agency.

1. Introduction

1.1 *Motivation*

If computational modeling is to become a widely used tool in social science research, we believe that a process we will call "alignment of computational models" will be an essential activity. Without such a process of close comparison, computational modeling will never provide the clear sense of "domain of validity" that typically can be obtained for mathematized theories. It seems fundamental to us to be able to determine whether two models claiming to deal with the same phenomena can, or cannot, produce the same results.

Alignment is essential to support two hallmarks of cumulative disciplinary research: critical experiment and subsumption. If we cannot determine whether or not two models produce equivalent results in equivalent conditions, we cannot reject one model in favor of another that fits data better; nor are we able to say that one model is a special case of another more general one—as we do when saying that Einstein's treatment of gravity subsumes Newton's.

Although it seems clear that there should be frequent efforts to show pairs of computer models to be equivalent, we are aware of only one such case (Anderson and Fischer 1986), and we know of no systematic analysis of the issues raised in trying to establish equivalence.

We have identified a few cases in which an older model has been reprogrammed in a new language, sometimes with extensions, by a later author. For example, Michael Prietula has reported[1] reimplementing a model from Cyert and March (1963), and Ray Levitt has reported a reimplementation of Cohen et al. (1972).[2] However, these procedures are not comparisons of different models that bear on the same phenomena. Rather they are "reimplementations," in which a later model is programmed from the outset to reproduce as closely as possible the behavior of an earlier model. Our interest is in the more general and troublesome case in which two models incorporating distinctive mechanisms bear on the same class of social phenomena, be it voting behavior, attitude formation, or organizational centralization.

This essay therefore aims to achieve two goals: (1) to report a novel set of results from aligning two different computer models of cultural transmission; and (2) to report an informative case study of the process used to obtain these novel results.

---

[1] Personal communication to Michael Cohen.
[2] Personal communication to Michael Cohen.

1.2 Overview

The essay is organized into six sections. After this brief introductory section, Section 2 provides more detailed background on the two models necessary for understanding the results. The third section reports our procedures in aligning the two models and in collecting information for this case report. The fourth contains results from two comparison experiments. The fifth reports our observations on the model alignment process. The conclusion is the sixth section.

2. Background on the Two Models

Our objective has been to determine if a set of results obtained in a model of cultural transmission built by Robert Axelrod (1997) could also be obtained in the different setting of the Sugarscape model of Joshua M. Epstein and Robert Axtell (1996).[3] Sugarscape differs from the Axelrod model in many ways. Most notably, culture is one of many processes that can be operative in the more general Sugarscape system, which has model agents who—among other things—move, eat, reproduce, fight, trade, and suffer disease. The Axelrod model has much simpler agents who do none of these things, but rather occupy fixed positions on a square plane, interacting only with their immediate neighbors to the north, south, east, and west.[4]

The two models are in this respect clear examples of different approaches to computational modeling: Sugarscape is designed to study the interaction of many different plausible social mechanisms. It is a kind of "artificial world" (Lane 1993). In contrast, the Axelrod Culture Model (ACM) was built to implement a single mechanism for a single process, with the aim of carrying out extensive experiments varying the parameters of that mechanism. It much more resembles the spirit of traditional

[3] Axelrod's source code is approximately 1,500 lines of Pascal for the Macintosh (Synamtec THINK Pascal version 4.0.1) and is available from the author. The Sugarscape source code is approximately 20,000 lines of Object Pascal and C for the 68K Macintosh (Symantec THINK Pascal version 4.0.2 and THINK C version 7.0.6 compilers). Agent objects are written in Pascal, whereas low-level and graphics routines are primarily written in C. This code is available from Robert Axtell. Executable versions of the code, configured with Axelrod's culture rule and capable of generating the data in this paper, are also available from Axtell.

[4] Other models of cultural transmission and social influence include Renfrew (1973), Sabloff (1981), Nowak et al. (1990), Friedkin and Johnsen (1990), Putnam (1966), March (1991), Harrison and Carroll (1991), Carley (1991), and Cavalli-Sforza and Feldman (1981). See also Axelrod (1997).

mathematical theorizing in its commitment to extreme simplicity and complete analysis of each model parameter.

We begin by describing briefly how the Axelrod model works.[5] The model studies a square array of agents all following a single rule. The agents are cultural entities that might be thought of as "villages." Each agent interacts with a fixed set of neighbors, four unless the agent is located on an edge or corner of the square. Each agent has several attributes and each of those attributes can take any one of several nominal-scale values. For the work reported here we have used five attributes, each taking one of fifteen values. The initial state of each agent is determined by randomizing the value of each attribute. Attributes might be interpreted as forms of dress, linguistic patterns, religious practices, or other culturally determined features.

The central aim of the ACM is to study the effects of a simple mechanism of cultural transmission that operates as follows. An agent is selected at random to be the next one active. One of the four neighbors is selected to be that agent's next contact. An attribute is selected among the five. If the two agents have the same value for that attribute, another attribute on which they differ, if there are any, is selected at random, and the active agent assumes the value for that attribute currently held by the contacted neighbor. Activity is allowed to continue until every agent differs from each of its neighbors either at every attribute or at none. At this point no further change is possible and the model run stops.

A key feature of this cultural change mechanism is that cultural change becomes more likely as two neighbors are more alike, and less likely as they differ. A central question of interest in the work with the model is whether this variability of interaction rate is itself sufficient to create stable diversity rather than eventual homogeneity—as one would expect with a model that allowed unlike neighbors to continue interacting no matter how different they were.

Whereas the ACM can be conveyed in a few paragraphs, and its results can be fully described in a short article, Sugarscape is a much more complex system that can be rendered fully only at book length (Epstein and Axtell 1996). This is not because individual mechanisms of Sugarscape are complex. On the contrary, each of its mechanisms is of about the same complexity as in the Axelrod model. However, the intent of Sugarscape is to investigate the interplay of many mechanisms as they operate simultaneously—as happens in actual social life. In particular, Sugarscape is intended as a tool in sufficiency testing of social theories, allowing theorists to ask if a stipulated set of mechanisms and conditions

---

[5] A complete account of the model structure and of results obtained from experiments can be found in Axelrod (1997).

(say, for a market to "clear") actually will produce the predicted phenomenon.

Sugarscape therefore has processes that allow its agents to look for, move to, and eat a resource ("sugar") that grows on its toroidal array of cells. Thus, whereas food growing cells are immobile, active agents are purposively mobile, and this is one of many fundamental differences with the Axelrod model.

Sugarscape agents also have cultural attributes. In typical studies with the model there are eleven cultural attributes, each of which takes one of two values. Cultural attributes change in Sugarscape as part of a larger cycle of agent activity.

In this model, the agents also become active in random order.[6] Each agent, when active, engages in a number of processes. For the present discussion, the most important of these is moving to a cell within its vision range that is richest in sugar. At that location an agent interacts culturally with all its neighbors. (Sugarscape agents typically do not populate all the landscape cells, so the active agent may have fewer than four other agents in its neighborhood.) In a cultural interaction, an attribute is selected at random, and if the neighbor differs from the agent, the value is changed to that of the agent.

In Sugarscape, attributes are aggregated (typically by a simple majority rule) and this determines an agent's cultural type, usually labeled as either "Red" or "Blue." Cultural type then enters into many other processes in which Sugarscape agents may engage, such as trade, combat, and sexual reproduction.

Whereas the Axelrod model was designed principally for intensive experimentation with parameter variation, the intended use of the Sugarscape model is quite different in design. In it, agents have many behavioral rules in addition to cultural ones, and although the model may be used for exploration of parameter spaces, it has heretofore been primarily used to generate "artificial histories," scenarios that display stylized facts of interest, such as cultural differentiation driven by resource availability, or recognizable patterns of migration, trade, and combat. The principal use of the generated scenarios is for sufficiency tests, showing that the implemented individual-level mechanisms are able to produce the collective-level phenomena of interest.

It should be apparent that the two models are vastly different in many important respects. Nonetheless, they have two central features in common that suggest that they could be meaningfully compared. The first is that both are "agent-based" models. They work by specifying properties of individual actors in the system and then studying the collective phe-

---

[6] The method is similar, but not identical, to that in ACM, as discussed below.

nomena that result as those individuals interact—in this case, in local neighborhoods of two-dimensional space. The second shared feature is that both represent cultural attributes of individual agents as strings of symbols and model cultural diffusion as a convergence process between neighbors.

3.   Procedures of Our Comparison

These two strong similarities suggested to Axelrod and Cohen, as they read a draft account of the Sugarscape project, that it might be possible to "dock" the two models—in analogy to orbital docking of dissimilar spacecraft. Thus it could be determined whether Sugarscape, under suitable conditions, would produce results equivalent to those already obtained for the ACM. Epstein and Axtell were contacted. They agreed such a test would be instructive. All four investigators believe that alignment of models will be necessary if computational modeling is to become a significant medium of theoretical expression. Equivalence testing could make an important contribution in the social sciences, though it would not replace external validity assessment.[7] None of the four could think of a case where such an equivalence test had been reported, or where the problem of equivalence testing had been analyzed in detail.[8]

3.1   *Making the Comparison and Preparing the Case Report*

The four investigators agreed on procedures for conducting the test, and for keeping records of the work done and problems encountered in the course of the testing. The aims were: (1) to determine if equivalent results were produced in equivalent conditions; (2) to demonstrate the effects of relaxing some of the equivalent conditions; and (3) to be able to report problems that occurred and their resolutions, thus taking first steps in establishing the practice of equivalence testing more generally in social science computational modeling.

The procedures followed were roughly analogous to those used when a second investigator in a laboratory science is attempting to reproduce results obtained in a first investigator's laboratory (Latour and Woolgar 1979).

Epstein and Axtell worked with a prepublication draft account of the

[7] On external validation see Dutton and Starbuck (1971), Knepell and Arangno (1993), and Burton and Obel (1995).

[8] Subsequent search did uncover one such report: Anderson and Fischer (1986). Thus far no systematic treatment of the conceptual issues has been found.

ACM to do their preliminary work. They considered what steps they would have to take in order to reproduce the key results identified by Axelrod. These results show how the number of culturally identical regions that exist when stability is reached varies as a function of three parameters: the number of attributes, the number of values per attribute, and the size of the square lattice. These results included the most surprising aspect of ACM's performance: that the equilibrium number of cultural "regions" produced by the model first increases, then decreases as a function of the number of agents.[9]

Axtell and Epstein then visited Axelrod and Cohen at the University of Michigan, where a conference clarified ambiguities. Further changes were made to Sugarscape, and then preliminary equivalence tests run. A fuller set of tests was run and analyzed when Epstein and Axtell returned to their work site at the Brookings Institution. Epstein and Axtell then continued by relaxing some of the factors that had been made equivalent to those of ACM in order to see what differences such changes would make.

3.2 Testing Model Equivalence

A central issue was the determination of how to assess "equivalence" of the two models. The plan required an effort to show that the Sugarscape model could behave comparably to the ACM, and this entails a standard by which to assess "equivalence" of measures made on the two models. This was discussed on the telephone and via email at an early stage. The conclusion was that for this case it would suffice if Sugarscape could be shown—when using a basic cultural transmission mechanism similar to the ACM's—to produce several distributions of measurements that were statistically indistinguishable from distributions produced by the ACM.

The four investigators agreed that this is a rather tight standard, since one might argue that Sugarscape was equivalent if it produced a set of results with the same ordinal patterns as those from the ACM. But a demanding test was felt to be appropriate because this was a first exercise of its kind, and because programming changes to Sugarscape could make its basic cultural transmission mechanism algorithmically equivalent to that in ACM. All the authors agreed that "equivalence" of models with stochastic elements must be defined in context, and further observations on this central and thorny issue are offered in the final section. In particular, we expand there on the difficult problem of giving a precise statistical content to the concept "statistically indistinguishable distributions."

[9] Axelrod defined a cultural region as a set of a contiguous sites with identical culture.

4. Results from the Two Experiments

We turn now to reporting our observations on the behavior of Sugarscape in comparison with that of ACM. We describe the changes made to Sugarscape in order to bring it into alignment with what were judged to be principal features determining ACM's results.

4.1 Changes Made to Dock Sugarscape with ACM

Vision range was reduced to the immediate four neighbors. Movement range was reduced to zero. The usual initialization of Sugarscape to a population sparsely distributed over its array of cells was altered to a distribution placing an agent on every cell. The toroidal topology of Sugarscape was altered to a bounded square. There was actually a discrepancy introduced in doing this, which we comment on below. The constant numbers of attributes and values per attribute in Sugarscape were made into variables that could be set to the three different levels used in the ACM runs shown in our Table A-1.

One difference was deemed small and not eliminated. Sugarscape activates agents one at a time from a random permutation of the list of agents. When the list is finished, it is repermuted and activation begins again. Axelrod, as mentioned, activates a new randomly chosen agent every time. Roughly the methods correspond to sampling agents for activation without and with replacement. Thus, for any given set of n agents, in Sugarscape a block of n activations will make each agent active exactly once, whereas in the Axelrod model most would be active once, but a few might be active either zero times or two or more times. Our decision not to eliminate this difference, small though it seemed, did have interesting consequences that we describe below.

We had decided that to reproduce Axelrod's results Epstein and Axtell should first try using exactly his rules for determining cultural change. They therefore programmed a substitute for their own cultural change rule, which took no account of interagent similarity in the diffusion of culture attributes among interacting neighbors, and which caused each agent to interact culturally with all its neighbors.

4.2 Sugarscape Reproduces Central Results of Axelrod's Culture Model

Table A-1a, with target data from Axelrod (1997), gives the number of stable cultural regions for a 10×10 lattice, averaged over ten runs, as a

TABLE A-1
Average Number of Stable Regions

a. Axelrod's Cultural Model

	VALUES/FEATURE		
FEATURES	5	10	15
5	1.0	3.2 ± 1.8	20.0 ± 10.1
10	1.0	1.0	1.4 ± 0.5
15	1.0	1.0	1.2 ± 0.4

b. Sugarscape Implementation

	VALUES/FEATURE		
FEATURES	5	10	15
5	1.0	5.3 ± 3.9	21.3 ± 12.6
10	1.0	1.0	1.5 ± 0.7
15	1.0	1.0	1.0

Note: Each cell is based on ten replications. Standard deviations are shown when they are not equal to zero. All data are for territories of 10 × 10 sites.

function of the number of cultural attributes and the values per attribute. Note that, other things being equal, the number of cultural regions present in equilibrium increases with the number of traits per feature and decreases with the number of cultural features. Of the nine tabulated values, only four are not equal to 1.0.

A directly analogous display, Table A-1b, has been generated with the Sugarscape implementation of the Axelrod cultural rule. The qualitative dependence of the number of stable cultural regions on the number of features and traits per feature is the same as in Axelrod's table. Notice that in this new table only three entries are not equal to 1.0.

Quantitative agreement between the two sets of data is clear for the five entries of 1.0 that the tables have in common. To test how well the remaining entries in the two tables agree quantitatively, nonparametric statistical comparisons were undertaken. The critical value of the two-sided Mann-Whitney U statistic at the 0.05 level of significance for samples of size ten is 23 (Siegel 1956). That is, one rejects the null hypothesis for a value of U at or below 23. For all comparisons between the two tables the U-statistics are greater than the critical value and thus one cannot reject the null hypothesis on nonparametric grounds. Overall, it seems very likely that the corresponding data in the two tables were drawn from the same distribution.

Figure A-1 gives the target data from Axelrod (1997) on the number of

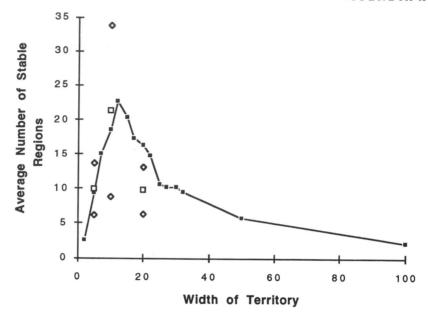

Figure A–1. Average Number of Stable Regions in Axelrod's Cultural Model and Sugarscape Implementation
Legend: Solid squares represent the target ACM data for five cultural features and fifteen traits per feature. Each territory size was replicated forty times, except the territories with 50 × 50 sites and 100 × 100 sites, which were replicated ten times.

Open squares represent the Sugarscape data for the same number of features and traits per feature. Each territorial size (5 × 5, 10 × 10, and 20 × 20) was replicated ten times.

Open diamonds represent Sugarscape means plus and minus a standard deviation.

stable cultural regions as a function of the lattice size for five cultural features with fifteen traits per feature. This figure has an interesting non-monotonic shape, a result discussed at some length by the author. Data for the 5 × 5, 10 × 10, and 20 × 20 lattices have been generated using the Sugarscape implementation of the Axelrod cultural rule. In each case, the sample size was forty, the same sample size used by Axelrod for these three cases. The means from the modified Sugarscape model and corresponding error bars are also displayed on Figure A-1. To determine to what extent this data agrees with Axelrod's original data, we employed the Kolmogorov-Smirnov (K-S) test of the goodness-of-fit of empirical cumulative distribution functions (cf. Hoel 1962)—a nonparametric test.[10]

[10] The Kolmogorov-Smirnov test was not used for the comparisons in Table A-1 because it has low power for small sample sizes.

The null hypothesis is that the corresponding data points are drawn from the same distribution. At the 5 percent significance level, the two-tailed critical value of the K-S statistic with forty observations is 0.304. That is, if the actual K-S value exceeds this critical value then the null hypotheses is rejected.

For the two sets of data corresponding to the 5×5 lattice the K-S statistic is 0.225. Therefore the null hypothesis cannot be rejected. In the 10×10 case the K-S statistic is 0.175, and so once again the null hypothesis cannot be rejected. Finally, the 20×20 lattice size reveals that the K-S statistic is $0.5 > 0.304$ and thus the null hypothesis is rejected—the data for this parameter value appear likely to have been drawn from different distributions. The ACM mean in this case was 16.25. The modified Sugarscape mean is 9.23.

1. In what sense may the computational models still be called "equivalent"? The modified Sugarscape model produces results that are numerically identical to those from ACM in some cases. It produces distributions of results that cannot be distinguished statistically from ACM distributions in eleven of the twelve comparions. In one case it produces a distribution that can be distinguished, although the mean is in the desired relationship to the other means. That is, the 20×20 lattice has a mean number of regions less than the 10×10 case. This nonmonotonicity was the important character of the result in Axelrod's view of his own results. In our conclusion we argue that these are three natural categories of model equivalence, which we call "numerical identity," "distributional equivalence," and "relational equivalence." We discuss implications of these distinctions in Section 6.

2. What is the likely cause of the observed difference? Because we had brought so many aspects of the two models into algorithmic agreement, we were surprised when this discrepancy occurred. But not all aspects of the two models agreed, and the statistically significant difference indicates that this mattered in the 20×20 case. We believe the difference arises from our decision not to convert the Sugarscape activation method to the ACM method. The Sugarscape method does not allow for the same agent to be occasionally active several times before other agents have had their "fair" share of influence. This additional uniformity of influence appears to be sufficient to induce greater ultimate convergence in cultures.[11] When we convert the activation code in Sugarscape to the "sampling with replacement" method of ACM, the 20×20 case no longer causes a problem. And when all the cases are rerun in Sugarscape with

---

[11] A possibly related result is obtained below in Section 4.3, where it is shown that allowing agents to mix with non-neighbors also reduces the eventual equilibrium number of cultures.

random activation, each one of them gives data that are indistinguishable from the ACM.[12]

3. What is the correct null hypothesis for statistical testing of equivalence? We have conformed in our statistical testing to the usual logic that formulates the problem as rejection of a null hypothesis of distributional identity. But the alert reader may have noticed that this is not entirely satisfactory in the special circumstances of testing model equivalence. With one exception discussed earlier, we have concluded that we cannot reject, at conventional confidence probabilities, the null hypothesis that the distributions are the same.

The unsatisfactory aspect of this approach is that it creates an incentive for investigators to test equivalence with small sample sizes. The smaller the sample, the higher the threshold for rejecting the null hypothesis, and therefore the greater the chance of establishing equivalence. We have resisted this temptation and used sample sizes typical of simulation studies. We feel satisfied in this case that, with the one exception noted, the models behave equivalently. In the long run, however, we see a need to formulate a more appropriate statistical logic.[13]

4.3 Sensitivity Analysis of Agent-Based Models

The literature on sensitivity analysis in agent-based models is, as yet, quite small.[14] How do alterations in local rules affect emergent macro-

[12] Sugarscape with random activation gives means and nonzero standard deviations as follows. For Table A-1, reading across, 1.2 ± 0.4, 4.10 ± 1.3, 18.8 ± 9.7, 1.0, 1.0, 1.9 ± 1.0, 1.0, 1.0, 1.0. The Mann-Whitney U statistics for these nine sets of data of ten data points each do not reject the null hypothesis that these data are drawn from the same underlying distributions as Table A-1, at the 0.05 level of significance. For Figure A-1, the data are 9.8 ± 2.8 (for 5 × 5 case), 20.4 ± 7.9 (for 10 × 10 case), and 14.8 ± 7.0 (for 20 × 20 case). The Kolmogorov-Smirnov statistics for these three data sets of forty points each do not reject the hypothesis that these data have the same distributions as the corresponding distributions from Axelrod's Culture Model shown in Figure A-1.

[13] Our current view of the most promising direction is to reverse the usual null hypothesis formulation and ask whether we can confidently reject the claim that the distributions are different. However, there are two complications in this approach. First, with stochastic models it will be extremely hard to conclude that all the observed difference in sample means is due to sampling fluctuation. This suggests that it will be necessary to use a null hypothesis such as "the two distributions differ by no more than X percent," with X chosen by convention or to be appropriate within the referent context. Second, with such a reversed and nonsimple null hypothesis, and with no solid reason to assume a convenient (e.g., Gaussian) form of the underlying distributions, it is unlikely that there will be a manageable analytic method of obtaining confidence levels for the statistics. This suggests that the problem will have to attacked with computational statistical tools, such as the bootstrap approach of Efron and Tibshirani (1993).

[14] For an example based on cellular automata see Wuensche and Lesser (1992).

scopic structures, such as cultural patterns? Dockings of the sort we have reported facilitate this new kind of sensitivity analysis. Here, we conduct two experiments involving agent movement rules.

4.3.1 A MOBILITY EXPERIMENT

As noted earlier, "agents" in the ACM occupy fixed positions on a square lattice, whereas in Sugarscape, agents are mobile. One natural question, therefore, is: what happens to the equilibrium number of cultures in the ACM if agents are permitted to move around the Sugarscape interacting with neighbors, with interaction governed by the ACM cultural transmission rule? Will we see greater equilibrium cultural diversity or less? In the ACM, there is zero probability that non-neighboring agents will directly interact, whereas in Sugarscape, depending on the landscape topography, any two agents might eventually interact directly. Because the effect of movement is therefore to "mix" the population, we would expect that eventually there would be less diversity than without movement. This is what we find.

In order to carry out the experiment, the Sugarscape was configured as a 50×50 grid having a single (Gaussian) "sugar mountain" in the center. One hundred mobile agents were given random initial locations on this landscape. Each agent engages in purposive behavior as follows: (1) it searches locally for the lattice location having the most sugar, (2) it moves to the nearest best site, and (3) it gathers (eats) the sugar on that site. The agent population is heterogeneous with respect to its vision, that is, how far each agent can "see" locally in the principal lattice directions (north, south, east, and west). In these runs vision was uniformly distributed between 5 and 10 in the agent population. After moving, agents engage in cultural exchange—here according to Axelrod's cultural exchange rule—with one of their neighbors. One important difference between the Sugarscape and the ACM is that agents may have anywhere from zero to four neighbors on the Sugarscape, whereas (nonboundary) agents always have exactly four neighbors in the ACM. Once sugar is "harvested" by the agents, it grows back at unit rate. The "termination criterion" employed had to be modified somewhat for this run. In the case of fixed agents, cultural transmission terminates when all neighboring agents are either completely identical or completely different. With mobile agents, it is necessary to check whether all agents are either completely the same or completely different, independent of whether or not they are neighbors. This "global" stopping criterion is computationally more expensive than the "local" one appropriate for fixed agents.

Because we expected movement to reduce the number of cultures present, it seemed natural to test the proposition using the parameters that yielded the most cultures in the ACM. In the case of 100 agents (10×10

grid) having five cultural features and fifteen traits per feature, the ACM produced an average of 20.0 (s.d. ±10.1) distinct cultures, whereas the Sugarscape version of the ACM (fixed agents) yielded 21.3 (±12.5). The introduction of movement dramatically reduces the number of cultures. Over a sample of ten runs in Sugarscape, the average was 1.1 (±0.3). When the experiment was repeated for the case of five features-thirty traits per feature, under the expectation that this larger "cultural space" would yield more distinct cultures in equilibrium, the average number of cultures present in Sugarscape increased somewhat to 2.2 (±1.2).

4.3.2 A "SOUP" EXPERIMENT

Movement mixes the population. The extreme form of this is the so-called "soup," in which agents are paired at random regardless of location, and then interact under the ACM rule. Because this results in more thorough mixing than movement, we would expect the "culturally homogenizing" effect to be even stronger. And it was.

For 100 agents having five cultural features and fifteen traits per feature, in ten runs there was never a case in which more than one culture remained. When the number of traits per feature was increased to thirty, a sequence of ten runs yielded seven runs that ended up with a single culture, two instances of two distinct cultures, and a single case of three equilibrium cultures; an average of 1.4 overall. Essentially, most of the ACM's cultural diversity disappears in soup. In summary, the more well-mixed the society, the lower is the equilibrium number of distinct cultures. Relatedly, multicultural equilibria in the ACM require that the probability of interaction between completely different agents be literally zero. If there is any probability of interaction (or if there is any point mutation rate) the long-run attractor is one culture. The above points concern the number of equilibria only; can we say anything about the rates at which these set in?

Recall the basic dynamic of the ACM: the greater the similarity between neighboring agents, the more rapidly does their similarity grow. Once similarity reaches a certain state, convergence is rapid—almost as if a phase transition occurs. Now, the counterintuitive result is that the more well-mixed the society, the later is this "phase transition." In the ACM model, local clusters of neighboring agents develop similarities. Their high spatial correlation permits these agents to arrive at "agreement" very quickly, whereas in the Sugarscape mobility case, agents "hop away" before agreement is possible; and in the extreme soup, where spatial correlation is zero, the "phase change" is later still. In summary, the lower the spatial correlation, the later is the onset of rapid convergence to equilibrium, and the lower is the equilibrium number of cultures.

5.   Results on the Docking Process Itself

5.1   The Docking Process

When Epstein and Axtell visited the University of Michigan, they brought their model with them on a portable computer. A portion of the work needed for the equivalence testing was done prior to their arrival. This encompassed most of the changes described in Section 4.1.

Fortunately, Sugarscape was programmed in Object Pascal and with considerable attention to generality. It was therefore possible to make most of these changes as substitutions of parameter values or by "throwing switches."

On their arrival in Ann Arbor, a meeting was held to resolve several ambiguities that remained on the basis of reading Axelrod's text. We note an implication of this: under current standards of reporting a simulation model, it will often not be possible to resolve all questions for an alignment exercise. Thus it will be necessary either to contact the author of the target model, to have access to the source code, or to have access to a documentation of the target model more complete than is generally provided in accounts published in contemporary journals.

The meeting also determined what steps were to be taken next. Axtell spent an evening doing additional programming. The next day it was possible to run a number of cases that would be needed to build a Sugarscape version of the Axelrod results.

Two months later, while preparing to write up the results, Axtell realized that another change was necessary for the docking. Whereas the ACM altered the active agent when a cultural borrowing happened, the original Sugarscape model altered the agent's neighbor. This made a subtle difference because agents on the edge of the territory have fewer neighbors than those in the interior. To be sure that every site had the same chance to change, the ACM method is needed. When this was realized, Axtell made the necessary change to the Sugarscape implementation, and generated the data shown in Table A-1 and Figure A-1.

5.2   Total Time Required

The various tasks entailed in this docking exercise and the experimental extensions of the ACM are listed in the Tables A-2 and A-3. These two tables provide a description of the specific tasks undertaken by Axelrod and Axtell respectively, along with the times required for each. All told, the work took about twenty-three hours for Axelrod and thirty-seven hours for Axtell.[15]

5.3 Factors Making This Case Relatively Easy

There are at least four factors that can be identified as contributing to the relative ease with which the equivalence test was accomplished. First, the Sugarscape program was written from the outset with the objective of maximizing generality and ease of change. These goals are not especially easy to attain in practice, but object-oriented programming certainly did help.[16]

A second positive contributing factor is the extreme simplicity of the Axelrod model. This allowed the prose description to be essentially complete. Had ACM contained as many processes as Sugarscape, it would have been considerably more difficult to bring the two so fully into alignment.

A third factor was the recency of the ACM project. The statistical comparison required the full 210 points underlying the results reported in the original article.[17] These were relatively easy for the original investigator to provide, but this might not be so in other cases.

A fourth factor, already mentioned briefly, is the underlying agreement of the two models on a basic, "agent-oriented" framework. In the absence of that, the architectures of the two models might have been so different as to make the project inconceivable.

5.4 Factors Making This Case Relatively Hard

On the other side of the ledger, there are several factors in this case study that probably made the exercise more difficult than future cases might be. Foremost among these is the probability that in the future models may be built with a prospect of equivalence testing clearly in view. ACM did not exist when Sugarscape was designed. Thus, demonstrating equivalence to the ACM was not among its design specifications. If it had been, the equivalence testing could have been simpler still.

Also, one can plausibly imagine that there may someday be a number of more standardized code modules available that are reused in succes-

[15] These numbers do not include the time spent by all four participants in writing this report.

[16] It should also be said that Axtell, the lead programmer on Sugarscape, is a relatively skilled practitioner. He does not have experience producing commercial quality code, but his training did include doctoral-level course work in computer science.

[17] There were ten runs for each of the nine cases in Table A-1, and forty runs from each of the three cases used for comparison from Figure A-1.

TABLE A-2
Axelrod's Work Log

Design of the Replication Study

1. Discussion with Cohen about the general idea of the replication experiment, including the suitability of my cultural model and Sugarscape for this purpose. (hours:minutes, 3:00)

2. Writing letter to Axtell and Epstein specifying what we came to call the docking experiment, including the choice of data points to be compared. (Cohen had already discussed the idea with them in Vienna.) (1:00)

3. Trip arrangements for Axtell and Epstein. (1:00)

4. Discussion among all four of us of the docking experiment and its motivation, especially the importance of doing what we came to call distributional equivalence, rather than relational equivalence. (1:00)

5. Discussion among all four of us about the details of Axelrod's cultural model. This included discussion about the sentence that said "the chance of interaction is proportional to the cultural similarity two neighbors already have," where cultural similarity is the proportion of attributes that have the same value. Axtell had implemented this literally, but I pointed out that I actually used a more efficient (and equivalent) method, namely, to allow interaction if a single randomly chosen attribute has the same value. (1:00)

6. Preliminary specification of what became the mobility experiment. See Section 4.3.1. (2:00)

SUBTOTAL: 9:00

Data Analysis

1. Extraction of key raw data from my old computer output for Axtell to use in comparing my data to his. (1:00)

2. Communications with Axtell about receiving his data, and updating it after he corrected for changing the agent rather than the neighbor. See Section 5.1. (2:30)

3. Discussions with Cohen and a statistical consultant, Pat Guire, on proper statistical testing. (3:00)

4. Putting Axtell's data in a format comparable to mine, and calculating basic statistics. (2:00)

5. Consideration of alternative possible reasons why the original attempt at docking did not succeed for the 20×20 case. Development of tests of these possibilities (e.g., a bug in my code or Axtell's code) and identification of the likely cause as differences in the activation methods. See Section 4.2. (5:30)

SUBTOTAL: 14:00
GRAND TOTAL: 23:00

TABLE A-3
Axtell's Work Log

Code Changes Accomplished in Ann Arbor

---

1. Generalize culture representation from type BOOLEAN to an enumerated type. (hours: minutes, 0:10)
   2. Change agent initialization:
      A. Fill lattice densely with agents. (0:20)
      B. Give agents random initial cultures. (0:20)
   3. Implement a version of Axelrod's culture rule. (1:00)
   4. Draw boundaries between agents not culturally identical. (0:30)
   5. New stopping criterion. (0:15)
   6. Count distinct cultures (surrogate for counting regions). (0:15)
   7. Switch landscape from torus to square. (negligible, <0:01)
   8. Turn off all other Sugarscape rules. (negligible, <0:01)
   9. Debugging all of above. (1:00)
      SUBTOTAL: 3:50

Subsequent Code Modifications

---

1. Modify neighborhood representation so that agents on the border of the lattice do not attempt to interact with nonexistent (NIL) neighbors. (0:30)
   2. Represent regions as social networks and then use "clique-size" of social network object to count regions. (this obviated the need for #6 above.) (0:30)
   3. File output of number of cultural regions. (0:10)
      SUBTOTAL: 1:10

Running the Model

---

1. Make executable files for various parameter settings. (0:40)
   2. 90 runs for comparison to Axelrod's data on features and values/feature. See Table A-1. (2:00)
   3. 120 runs for comparison to Axelrod's data on lattice size. See Figure A-1. (8:00)
      SUBTOTAL: 10:40

Statistical Comparison

---

1. Development of Mann-Whitney U test in Mathematica. (2:00)
   2. Analysis of data using the Mann-Whitney U test. (1:00)
   3. Development of Kolmogorov-Smirnov (K-S) analysis routines in Mathematica. (4:00)
   4. Analysis of data using K-S test. (2:00)
      SUBTOTAL: 9:00

(Continued)

TABLE A-3
(*Continued*)

Mobility Experiment (see Section 4.3.1)

---

1. Modify the stopping criteria to consider agent interactions with the entire population. (0:10)
2. Time series plot for the distinct number of cultures. (1:00)
3. Instantiate a standard version of the Sugarscape with the Epstein-Axtell culture rule replaced by Axelrod's. (0:10)
4. Make executable file. (0:05)
5. Perform multiple runs of this model. (1:00)
  SUBTOTAL: 2:25

"Pure Soup" Experiment (see Section 4.3.2)

---

1. Instantiate soup version of the Sugarscape with Axelrod's culture rule. (0:10)
2. Make executable file. (0:05)
3. Perform multiple realizations of this model. (1:00)
  SUBTOTAL: 1:15

Re-docking (see Section 4.2)

---

1. Change agent activation from sequential to random. (0:10)
2. Re-run the model (40 runs). (8:00)
3. Analysis of new data. (0:20)
  SUBTOTAL: 8:30
  GRAND TOTAL: 36:50

---

sive modeling projects. Random number generators meet this criterion today, and more substantive model elements may do so in the future. This, too, could substantially decrease costs of equivalence testing.

Overall, we would say that we did not find it completely straightforward to align the two models. But we were able to accomplish it in the end. And although the difficulties we encountered in reconciling them may seem disquieting, we should recall that they are not without precedent. Differential and integral calculus produced different results in the hands of different investigators until the foundations were solidified in the nineteenth century by the work of Cauchy and Weierstrass (Kramer 1970). And what is the alternative to confronting these difficulties, to look away and rest our theorizing on unverified assumptions of equivalence?

6.   Observations on the Value and Difficulties of Alignment

We conclude with some further observation on three matters: whether the face-to-face meeting we used in this alignment effort is likely to be typical; how we might label different approaches to defining "equivalence"; and a brief proposal for the use of equivalence tests in evaluations made of journal submissions and research funding proposals.

There is one point at which the process we report might not be typical of alignments that would be done in the future, if this kind of analysis were to become more common. A meeting, such as Epstein and Axtell had with Axelrod, might not be necessary in general. The meeting that was held served two functions: establishing details about the procedure of alignment and clarifying ambiguous aspects of the ACM. If the situation were one of comparison to a published model situated in an established line of research, the former issues might be decided entirely by the author of a new model who seeks to establish its equivalence to an older one. This situation is one that we imagine might become more usual.

The second function of the meeting, resolving ambiguities about the construction of the target model, is not one that we imagine is likely to go away. On the contrary, many target models will be considerably more complex than the ACM. However, it may also be true that those attempting to show a new model equivalent to an old one will have source code for the old one—a resource that was deliberately not employed in this case. It may also be true that the criteria of equivalence may be looser than they were in this case, a point we discuss below.

Considering all these factors, our impression is that good alignments can be made without actual meetings of model authors. This will be all the more likely if authors who report their models begin to assume that alignments may later be tried and thus become careful about providing information that may be essential to such efforts. We emphasize that (1) a precise, detailed statement of how the model works is critical, and (2) distributional information about reported measurements is necessary if statistical methods to test equivalence are to be employed by a later investigator.

As we noted above, the problem of specifying what will be taken as "equivalent" model behavior is by no means trivial. Our reflections on it suggest that there are at least two categories of equivalence beyond the obvious criterion of numerical identity, which will not be expected in any models that have stochastic elements. We call these two categories "distributional" and "relational" equivalence. By distributional equivalence we mean a showing that two models produce distributions of results that cannot be distinguished statistically. This is the level of equivalence we eventually chose to test for in our case. By "relational equivalence" we mean that the two models can be shown to produce the same internal relationship among their results. For example, both models might show a particular variable is a quadratic function of time, or that some measure on a population decreases monotonically with population size.

Clearly, relational equivalence will generally be a "weaker," less demanding test. But for many theoretical purposes it may suffice. And distributional equivalence may sometimes be possible only with alignment of parametric details of the two models that would be quite laborious to achieve.

Finally, our generally positive experience in this enterprise has suggested to us that it could be beneficial if alignment and equivalence testing were more widely practiced among computational modelers. It can be done within the reasonable effort level of a few days' or weeks' work—possibly less if it is planned for from the outset. And the consequences are quite large. The Sugarscape group can now say with confidence that their model can be modified to reproduce the ACM results, and they can point to specific mechanisms of Sugarscape that are sufficient to change the effect of the ACM transmission mechanism. This begins to build confidence that other results with Sugarscape may be robust over potential variation in the specifics of its cultural transmission process.

Readers of papers on Sugarscape and the ACM can now have a clearer conception of how they relate to each other. And future modelers of cultural transmission will have a clearer understanding of the likely consequences of different transmission mechanisms. In short, the interested community obtains from such an exercise an improved sense of the robustness, the range of plausibility, of model results. And points of difference have been established that could allow empirical evidence to discriminate between the models. These are major hallmarks of cumulative disciplinary theorizing that are unavailable without alignment of models.

We are led to the suggestion that it might be valuable if authors of computational models knew they would receive credit for having made such alignments. If reviewers of journal and research grant submissions were encouraged to give substantial positive weight to such demonstrations, and authors knew of this policy, the effects could be dramatic. Among other things, this would create an incentive to establish a model in an area of inquiry that could readily serve as a "benchmark" for comparisons by later models. The result might well be more—and more extensive—families of computational models displaying an explicit and clear network of relations to each other. This would be an important gain over the current situation in which, with a small number of exceptions, each model has been constructed entirely de novo.

Computational modeling offers a striking opportunity to fashion miniature worlds, and this appeals to powerful creative impulses within all of us. William Blake expressed this deep need, writing in his *Jerusalem* ([1804] 1974, pl. 10, 1.20): "I must Create a System, or be enslav'd by another Man's; / I will not Reason and Compare: my business is to Create." But if these wonderful new possibilities of computational modeling are to become intellectual tools well harnessed to the requirements of advancing our understanding of social systems, then we must overcome the natural impulse for self-contained creation and carefully develop the methodology of using them to "Reason and Compare."

References

Anderson, Paul A., and Gregory W. Fischer. 1986. "A Monte Carlo Model of a Garbage Can Decision Process." In *Ambiguity and Command: Organizational Perspective on Military Decision Making,* ed. James March and Roger Weissinger-Baylon, 140–64. Marshfield, Mass.: Pitman Publishing, Inc.

Axelrod, R. 1997. "The Dissemination of Culture: A Model with Global Polarization." *Journal of Conflict Resolution* 41: 203–26, and included as Chapter 7 of this volume.

Blake, W. [1804] 1974. *Jerusalem, the Emanation of the Giant Albion.* London: B. Quarich.

Burton, R. M., and B. Obel. 1995. "The Validity of Computational Models in Organization Science: From Model Realism to Purpose of the Model." *Computational and Mathematical Organization Theory* 1: 57–71.

Carley, K. 1991. "A Theory of Group Stability." *American Sociological Review* 56: 331–54.

Cavalli-Sforza, L. L., and M. W. Feldman. 1981. *Cultural Transmission and Evolution: A Quantitative Approach.* Princeton, N.J.: Princeton University Press.

Cohen, M. D., J. G. March, and J. P. Olsen. 1972. "A Garbage Can Model of Organizational Choice." *Administrative Science Quarterly* 17: 1–25.

Cyert, R. M., and J. G. March. 1963. *A Behavioral Theory of the Firm.* Englewood Cliffs, N.J.: Prentice-Hall.

Dutton, J. M., and W. H. Starbuck. 1971. *Computer Simulation of Human Behavior.* New York: Wiley.

Efron, B., and R. J. Tibshirani. 1993. *An Introduction to the Bootstrap.* New York: Chapman and Hall.

Epstein, J. M., and R. Axtell. 1996. *Growing Artificial Societies: Social Science From the Bottom Up.* Washington, D.C.: The Brookings Institution; and Cambridge, Mass.: MIT Press.

Friedkin, N. E., and E. C. Johnsen. 1990. "Social Influence and Opinions." *Journal of Mathematical Sociology* 15: 193–205.

Harrison, J. R., and G. R. Carroll. 1991. "Keeping the Faith: A Model of Cultural Transmission in Formal Organizations." *Administrative Science Quarterly* 36: 552–82.

Hoel, P. G. 1962. *Introduction to Mathematical Statistics.* 3d ed. New York: Wiley.

Knepell, P. L., and D. Arangno. 1993. *Simulation Validation, A Confidence Assessment Methodology.* Los Alamitos, Calif.: IEEE Computer Society Press.

Kramer, E. E. 1970. *The Nature and Growth of Modern Mathematics,* vol. 2. Greenwich, Conn.: Fawcett.

Lane, D. 1993. "Artificial Worlds and Economics, Parts 1 and 2." *Journal of Evolutionary Economics* 3: 89–107, 177–97.

Latour, B., and S. Woolgar. 1979. *Laboratory Life: The Social Construction of Scientific Facts.* Beverly Hills, Calif.: Sage Publications.

March, J. G. 1991. "Exploration and Exploitation in Organizational Learning." *Organization Science* 2: 71–87.

Nowak, A., J. Szamrej, and B. Latane. 1990. "From Private Attitude to Public Opinion: A Dynamic Theory of Social Impact." *Psychological Review* 97: 362–76.

Putnam, R. 1966. "Political Attitudes and the Local Community." *American Political Science Review* 60: 640–54.

Renfrew, C., ed. 1973. *The Explanation of Social Influence: Models in Prehistory.* Pittsburgh: University of Pittsburgh Press.

Sabloff, J. A., ed. 1981. *Simulations in Archeology.* Albuquerque: University of New Mexico Press.

Siegel, S. 1956. *Nonparametric Statistics for the Behavioral Sciences.* New York: McGraw-Hill.

Wuensche, A., and M. J. Lesser. 1992. *The Global Dynamics of Cellular Automata: An Atlas of Basin of Attraction Fields of One-Dimensional Cellular Automata.* Reading, Mass.: Addison-Wesley.

B

Resources for Agent-Based Modeling

COMPLEXITY THEORY and agent-based modeling are relatively new to the social sciences. For this reason, there are no comprehensive textbooks and few university courses on the subject. People who want to learn the research techniques of agent-based modeling are generally on their own.

At the University of Michigan, I recently taught a "hands-on" course on Complexity Theory in the Social Sciences. The primary focus was on learning how to do agent-based modeling by studying examples and doing projects. The course attracted undergraduate and graduate students from political science, economics, anthropology, biophysics, and computer science. It also attracted faculty auditors from political science, mathematics, business, and psychiatry. Preparing this course gave me an opportunity to collect a variety of resources in the field, and forced me to decide what is really worth learning. Teaching the course gave me a sense of what questions and problems students are most likely to have.

Listening to students from such a wide range of backgrounds reinforced my appreciation of just how important our traditional disciplines are for shaping our understanding of the universe. For example, an economics student implicitly equated "behavior" with "choice," and "choice" with "rational choice." This is quite a leap. A political science student wondered whether the leap is warranted, and an anthropologist was quite certain that it was not. People from biophysics or computer science considered "choice" as simply a matter of optimization or adaptation, depending on the problem.

Despite such huge differences in perspective, the concepts of complexity theory and the techniques of agent-based modeling can indeed serve as effective research tools for all of these disciplines. Even better, they allow people to learn from each other despite their differences. Just as game theory has served to unite studies of strategy across the social sciences and evolutionary biology, so complexity theory and agent-based modeling may serve to unite studies of emergent phenomena across an equally wide range of fields. For example, the student projects in my course ranged from the design of institutions for fishing rights and digital libraries, to the understanding of traffic congestion and protein folding.

The material offered here is intended for either teachers or independent students of agent-based modeling.

If you undertake to build and run an agent-based model, rather than just read about them, you are in for some real fun. It is delightful to watch a creation of your own perform. The agents sometimes seem to just get up and walk around. A society of agents very often does things that you as its creator never dreamed it would or even could do. As Kelly (1994, 351) points out, it is human to want to give life and freedom—to say, "Here's your life *and* the car keys."

Reference

Kelly, Kevin. 1994. *Out of Control: The Rise of Neo-Biological Civilization.* Reading, Mass.: Addison-Wesley.

Resources for Agent-Based Modeling

This appendix offers resources to learn more about complexity theory and agent-based modeling in the social sciences. The three sections provide:

advice on computer simulation techniques,
exercises for learning how to do agent-based modeling, and
a syllabus for a short course in agent-based modeling in the social sciences.

Associated with this volume is an Internet site.[1] The site provides links to the source code and documentation for most of the models in this book, as well as the exercises in this Appendix. The site also provides links to information about literature, people, organizations, software, and educational opportunities related to complexity, agent-based modeling, and cooperation.

Computer Simulation for Agent-Based Modeling

Programming Your Own Agent-Based Model

There are several programming environments specifically designed for agent-based models.

1. StarLogo is a programmable modeling environment for exploring the behaviors of decentralized systems, such as bird flocks, traffic jams, and ant colonies. It is designed especially for use by students. Resnick (1994) provides an excellent introduction. Although not designed for serious research, StarLogo does provide an easy way to get started in agent-based modeling for someone who has never done any programming. StarLogo is available for Macintosh computers free of charge on the Internet. Another version of the Logo family that can run many agents at once is available commercially as Microworlds Project Builder. It comes with an excellent user interface, and is available in both PC and Macintosh versions.

2. For advanced programmers, the Swarm programming environment provides a very rich set of tools for agent-based modeling. It allows nested hierarchies of agents, full control of the scheduling of events, and probes to report the current state of the agents and their environment. The Swarm system is available free from the Web site of the Santa Fe

---

[1] http://pscs.physics.lsa.umich.edu/Software/ComplexCoop.html

Institute. The system runs in UNIX, and requires programming in Objective C. The aspiration of the designers is that the community of Swarm users will be able to share each other's ever-expanding set of simulation tools. For those familiar with UNIX and any object-oriented version of C, Swarm is a good choice because its powerful tools make it easy to implement a new model and to analyze its dynamics.

Selecting a Programming Language

Because StarLogo is not designed for serious research, and Swarm requires considerable programming sophistication, many modelers prefer to work with the general-purpose tools that come with the compiler of a standard programming language. This leads to the question of which programming language to use. My answer is that although many types of programming languages exist, a beginner should select a procedural language.[2] The most common procedural languages are Basic, FORTRAN, Pascal, and C. These languages have different histories and characteristics.

1. Basic is designed for beginners, and is perhaps the simplest to learn and use. It is suitable for small projects, but usually runs slower than the other languages for projects involving large amounts of computation. The early versions of Basic were quite rudimentary, but recent versions are a delight to use. For example, Visual Basic has tools for constructing good user interfaces, as well as tools for debugging. Visual Basic is available within some spreadsheet programs such as Excel. The integration of a programming language within a spreadsheet is a very convenient way to combine the full control of a programming language with the intuitive look and feel of a spreadsheet.

2. FORTRAN is an old language that is not as convenient to use as the others. Because of its age and prior popularity, many programmers are familiar with it, and many old programs are available in FORTRAN.

---

[2] Among the alternatives to the common procedural languages are the following: LISP is a functional language preferred by many researchers in artificial intelligence, and is especially good for handling data structures and programs interchangeably. Unfortunately, LISP is relatively difficult to learn, and typically runs much slower than compiled procedural languages.

Mathematica and Maple are functional languages that are especially good for data analysis and graphics.

Stella is designed for problems involving systems of difference or differential equations. Unfortunately, it is usually not easy to represent an agent-based model in this framework.

Gauss is designed for advanced statistical problems. It makes it easy to do matrix manipulation, for example. Unfortunately, most agent-based models cannot be easily represented in ways that exploit Gauss's strengths.

A beginner, however, should definitely pick one of the more modern languages.

3. Pascal was designed to be a first language for serious programmers. It is easy to learn, and is structured to encourage good programming habits. Most of simulations in this volume were programmed in Pascal.

4. C is the most common procedural language among serious programmers. It is designed to allow relatively easy conversion between one type of computer and other. It includes many shortcuts that a beginner need not learn. Unfortunately, the availability of these shortcuts can make understanding someone else's C code difficult. Besides the popularity and compatibility of C, another advantage is that it is the basis of the most popular object-oriented language, C++. An object-oriented language makes really large projects easier to program. It also makes it much easier to use portions of an old program in a new context. For all these reasons, C++ was chosen as the foundation for the Java programming language designed to be used over the World Wide Web.

Where do all these options leave the beginner? If you are a beginner to programming, my advice is to avoid FORTRAN and pick one of the others based upon what help is readily available. What you will need most is someone who can answer questions when you get stuck. If a friend or coworker is available to answer questions about Pascal, for example, pick Pascal. Alternatively, if you want to take a programming course and there is one available on C, then that would be a good choice. If the availability of help or instruction does not lead to a clear choice, then you can make a decision based on how serious you plan to be about programming. If you just want to try it out to get a feel for doing your own programming or because you have a simple idea you want to test, then Visual Basic is a good choice. If you are fairly sure that you will be doing programming for some time and want to start with a language that you can grow with, then C or C++ is the best choice.

Goals of Good Agent-Based Programming

The programming of an agent-based model should achieve three goals: validity, usability, and extendability.

The goal of validity is for the program to correctly implement the model. (Whether or not the model itself is an accurate representation of the real world is a different kind of validity, which is not considered here.) Achieving validity is harder than it might seem. The problem is knowing whether an unexpected result is a reflection of a mistake in the programming or a surprising consequence of the model itself. For example, in the model of social influence presented in Chapter 7, there were fewer stable regions in very large territories than there were in middle-sized territories. Careful analysis was required to confirm that this result was a consequence of the model, and not due to a bug in the program.[3]

The goal of usability is to allow you and those who follow to run the program, interpret its output, and understand how it works. You may be changing what you want to achieve while you do the programming. This means that you will generate whole series of programs, each version differing from the others in a variety of ways. Versions can differ, for example, in which data are produced, which parameters are adjustable, and even which rules govern agent behavior. Keeping track of all this is not trivial, especially when one tries to compare new results with output of an earlier version of the program to determine exactly what might account for the differences.

The goal of extendability is to allow a future user (including your future self) to adapt the program for new uses. For example, after writing a paper using the model, the researcher might want to respond to a question about what would happen if a new feature were added. In addition, another researcher might someday want to modify the program to try out a new variant of the model. A program is much more likely to be extendable if it is written and documented with this goal in mind.

Project Management

In order to be able to achieve the goals of validation, usability, and extendability, considerable care must be taken in the entire research enterprise. This includes not just the programming, but also the documentation and data analysis. I often find myself wanting to get on with the programming as quickly as possible to see the output of the simulation. Whether I do the programming and documentation myself or use a research assistant, I tend to be too eager to see results. I have learned the hard way that haste does indeed make waste. Quick results are often unreliable. Good habits slow things down at first, but speed things up in the long run. Good habits help by avoiding some costly mistakes and confusion that can take a great deal of effort to unravel.

If you are just beginning to do computer simulation, it pays to build good habits. Your own needs will depend upon your programming experience and the demands of the project. The aim is to develop a set of

---

[3] Indeed, one of the contributions of the alignment exercise of Appendix A was to confirm the validity of the original program.

habits that are effective, with a minimum of administrative overhead. Here are some recommendations based upon my own experience:

1. Use long names for almost all of the variables rather than short names that will be incomprehensible a month later. It is fine to use i and j, or x and y for a few really common variables. Beyond that, however, the clarity of long names is worth the extra typing or cutting and pasting.

2. List all the variables at the start of the program. Some languages, such as Pascal and C, require you to declare all the variables and their type (e.g., integer or floating point) before you use them. Other languages, such as Visual Basic, make explicit declaration of variables optional. Force yourself to be explicit about declaring variables in advance of their use. This will save you many hours of debugging by warning you that a misspelled variable name deep in the code is illegal, rather than letting the compiler make the false assumption that it is meant to be a new variable.

3. Write helpful comments. For example, when you declare a variable, write a comment about what the variable is intended to represent, and how it is distinguished from related variables. Likewise, write comments in the body of the code to describe what each subroutine does and how it fits into the main program. It is a good idea to have as much text in comments as in code. Days or months later, these comments can be very useful.

4. Develop the sequence of programs so that they are upwardly compatible. This means that later versions should include all the useful features of old versions. Suppose, for example, that you start with a model that employs a 10×10 array of cells, each with exactly four neighbors. You can do this by having the map "wrap around," thereby making cells on the north and south edges into neighbors, and doing the same for cells on the east and west edges. Suppose that you later wanted to have a flat map with boundaries at the edges. You should not delete the portion of the code that deals with the neighborhoods on the original map. Instead, you should isolate that portion as a subroutine, and write another subroutine dealing with the neighborhoods on the new map. Then add a control parameter to serve as a switch specifying whether a given run uses the wrap-around map or the flat map. Doing it this way gives you the option to return to a wrap-around map at a later time.

5. Fully label the output. The output should include the time and date of the run, a sequential run number, the version number of the program, the settings of all the parameters that specify the nature of the run, and the random number seed if there is one. The output should allow you to replicate a run precisely. If the versions are upwardly compatible, as suggested earlier, then you will be able to replicate a previous run using any later version of the program.

6. Practice defensive programming. Taking a few minutes to be cautious can save hours of searching for a mysterious bug. As already mentioned, it pays to explicitly declare all variables so that some typos can be caught early, and it pays to use long variable names so that a month later you do not get confused about what a mysterious "XKLT" might mean. Another defensive move is to declare the intended limits of your variables so that you can use the automatic debugging features of your compiler. For example, if the Agent_X_Location should be between 1 and Max-_X_Coordinate, then be sure that your compiler knows this, or that you confirm it in your code. Finally, using a programming technique called pointers is dangerous. Although pointers can be the most efficient way to program certain relationships, they should be used with great care because a mistake with a pointer can often cause bizarre symptoms that can be hard to isolate and repair.

7. Document each version of the code as you go. The documentation should include the exact specification of the model, a description of the algorithms used in the calculations, details about the inputs needed, and information about how to read the output. Explaining the output is particularly important because a column of data typically has such a brief label that you may not be sure what it means a month later. In many cases, the documentation of a new version can be as simple as the following: "Version 2.3 is the same as version 2.2 except an option is added to have a flat map. This is implemented by setting Flat_Map to True. If Flat_Map is False, then the map is wrap around as in previous versions." The documentation need not be elegant or concise. It does need to be complete and accurate. It pays to put some documentation into the program itself, but usually full documentation is more easily managed as a memo written with your word processor.

8. Use a commercial program to do most of the data analysis. Within your program do only simple data analysis, such as the calculations of averages, to reduce the amount of output that is required. Beyond that, it pays to use reliable software developed by others. For example, a good spreadsheet will allow you to manipulate the variables, do simple statistical analysis, and graph the data in different ways. An alternative to a spreadsheet is a program like Mathematica that includes not only statistical and graphics capability, but also a well-organized notebook structure to keep track of your work.

9. In validating the program, check the microdynamics, not just the aggregate results. Because agent-based models often have surprising results, you typically cannot confirm the code by checking its output against known results, as you could with a prime number generator, for example. Instead you need to confirm that your program is correctly handling the details. For example, you should check how a given agent be-

haves in the various possible circumstances. This will require interim reports that are much more detailed than you will usually need for the main data analysis.

10. If the modeler and the programmer are two different people, make sure the two of you understand each other at each step. It is surprisingly easy for two people to be confident they understand each other, and then find out much later that there was a subtle difference in what each thought they had agreed upon. Because it is not easy to validate an agent-based model, it is especially important that this sort of programming be based on thorough and accurate communication between the modeler and the programmer.

There is more to project management than good programming. You also need to develop systematic methods for archiving the output, analyzing the data, and interpreting the results. For example, it is a good idea to write memos to yourself as you go about your interpretation of particular runs. Like the documentation, these memos need not be concise or elegant, but they do need to be accurate. For example, suppose you are doing sets of runs to see what difference it makes whether the map is flat or wrap-around. When you get the results you can write a brief memo comparing a set of runs done one way with a set of runs done the other way. The memo should include the identifying information from the output, such as the version number of the program, the parameter settings, and the run numbers. This can easily be done by opening the output file from your word processor, selecting the required information, and pasting it into the memo you are writing. Then you can write your interpretation of the data, including a graph or two copied from your analysis of the comparative data. A series of memos such as these can serve as a "lab notebook" recording your progress in understanding the implications of your modeling decisions. Eventually, the memos can provide the basis for the data analysis section of your final report.

Exercises

The best way to learn about agent-based modeling is to build and run some model. Here is a set of exercises that can help you get started. Each one can be done in a few days once you have mastered a programming language. These exercises are suitable for classroom use or independent study. The first three exercises can be done by relatively simple modifications of source code available on the Internet.[4]

---

[4] See the first footnote of this Appendix.

Exercise 1. Schelling's Tipping Model

Thomas Schelling, who is best known for his work on deterrence theory, was also one of the pioneers in the field of agent-based modeling. He emphasized the value of starting with rules of behavior for individuals and using simulation to discover the implications for large-scale outcomes. He called this "micromotives and macrobehavior" (Schelling 1978).

One of his models demonstrates how even fairly tolerant people can behave in ways that can lead to quite segregated neighborhoods. This is his famous tipping model (Schelling 1978, 137–55). It is quite simple. The space is a checkerboard with sixty-four squares representing places where people can live. There are two types of actors, represented by pennies and nickels. One can imagine the actors as Whites and Blacks. The coins are placed at random among the squares, with no more than one per square. The basic idea is that an actor will be content if more than one-third of its immediate neighbors are of the same type as itself. The immediate neighbors are the occupants of the adjacent squares. For example, if all the eight adjacent squares were occupied, then the actor is content if at least three of them are the same type as itself. If an actor is content, it stays put. If it is not content, it moves. In Schelling's original model, it would move to one of the nearest squares where it would be content. For the purposes of this exercise, it is easier to use a variant of the model in which a discontented actor moves to one of the empty squares selected at random.

The exercise is to implement this model and explore its behavior. In particular, test one of Schelling's speculations about his tipping model. His speculation was, "Perhaps . . . if surfers mind the presence of swimmers less than swimmers mind the presence of surfers . . . the surfers will enjoy a greater expanse of water" (Schelling 1978, 153).

To make things concrete, assume there are twenty surfers and twenty swimmers.[5] Let the surfers be content if at least a third of their neighbors are surfers, and let the swimmers be content if at least half of *their* neighbors are swimmers. The actors can be numbered 1 to 40, and activated in the same order each cycle. Run the model for fifty cycles. Then for each of the twenty-four empty cells, write an A in the cell if more of its neighbors are surfers than swimmers, and write a B in the cell if more of its neighbors are swimmers than surfers. (It will probably be easier to do this step by hand than to automate it.) Then see if the surfers enjoy a greater expanse of water by seeing if there are more A's than B's. Do ten runs to get some idea of the distribution of results.

[5] Schelling made his speculation in the context of unequal numbers for the two types, but equal numbers are a good place to start.

If you are a beginner, you might want to take advantage of source code and documentation I have written to implement this variant of Schelling's model. The source code is available both in Visual Basic and Pascal. Doing the exercise would then require making some simple modifications in the code to allow the two types of actors to have different requirements to be content.

Exercise 2. Schelling's Tipping Model, Continued

The purpose of this exercise is to study some of the effects of having unequal numbers of the two types of actors. You should use the variant of Schelling's model described in the first exercise. The exercise is to answer these two questions and explain why things worked out as they did:

1. Do minorities get packed in tighter than majorities?
2. Does the process settle down faster when the numbers are unequal?

To make things concrete, use thirty Whites and ten Blacks, both with the original (and equal) requirements for contentment. For density studies, use the A and B measures described for the first exercise.

You should arrange to stop a run when no further change is possible. An easy way to do this is use periods of at least forty events to allow each actor to be checked at least once. If there has been no movement in the current period, that would imply that everyone is content and no will ever move again. As in the first exercise, a beginner may choose to use the source code provided, and make the necessary changes.

Exercise 3. Extending the Social Influence Model

To gain practice in extending an existing model, here is an exercise based on the model of social influence described in Chapter 7. The model is simple enough that even adding an extension keeps it quite manageable. The purpose of this exercise is to implement a particular extension of the model to see what insights can be gleaned.

A dozen suggestions are briefly outlined in the section of Chapter 7 on "Extensions of the Model." Here are some more details about two of these possibilities.

Early Geographic Differences. The initial values of cultural features are assigned at random in the basic model. A wide variety of interesting experiments could be conducted by having some or all of the features given particular values. For example, suppose one wanted to study the effects of the seemingly universal phenomenon that "things are different in the south." An easy way to do this would be to give one or two of the cultural features one value in the northern sites, and a different value in the southern sites. Would regions tend to form based on these small initial differences? If so, would the eventual boundary between the regions closely correspond to the initial line between the north and the south? Another example of an interesting experiment would be to see how easy or hard it is for an initial advantage in numbers to take over the entire space. A simple way to study this is by giving a slight bias in the original assignment of values to features throughout the space, and then seeing how much bias it takes to overcome the tendency to get swamped by random variations, and eventually to dominate the entire space.

Cultural Attractiveness. Some cultural features might be favored in the adoption process over others. For example, Arabic numbers are more likely to be adopted by people using Roman numerals than the other way around. This differential attractiveness of cultural features might be due to superior technology (as in this case of number systems), or it might be due to seemingly arbitrary preferences. One way to model this process would be to favor higher values of a given cultural feature over lower values. Presumably, features that are culturally attractive would tend to drive out less attractive features. Just how attractive does a feature have to be to dominate? Does the process of differential attractiveness lead to larger (and thus fewer) regions?

Incidentally, I do not have good answers to the questions raised by these two suggested extensions or any of the others mentioned in Chapter 7. These are open research topics.

Source code and documentation for the social influence model is available on the Internet in both Visual Basic and Pascal.[6]

Exercise 4. Standing Ovation

Consider the situation in which people are seated in an auditorium listening to a brilliant performance. At the end, the applause begins, and perhaps a standing ovation ensues. The exercise is to model the process of a standing ovation. You should consider potentially interesting future directions for your model. You should also consider whether there are some economic or social scenarios that could be usefully modeled using such a process.[7]

---

[6] See the first footnote of this Appendix.

[7] This exercise is adapted from a homework problem given in the 1995 Santa Fe Institute Graduate Workshop in Computational Economics. It was placed on the Internet with some original answers at http://zia.hss.cmu.edu/econ/homework95.

Exercise 5. Human Waves

People are seated in a football stadium. Someone gets up and shouts, "Wave." A human wave can be formed if everyone follows rule A: stand up for one second if either (or both) immediate neighbors are standing.

To keep things simple, suppose there are only twenty people, and they are seated in a circle around the field. These people can be represented as being on a line, with the understanding that person 20 is adjacent to person 1 as well as person 19.

Now suppose that people also follow rule B, which says that regardless of rule A, once a person sits down, he or she stays seated for at least two seconds.

The first part of the exercise is to compare what will happen under rule A alone, and under the combination of rules A and B.

The second part of the exercise is to modify the A-B model to take into account some or all of the following observations:

1. A human wave actually moves in one rather than two directions.
2. A human wave can continue even if there is one person who never stands.
3. A human wave eventually dies out.
4. Some people need to stay seated for more than two seconds.

A Short Course in Agent-Based Modeling in the Social Sciences

If you want a structured way to learn more about applications of complexity theory in the social sciences, here is the outline of a short course that you can do on your own. It is designed for advanced undergraduates or graduate students. The only prerequisite is knowledge of some programming language if you want to do the exercises.

The fact that complexity theory is a new and rapidly evolving field has two important implications for how the course is designed. First, there is not yet a comprehensive textbook for complexity theory. Therefore, the best way to learn the field is to read mainly original research. Second, because the principal methodology of complexity theory in the social sciences is agent-based modeling, the best way to learn the field is to study a variety of specific models. Each of the reports on specific models contains not only ideas for how to do modeling, but also useful techniques for the analysis of simulation data, and examples of how to draw inferences from the performance of the models for the understanding of real social problems. Even if you are interested primarily in a single discipline, you will find that readings on many of the topics contain ideas that can be used in your own field of interest.

The course considers a wide variety of applications of agent-based models to the social sciences, including elections, markets, residential segregation, social influence, war, alliances, nation formation, and organizational change. Among the issues examined across models are path dependence, sensitivity to initial conditions, emergence of self-organized structure, adaptation to a changing environment, and criteria for judging the value of an agent-based model.

The exercises described above can be done in tandem with the readings. The first three exercises can be done within the first four weeks. Either or both of the other two exercises can be done by the seventh week.

If you are an instructor interested in developing a semester-long course, I would suggest adding a major project to the readings and exercises. The project could be the development and analysis of an original agent-based model (perhaps one based in part on someone else's model), or the project could be a review and criticism of an application of complexity theory to a specific domain. The projects could be done by individuals or small groups. The last few weeks of the class could be devoted mainly to student reports on their projects.

Additional suggested readings are available on the Internet.[8]

Course Outline

1. Introduction to Complexity Theory
   Chapter 1 of this volume.
   Schelling, Thomas. 1978. *Micromotives and Macrobehavior.* New York: Norton, pp. 137–55.

2. Agent-Based Models
   Resnick, Mitchel. 1994. *Turtles, Termites, and Traffic Jams: Explorations in Massively Parallel Microworlds.* Cambridge, Mass.: MIT Press, pp. 3–19, on decentralization.
   Epstein, Joshua M., and Robert Axtell. 1996. *Growing Artificial Societies: Social Science from the Bottom Up.* Washington, D.C.: Brookings Institution Press; and Cambridge, Mass.: MIT Press, introduction.
   Poundstone, William. 1985. *The Recursive Universe: Cosmic Complexity and the Limits of Scientific Knowledge.* Chicago: Contemporary Books, pp. 24–37, on the Game of Life. Programs to run the Game of Life are available on the Internet.

---

[8] The Internet site associated with this volume includes links to a wide variety of additional source material on complexity theory. See the first footnote of this Appendix.

3. Social Influence

Axelrod, Robert. 1997. "The Dissemination of Culture: A Model with Local Convergence and Global Polarization." *Journal of Conflict Resolution* 41: 203–26. Included as Chapter 7 of this volume.

Axtell, Robert, Robert Axelrod, Joshua Epstein, and Michael D. Cohen. 1996. "Aligning Simulation Models: A Case Study and Results." *Computational and Mathematical Organization Theory* 1: 123–41. Included in this volume as Appendix A.

4. Organization Theory

March, James G. 1991. "Exploration and Exploitation in Organizational Learning." *Organization Science* 2: 71–87.

Simon, Herbert. 1982. *The Sciences of the Artificial.* 2d ed. Cambridge, Mass.: MIT Press, pp. 193–230.

5. Politics

Kollman, Ken, John H. Miller, and Scott E. Page. 1992. "Adaptive Parties in Spatial Elections." *American Political Science Review* 86: 929–37.

Cederman, Lars-Erik. Forthcoming. *Emergent Actors in World Politics: How States and Nations Develop and Dissolve.* Princeton, N.J.: Princeton University Press, chapters 8 and 9.

6. Genetic Algorithm and the Prisoner's Dilemma

Holland, John H. 1992. "Genetic Algorithms." *Scientific American* 267 (July): 66–72.

Riolo, Rick. 1992. "Survival of the Fittest." *Scientific American* 267 (July): 114–16, on how to make your own genetic algorithm.

(If you are not familiar with the Prisoner's Dilemma, read Axelrod, Robert. 1984. *The Evolution of Cooperation.* New York: Basic Books, pp. 3–69 and 158–68.)

Axelrod, Robert. 1987. "The Evolution of Strategies in the Iterated Prisoner's Dilemma." In *Genetic Algorithms and Simulated Annealing,* ed. Lawrence Davis, 32–41. London: Pitman; Los Altos, Calif.: Morgan Kaufman. Included in revised form as Chapter 1 of this volume.

7. Genetic Algorithm and the Prisoner's Dilemma, cont.

Lindgren, Kristian. 1991. "Evolutionary Phenomena in Simple Dynamics." In *Artificial Life II,* ed. C. G. Langton et al. Reading, Mass.: Addison-Wesley.

8. Economics

Arthur, W. Brian. 1988. "Urban Systems and Historical Path Dependence." In *Cities and Their Vital Systems,* ed. Jesse H. Ausubel and Robert Herman, 85–97. Washington D.C.: National Academy Press.

Arthur, W. Brian. 1993. "Why Do Things Become More Complex?" *Scientific American* (May): 144.

Epstein, Joshua M., and Robert Axtell. 1996. *Growing Artificial Societies: Social Science from the Bottom Up.* Washington D.C.: Brookings Institution Press; and Cambridge, Mass.: MIT Press, chapters II and IV.

Albin, Peter, and Duncan K. Foley. 1992. "Decentralized, Dispersed Exchange Without an Auctioneer: A Simulation Study." *Journal of Economic Behavior and Organization* 81: 27–51.

9. Concepts of Complexity

Resnick, Mitchel. 1994. *Turtles, Termites, and Traffic Jams: Explorations in Massively Parallel Microworlds.* Cambridge, Mass.: MIT Press, pp. 129–44, on decentralized mind-set.

Todd, Peter M. 1995. "Unsettling the Centralized Mindset." *Adaptive Behavior* 3: 225–29. A useful review of Resnick's book.

Gell-Mann, Murray. 1995. "What Is Complexity?" *Complexity* 1: 16–19, on measuring the degree of complexity in a system.

Holland, John. 1995. *Hidden Order.* Reading, Mass.: Addison-Wesley, pp. 1–40, on elements of a complex adaptive system.

Bak, Per, and Kan Chen. 1991. "Self-Organized Criticality." *Scientific American* (Jan.): 46–53.

10. Adaptive Landscapes

Axelrod, Robert, and D. Scott Bennett. 1993. "A Landscape Theory of Aggregation." *British Journal of Political Science* 23: 211–33. Included in this volume as Chapter 4.

Kauffman, Stuart. 1995. *At Home in the Universe: The Search for Laws of Self-Organization and Complexity.* New York and Oxford: Oxford University Press, pp. 252–71, on his patches model.

Coveney, Peter, and Roger Highfield. 1995. *Frontiers of Complexity: The Search for Order in a Chaotic World.* New York: Fawcett Columbine, pp. 130–49, on neural nets.

References

Poundstone, William. 1985. *The Recursive Universe: Cosmic Complexity and the Limits of Scientific Knowledge.* Chicago: Contemporary Books.

Resnick, Mitchel. 1994. *Turtles, Termites, and Traffic Jams: Explorations in Massively Parallel Microworlds.* Cambridge, Mass.: MIT Press.

Schelling, Thomas. 1978. *Micromotives and Macrobehavior.* New York: Norton.

Index

Roberts, Marc J., 119
Rocke, David M., 32
Rogers, Everett M., 151–52, 176
Rokkan, Stein, 92n. 51
Romania, 90; predicted alignment of in
World War Two, 81–90
Rome, 127
Ross, Edward Alsworth, 92n. 49
Rousseeuw, Peter J., 81nn. 13–14,
87n. 36
Rubinstein, Ariel, 14, 29
Rueschemeyer, D. H., 144
rules. See strategies
Russett, Bruce, 83n. 26
Russia, xiii
Rutter, Owen, 40, 43

Sabloff, Jeremy A., 152, 177, 185n. 4,
205
Saldinger, Amy, 44n
Saloner, G., 96, 98, 98n. 1, 99, 102, 107,
119–20, 152, 168, 177
Samuelson, Larry, 14, 28
Sanders, David, 72n
Sanders, Lynn, 44n, 59n. 4
Santa Fe Institute, 69, 124, 208–9,
217n. 7
Schaefer, Phil, 84n. 28
Schelling, Thomas, 41, 43, 48, 67,
131n. 7, 144, 150, 153, 177, 215–16,
219, 221
Schendel, D., 119
Schepple, Kim, 44n
Schofield, Norman, 91n. 45
Schotter, Andrew, 45, 67
Schrodt, Philip A., 153n. 3, 156n. 6, 177
Schwartz-Shea, Peregrine, 67
Scott, John E., 57, 67
segregation, 150, 215–16
Selten, R., 47, 67, 103, 120
sensitivity analysis: of Axelrod Culture
Model, 194–96; of landscape approach
to alliance formation, 113–14
sexual reproduction, 12, 14, 22, 24,
24n. 7, 26
Shapely, L. S., 103, 120
Shapiro, C., 98, 99, 102–3, 117, 120
Shapiro, Michael J., 147
shared culture, 6, 8. See also Axelrod Cul-
ture Model; cultural regions; culture;
social influence, model of; Sugarscape

Shaw, Christopher D., 77, 79n. 6,
106n. 8, 118
Shepsle, Kenneth, 69, 71
Sherif, Muzafer, 45, 59, 67
Shubik, M., 103, 120
Siegel, S., 191, 205
Sigmund, Kari, 31–32, 33n. 1, 34, 39
signaling principle, in norms game, 62,
62n. 8
Simmel, Georg, 150, 177
Simmons, Randall T., 67
Simon, Carl, 72n, 124n, 148n
Simon, Herbert A., 6, 9, 81n. 16, 220
Simpleton. See Pavlov strategy
Singer, J. David, 83nn. 25–26
Sirbu, M., 97, 100, 109, 120
Siverson, Randolph M., 32
size, importance of for alliance formation,
76, 80–82, 100
Skocpol, T., 144
slavery, 41, 65
Small, Melvin, 83n. 25
Smith, Robert E., 13
smoking in public, norms regarding, 46,
60
Snell, J. Laurie, 176
Snyder, Glenn H., 82, 82n. 19
Sobel, Andrew, 44n
social differentiation, 150
social influence, 8, 145–46, 148; genetics
in, 152; model of, 153–55; time in
models of, 165, 167, 181. See also Ax-
elrod Culture Model; culture;
Sugarscape
social networks, 91–92
social proof, 44, 58–59
socialization, norms and, 45
Solidarity (Poland), 53
Solomon Islands, number of languages on,
169
South Korea, 130
Soviet Union. See U.S.S.R.
specialization, 151
speciation, 27
Spence, A. Michael, 62n. 7, 67
Sperber, Dan, 148n
spin-glass models, 69–70, 79–80
Sprague, John, 152, 153n. 3, 176
Stacchetti, Ennio, 66
Starbuck, W. H., 188n. 7, 204
state, formation of, 149, 172

About the Author

Robert Axelrod is the Arthur W. Bromage Distinguished University Professor of Political Science and Public Policy at the University of Michigan. His work on cooperation and norms has received awards from the American Association for the Advancement of Science, the American Political Science Association, the MacArthur Foundation, and the National Academy of Sciences.